Indicators of the
Quality of Life in
New Communities

New Communities Research Series

Shirley F. Weiss and *Raymond J. Burby, III*, series editors
Center for Urban and Regional Studies,
The University of North Carolina at Chapel Hill

- Access, Travel, and Transportation in New Communities by Robert B. Zehner

- Economic Integration in New Communities: An Evaluation of Factors Affecting Policies and Implementation by Helene V. Smookler

- Health Care in New Communities by Norman H. Loewenthal and Raymond J. Burby, III

- Indicators of the Quality of Life in New Communities by Robert B. Zehner

- Recreation and Leisure in New Communities by Raymond J. Burby, III

- Residential Mobility in New Communities: An Analysis of Recent In-movers and Prospective Out-movers by Edward J. Kaiser

- Schools in New Communities by Raymond J. Burby, III and Thomas G. Donnelly

Indicators of the Quality of Life in New Communities

Robert B. Zehner

Ballinger Publishing Company • Cambridge, Massachusetts
A Subsidiary of J.B. Lippincott Company

This book is printed on recycled paper.

NSF−RA−E '75−030

All of the material incorporated in this work was developed with the support of National Science Foundation grant number APR 72−03425. However, any opinions, findings, conclusions or recommendations expressed herein are those of the author and do not necessarily reflect the views of the National Science Foundation.

International Standard Book Number: 0−88410−461−3

Library of Congress Catalog Card Number: 77−3353

Printed in the United States of America

Library of Congress Cataloging in Publication Data

Zehner, Robert B
  Indicators of the quality of life in new communities.

  (New communities research series)
  Bibliography: p. 233
  Includes index.
  1. New towns—United States. 2. Social indicators—United States.
I. Title.
HT167.2.Z44   301.36'3'0973   77−3353
ISBN 0−88410−461−3

Dedication

For my family,
Ruth, David, and my parents,
the main contributors to my quality of life

Contents

✳

List of Figures and Tables

Preface

This volume is one of a series of books that summarizes the results of a nationwide study and evaluation of new community development in the United States. The study was initiated in May 1972 under the direction of Dr. Shirley F. Weiss, principal investigator, and coprincipal investigators, Dr. Raymond J. Burby, III, Dr. Thomas G. Donnelly, Dr. Edward J. Kaiser, and Dr. Robert B. Zehner, at the Center for Urban and Regional Studies of The University of North Carolina at Chapel Hill. Financial support for the project was provided by the Research Applied to National Needs Directorate of the National Science Foundation.

The New Communities Study grew out of our concern for the lack of information about the outcomes of new community development in this country. When the original prospectus for the study was prepared, new community development was attracting an increasing amount of attention from both the private and the public sectors. Beginning with a few pioneering new community projects started in the 1940s and 1950s, such as Park Forest and the Levittowns, the 1960s saw a significant expansion in community building. By the end of the decade, over 60 private new community ventures were reported to be under development in eighteen states. The prospect for further expansion in new community development was greatly enhanced by the passage of Title IV of the 1968 Housing and Urban Development Act and the Urban Growth and New Community Development Act of 1970, which provided federal loan guarantees and other forms of assistance for approved new community projects. In the early 1970s, officials of the Department of Housing and Urban

Development were confidently projecting that 10 new communities per year would be started under the federal new communities program.

Increasing public involvement in community building was accompanied by heightened expectations about the public benefits that would result from new community development. The Urban Growth and New Community Development Act of 1970 indicated that the Congress expected new communities to improve the quality of life in the nation by (1) increasing for all persons, particularly members of minority groups, the available choices of locations for living and working; (2) helping to create neighborhoods designed for easier access between the places where people live and the places where they work and find recreation; and (3) providing adequate public, community, and commercial facilities (including facilities needed for education, health and social services, recreation, and transportation). Congressional expectations about the benefits from new community development, however, were not shared by all observers of the new communities movement.

On the basis of an in-depth study of new communities in California conducted in the mid-1960s, Edward P. Eichler and Marshall Kaplan (1967, p. 160) concluded that, ". . . community building, even with public aid or under public sponsorship, can do little to solve the serious problems confronting American society." Three years later, William Alonso reviewed many of the potential benefits of new community development, but ended up by concluding that, "On the whole, a national policy of settling millions of people in new towns is not likely to succeed and would not significantly advance the national welfare if it could be done" (1970, p. 16). The Twentieth Century Fund Task Force on the Governance of New Towns, which reported its findings in 1971, felt that few large-scale developments in the United States were living up to the promise of the new community concept, and Clapp (1971, p. 287) concluded that existing public programs ". . . to date appear inadequate to further the satisfaction of the major objectives of the new town concept."

Obviously, whether the benefits from new community development are real or imagined is a matter of crucial importance in the formulation of national urban growth policies. Since passage of the 1968 and 1970 federal new communities legislation, seventeen new communities have been approved for assistance. Loan guarantee commitments by the federal government now total $361 million. When completed in about 20 years, these new communities are expected to house almost one million persons, with private investments running into the billions of dollars. Given the conflicting opinions about the benefits of new communities and the major public and private investments involved in their development, it seemed appropriate to propose, and for the National Science Foundation to support, a full-scale evaluation of new communities now under development in the United States.

The need for objective information about the performance of new communities has been further underscored by the devastating impacts of the national economic recession, which has produced severe financial problems for the projects participating in the federal new communities program. During 1974, no new loan guarantee commitments were made by the New Communities Administration in the Department of Housing and Urban Development, and on January 14, 1975 the Department suspended further processing of applications for assistance. Faced with mounting financial difficulties with assisted projects, attention within the federal government and the new communities industry has shifted away from the outputs of the program to more pressing concerns for the economic viability of assisted new community ventures. However, the outputs of the program cannot be ignored. If new communities are to receive continued and expanded federal support, they not only must survive as financially viable undertakings, they must also produce benefits that could not be as readily achieved through conventional urban growth.

THE NEW COMMUNITIES STUDY

The University of North Carolina New Communities Study was undertaken to provide federal, state, and local officials, as well as public and private developers, with an improved information base to use in judging the merits of new community development as an urban growth alternative. To assure that new communities do, in fact, realize the "quality of life" objectives set forth by the Congress, the study also sought to determine the critical factors affecting the success or failure of new communities in attracting socially balanced populations and meeting the needs of all of their residents.

In pursuing these two goals, the new communities study was designed to provide answers to five major policy questions: (1) Are federally guaranteed new communities contributing more to residents' quality of life than nonguaranteed new communities and less planned environments? (2) Which characteristics of housing, neighborhood design, community facilities, and governmental mechanisms contribute most to the quality of life of new community residents, including minorities, low-income families, the elderly, and teenagers? (3) Which factors in the developer decision process lead to new community characteristics that contribute most to the quality of life of new community residents? (4) How has the federal new community development program influenced developer decisions regarding housing, neighborhood design, community facilities, and governmental mechanisms? (5) How can the federal new community development program be applied most effectively to produce communities that promise to improve the quality of life of their residents?

The research design that was formulated to answer these questions is based on the belief that an evaluation of new community development must involve more than a study of new communities. To provide a sound basis for conclusions about new community performance, comparisons using the same measurement techniques must be made between new communities and alternative conventional forms of urban development. This research strategy led to the selection of a sample of seventeen communities to represent different types of new communities under development in the United States and nineteen conventional communities. The new community sample includes two communities that are participating in the federal new communities program, thirteen nonfederally assisted new communities that were initiated prior to the federal program, and two retirement new communities designed specifically for older households. Fifteen of the conventional communities were selected by pairing each of the two federally assisted and thirteen nonfederally assisted new communities with a nearby community containing housing similar to that available in the new community in terms of age, type, and price range. Because the paired conventional communities did not have sufficient black and low- and moderate-income populations for comparison with the new communities, four additional conventional communities were selected. These included two suburban communities with subsidized housing and two suburban communities with predominantly black residential areas.

Data collection in the sample new and conventional communities was begun during the spring of 1973 and continued through the summer of 1974. Four types of information were assembled to answer the research questions. First, data on people's attitudes and behavior were collected through 90-minute interviews with 5511 new and conventional community adult residents and self-administered questionnaires returned by 974 young adults (age 14 to 20) living in the sample communities. Second, data about community characteristics, including the number, accessibility, and quality of facilities and services available and selected housing and neighborhood characteristics, were obtained from community inventories completed for all 36 sample communities and from interviews with professional personnel serving the communities. Third, professionals' observations about the communities, as well as factual information about community service systems, were collected through interviews with 577 professional personnel, including school district superintendents, school principals, health officials and practitioners, recreation administrators, and community association leaders. Finally, the plans and activities of developers, governments, and other institutions involved in the development of the new and conventional communities were secured during preliminary reconnaissance interviews in each community, two waves of interviews with developer personnel, accounts published in newspapers and other secondary sources, discussions with local governmental officials, and also from the professional personnel survey.

NEW COMMUNITIES U.S.A.

The major findings and conclusions emerging from the new communities study are summarized in *New Communities U.S.A.* (D.C. Heath, Lexington Books, 1976). Capsuling three years of research, the summary report focuses on the strengths and weaknesses of new community development in the United States, key factors which account for variation in new community performance, and public policy options.

In comparison with conventional modes of suburban growth and development, new communities were found to be superior in five major respects. *First*, better land use planning and community design resulted in the provision of a wider choice of housing types for purchase or rent, more neighborhood amenities and services, and safer access to them. *Second*, new community households tended to accumulate less annual automobile mileage, in part because of consistently better access to community facilities and services. *Third*, new communities were characterized by better recreational facilities and services, which resulted in somewhat higher participation in outdoor recreational activities and much higher levels of resident satisfaction with community recreational service systems. *Fourth*, new community residents tended to give higher ratings to the overall livability of their communities and were more likely than conventional community residents to recommend their communities as particularly good places to which to move. *Fifth*, new communities were found to provide more satisfying living environments for target populations—

black households, low- and moderate-income residents of subsidized housing, and older persons—than the comparison conventional communities.

Given these benefits and assuming that the costs of new community development are no greater than those incurred in conventional urban growth, the study findings provide ample justification for federal efforts to encourage the increased production of new communities in this country. In fact, federal participation in the new communities field appears to be necessary if new communities are to serve as one means of achieving the goals set forth by the Congress in the Urban Growth and New Community Development Act of 1970.

While producing substantial benefits, new community development in the United States has fallen short of achieving the full potential of the new community concept for solving urban problems and creating a better urban environment. Aspects of community development and life where few overall differences were found between the new and conventional communities studied included: evaluations of housing and neighborhood livability; residents' social perspectives, rates of participation in neighboring, community organizations, and community politics, and satisfaction with various life domains and with life as a whole; the provision of some community services; and the organization and operation of community governance. Clearly, in some cases planners have been overly optimistic about the influence of improvements in the physical environment on people's attitudes and behavior. However, in many cases, including the attainment of population balance and the provision of superior public services, the gap between concept and reality can be traced to a variety of factors subject to change through public policy.

In order to optimize the potential that new communities offer for a quantum improvement in the character of urban growth and development, some means must be found to overcome the private developer's limited ability to assume public sector responsibilities and local government's inability to cope with fragmented urban service responsibilities and the debilitating effects of insufficient financial resources. The need to assist developers and local governments in the provision of public and community services was recognized in the Urban Growth and New Community Development Act of 1970, but many of the provisions of the act designed to achieve this purpose were never implemented.

With the federal new communities program at a standstill, two basic, though not mutually exclusive, policy options are available. First, given waning developer interest in larger scale new communities, the program could be reoriented toward smaller scale planned

unit developments, villages, and experimental new communities. At
the same time that assistance is directed toward smaller scale development, the existing new communities legislation could be amended
to recharge those new communities already participating in the federal program. This would require expanded support for low- and
moderate-income housing in new communities and the design of new
incentives for the provision of high quality and innovative community service systems. In addition, eligibility for such assistance could
be extended to new communities not now federally assisted, if they
subscribe to the goals of the program.

Another option, not excluded by the first, would be to return to
the basic purposes embraced in the 1970 Urban Growth and New
Community Development Act and link the production of new communities to the implementation of a national urban growth policy.
If new communities are to be an integral part of a national urban
growth policy, stronger measures than those found in current legislation for private developer and state and local government participation in new community development must be provided. This would
require full funding and implementation of the 1970 new communities legislation as a first step. Beyond this, federal incentives are
needed to encourage state government participation in new community projects, including state oversight of land use and development
regulations, state initiatives to establish new governmental structures
for new communities, and state financial assistance in meeting the
public overhead and front-end costs of new community development
projects.

NEW COMMUNITIES RESEARCH SERIES

The seven volumes in the *New Communities Research Series*, published by Ballinger Publishing Company, explore in depth key facets
of new community development in the United States. The books in
this series are designed to give community development professionals
and researchers in architecture, design, education, health care, housing, planning, recreation, social services, transportation, and allied
professions a fuller and more detailed description and analysis of the
new community experience than could be provided in a summary
report. In addition to their utility to persons concerned with new
community development, these books summarize the results of a
pioneering social science research effort. They report the findings of
one of the first, and probably the most comprehensive, attempts to
trace through sequences of actions and consequences in the community development process—from the decisions which led to the

provision of housing and the production of facilities and services through their effects on individual and household attitudes and behavior.

A central premise of the new community concept has been that through comprehensive planning better relationships can be attained among many of the key variables that influence travel behavior. In *Access, Travel, and Transportation in New Communities*, Robert B. Zehner examines the availability of transportation and other community facilities and services in new communities and how they influence travel behavior. Particular attention is given to alternatives to the automobile, including walking and community transit, the journey to work, automobile ownership rates, and annual household automobile mileage. By analyzing relationships between demographic and community characteristics on the one hand, and residents' travel behavior on the other, Dr. Zehner shows how community design can result in reduced travel and potential energy savings.

In *Economic Integration in New Communities: An Evaluation of Factors Affecting Policies and Implementation*, Helene V. Smookler describes the processes of income and racial integration (and nonintegration) in 15 new communities. The communities are analyzed to determine what factors made integration possible and how they contributed to the effectiveness of the integration programs and strategies that were utilized. The early effects of federal involvement in new community development are described. Dr. Smookler also examines the correlates of residents' integration attitudes, showing that significant differences in attitudes characterize communities with varying amounts of income and racial integration. Finally, the benefits of integration are analyzed in terms of the actual attitudes and perceptions of low-income and black residents living in integrated new communities.

Planned new communities have been viewed as ideal settings in which to develop better ways of organizing and delivering health care services. As described in *Health Care in New Communities*, by Norman H. Loewenthal and Raymond J. Burby, III, however, a number of factors have prevented many new communities from achieving this potential. In addition to describing the approaches to health care that have characterized community building in the United States, the authors examine the impacts of available health care resources on residents' satisfaction with and utilization of health care facilities and services. Health care resources analyzed in the study include the provision of physicians' services, hospital care and ambulance service, social service programs, nursing and convalescent care facilities, public health facilities, and health maintenance programs. Objective characteristics of health care systems, residents' attitudes and behavior, and health professionals' evaluations are interrelated and used as a basis for the formulation of health care policies for the next generation of new communities to be built in this country.

During the past five years increasing interest has been expressed in the quality of life in the United States and how it can and should be measured. The strategy used to assess the quality of life of new and conventional community residents, reported in *Indicators of the Quality of Life in New Communities* by Robert B. Zehner, is eclectic, ranging from measures focused on specific functional community service areas to more general concepts, such as residents' overall life satisfaction. A unique aspect of the data presented in this book is the discussion of residents' individual perceptions of the factors that influence the quality of life as they have defined it for themselves. Dr. Zehner also explores residents' satisfactions with a number of life domains—standard of living, use of leisure time, health, family life, marriage, and work, among others. He also shows how satisfaction with each domain relates to satisfaction with life as a whole. Differences in the quality of life among nineteen classifications of residents, including blacks, low- and moderate-income persons, and the elderly, are highlighted, as well as observed differences in the quality of life between new and conventional communities.

Recreation and Leisure in New Communities by Raymond J. Burby, III provides a comprehensive description and analysis of this key community service system. A comparative evaluation of the experiences of fifteen new communities in developing recreational service systems is presented. Key agents and their roles in developing community recreational resources are identified. Dr. Burby also discusses the administration of recreational service systems, including their governance, approaches to recreational planning, and methods of financing facilities and services. The effectiveness of alternative approaches to organizing the provision of recreational services is evaluated in terms of recreational resources produced and residents' use of and satisfaction with facilities and services. Particular attention is given to how the recreational needs of young adults, elderly persons, women, blacks, and subsidized housing residents have been met. Recreational service system characteristics that influenced residents' participation in outdoor recreational activities, satisfaction with the facilities and services used most often, and overall evaluations of community recreational resources are identified and used as a basis for suggestions about the best approaches to the design and development of community recreational facilities and services.

Who moves to new communities and why? Why are families considering moving from new communities? What factors attract black families and low- and moderate-income households to new and conventional suburban communities? How do residential mobility processes shape the population profiles of new communities? These and related questions are addressed in *Residential Mobility in New Communities: An Analysis of Recent In-movers and Prospective Out-movers* by Edward J. Kaiser. In this book, Dr. Kaiser examines the inflow of residents to new communities, paying particular attention to the characteristics of recent in-movers, their reasons for selecting a home in a new community, and the improvements that were realized as a result of the move. Because the number and profile of out-movers influence the profile of residents left behind, Dr. Kaiser also examines the rate and type of household being lost to new communities through out-mobility. The characteristics of those households most likely to move are identified, together with the key reasons for their moving intentions. Separate chapters are devoted to the retrospective residential choices and prospective mobility of black households, subsidized housing residents, and the residents of federally assisted new communities.

The last book in the series, *Schools in New Communities* by Raymond J. Burby, III and Thomas G. Donnelly, examines school development processes and outcomes in the sample of new and conventional communities. Five topics are covered in this study. First, the capacity of school districts to cope with large-scale community development projects is examined through an analysis of the experiences of 27 school districts in developing educational programs for and building new schools in nonfederally and federally assisted new communities. School districts' experiences in serving new communities are traced from each district's initial contacts with developers, through various phases of the school development process, to current issues in the operation of new community schools. Second, school development outcomes are evaluated in terms of both the objective characteristics of school plants and educational programs and the subjective attitudes of educators and parents. Third, links between characteristics of the schools and parents' evaluations of the schools attended by their children are identified. Fourth, the impact of school availability on the attractiveness of new communities to various population groups is reported, including the contribution of public schools to households' decisions to move to new communities and their satisfaction with the community as a place to live after they have occupied their homes. Finally, suggestions for increasing the effectiveness of school development are offered.

THE RESEARCH TEAM

The New Communities Study, summary report, and monographs in the *New Communities Research Series* were made possible by the combined efforts of a large team of researchers and supporting staff assembled at the Center for Urban and Regional Studies of The University of North Carolina at Chapel Hill. The team members and their roles in the study were the following:

Dr. Shirley F. Weiss, principal investigator and project director, who had primary responsibility for management of the study and coordination of the research efforts of the team of coprincipal investigators and research associates. Dr. Weiss's research focused on the overall new community development process, implementation, fiscal concerns, and federal assistance, as well as shopping center and other commercial facilities.

Dr. Raymond J. Burby, III, coprincipal investigator and deputy project director, who assumed primary responsibility for implementation of the research design and preparation of the project summary report. Dr. Burby's research focused on new community planning and governance, the recreation and leisure service system, schools, and health care planning and delivery.

Dr. Thomas G. Donnelly, coprincipal investivator, who assumed primary responsibility for the extensive data processing for the study. Dr. Donnelly's research focused on the development and utilization of efficient computation routines for the data analyses and on educational development processes in new communities.

Dr. Edward J. Kaiser, coprincipal investigator, who helped formulate the original research design and research management strategy, and offered invaluable advice throughout the study. Dr. Kaiser's research focused on residential mobility processes in new communities.

Dr. Robert B. Zehner, coprincipal investigator, who assumed primary responsibility for the design and conduct of the household survey. Dr. Zehner's research focused on transportation and travel in new communities, neighborhood and community satisfaction, and the quality of life of new community residents.

David F. Lewis, research associate, who prepared a comparative analysis of the population characteristics of new communities, their host counties, and host SMSAs, and contributed to the analysis of housing and neighborhood satisfaction in new communities.

Norman H. Loewenthal, research associate, who undertook a major portion of the professional personnel survey design and field work and assumed primary responsibility for the analysis of health care service systems in new communities.

Mary Ellen McCalla, research associate, who assumed responsibility for immediate supervision of the household survey sampling, field work, and coding operations, supervision of the community inventory map measurement and professional personnel survey coding, and contributed to the analysis of the social life of new communities.

Dr. Helene V. Smookler, research associate, who assumed primary responsibility for the design and conduct of developer decision studies and the analysis of economic integration in new communities.

Invaluable assistance throughout the study was provided by Barbara G. Rodgers, who served as administrative aide, research assistant, and publications manager.

The research work was supported by a staff of technical specialists, research assistants, interviewers, coders, and office personnel too extensive for a complete listing. In particular, the efforts of the following persons should be recognized: research assistants Jerry L. Doctrow, Mary C. Edeburn, Leo E. Hendricks, Christopher G. Olney, and Raymond E. Stanland, Jr., and, secretaries Cathy A. Albert, Lisa D. McDaniel, Linda B. Johnson, Lucinda D. Peterson, and Diana Pettaway.

THE NATIONAL SCIENCE FOUNDATION

The new communities study was made possible by research grant APR 72−03425 from the Research Applied to National Needs Directorate of the National Science Foundation. Throughout the course of the study, the research team benefited greatly from the continuing interest and constant encouragement of Dr. George W. Baker, the project's program manager. Dr. Baker worked with the research team to achieve scientific excellence in each phase of the study.

Of course, the findings, opinions, conclusions, or recommendations arising out of this research grant are those of the authors, and it should not be implied that they represent the views of the National Science Foundation.

SITE AND ADVISORY COMMITTEES

The process of refining the initial research design was aided by the expert advice of the Site Visit Committee and the panel of anonymous peer reviewers whose ideas were synthesized by Dr. George W. Baker.

An important source of guidance and consultation was made possible by the project's advisory committee, drawn from experts in new community development, city planning, economics, political science, and sociology. Jonathan B. Howes, Director, Center for Urban and Regional Studies, The University of North Carolina at Chapel Hill, ably served as chairman of the advisory committee which included Dr. George W. Baker, National Science Foundation; Professor F. Stuart Chapin, Jr., The University of North Carolina at Chapel Hill; Dr. Amos H. Hawley, The University of North Carolina at Chapel Hill; Morton Hoppenfeld, The Rouse Company (resigned March 5, 1975); Dr. Richard M. Langendorf, University of Miami; Floyd B. McKissick, McKissick Enterprises, Inc.; Dr. Frederick A. McLaughlin, Jr., New Communities Administration, Department of Housing and Urban Development (appointed in 1973); Dr. Peter H. Rossi, University of Massachusetts; Dr. Joseph J. Spengler, Duke University; Dr. Lawrence Susskind, Massachusetts Institute of Technology; Dr. Dorothy S. Williams, Department of Housing and Urban Development (1972–73); and Dr. Deil S. Wright, The University of North Carolina at Chapel Hill.

While their collective and individual contributions to the conduct of the study are gratefully acknowledged, it goes without saying that neither the Site Committee, the Advisory Committee, nor any individual members bear responsibility for the findings and interpretations in the *New Communities Research Series* and other publications of the project.

NEW COMMUNITIES POLICY APPLICATIONS WORKSHOP

A New Communities Policy Applications Workshop was held in Chapel Hill at The University of North Carolina from November 17 to 19, 1974. The workshop brought together invited representatives of federal, state, local, private, and academic user communities to review the methodology and preliminary findings of the study. The workshop was structured to assure that critical feedback to the research team would be secured from formal and informal discussion sessions and to provide a forum for the consideration of broad issues in new community development.

The Policy Applications Workshop was an invaluable part of the research process. The following participants offered many astute observations and critical comments which were helpful to the research team.

Representing the federal government: Dr. Harvey A. Averch, National Science Foundation; Dr. George W. Baker, National Science

Foundation; Bernard P. Bernsten, U.S. Postal Service; Larry W. Co-law, Tennessee Valley Authority; Dr. James D. Cowhig, National Science Foundation; Dr. Frederick J. Eggers, U.S. Department of Housing and Urban Development; Richard L. Fore, U.S. Department of Housing and Urban Development; James L. Gober, Tennessee Valley Authority; George Gross, House Budget Committee, U.S. House of Representatives; Charles A. Gueli, U.S. Department of Housing and Urban Development; Benjamin McKeever, Subcommittee on Housing of the Committee on Banking and Currency, U.S. House of Representatives; Dr. Frederick A. McLaughlin, Jr., U.S. Department of Housing and Urban Development; Paul W. Rasmussen, U.S. Department of Transportation; Dr. Salvatore Rinaldi, U.S. Office of Education; Ali F. Sevin, Federal Highway Administration; Dr. Frederick T. Sparrow, National Science Foundation; Otto G. Stolz, U.S. Department of Housing and Urban Development; Jack Underhill, U.S. Department of Housing and Urban Development; Margaret L. Wireman, U.S. Department of Housing and Urban Development; and Theodore W. Wirths, National Science Foundation.

Representing state, local, and community government: D. David Brandon, New York State Urban Development Corporation; W.C. Dutton, Jr., The Maryland–National Capital Park and Planning Commission; Brendan K. Geraghty, Newfields New Community Authority; James L. Hindes, Office of Planning and Budget, State of Georgia; Mayor Gabrielle G. Pryor, City of Irvine, Calif.; Roger S. Ralph, Columbia Park and Recreation Association; Anne D. Stubbs, The Council of State Governments; and Gerald W. von Mayer, Office of Planning and Zoning, Howard County, Md.

Representing new community developers: James E. Bock, Gerald D. Hines Interests; Dwight Bunce, Harbison Development Corporation; David J. Burton, Harbison Development Corporation; Gordon R. Carey, Warren Regional Planning Corporation; David Scott Carlson, Riverton Properties, Inc.; Eva Clayton, Soul City Foundation; Mark H. Freeman, League of New Community Developers; Morton Hoppenfeld, DEVCO—The Greater Hartford Community Development Corporation; Joseph T. Howell, Seton Belt Village; Floyd B. McKissick, The Soul City Company; Richard A. Reese, The Irvine Company; Jeffrey B. Samet, Harbison Development Corporation; Elinor Schwartz, League of New Community Developers; Michael D. Spear, The Rouse Company; and Francis C. Steinbauer, Gulf-Reston, Inc.

Representing public interest groups and new community and urban affairs consultants: Mahlon Apgar, IV, McKinsey and Company; Evans Clinchy, Educational Planning Associates; Ben H. Cunningham,

The Hodne-Stageberg Partners; Harvey B. Gantt, Gantt/Huberman
Associates; John E. Gaynus, National Urban League, Inc.; James J.
Gildea, Barton-Aschman Associates; Nathaniel M. Griffin, Urban
Land Institute; Guy W. Hager, Planning and Management Consultant;
William H. Hoffman, National Corporation for Housing Partnerships;
Jack Linville, Jr., American Institute of Planners; Hugh Mields, Jr.,
Academy for Contemporary Problems; William Nicoson, Urban Af-
fairs Consultant; Dr. Carl Norcross, Advisor on New Communities;
Robert M. O'Donnell, Harman, O'Donnell and Henninger Associates;
Donald E. Priest, Urban Land Institute; Edward M. Risse, Richard P.
Browne Associates; George M. Stephens, Jr., Stephens Associates;
Eugene R. Streich, System Development Corporation; and Doris
Wright, REP Associates.

Representing the academic community: Dr. Allen H. Barton, Co-
lumbia University; Professor David L. Bell, North Carolina State
University; Professor Richard D. Berry, University of Southern Cali-
fornia; Donald W. Bradley, Michigan State University; William A.
Brandt, Jr., University of Chicago; David J. Brower, The University
of North Carolina at Chapel Hill; Lynne C. Burkhart, University of
Massachusetts; Professor F. Stuart Chapin, Jr., The University of
North Carolina at Chapel Hill; Dr. Lewis Clopton, The University of
North Carolina at Chapel Hill; Dr. Robert H. Erskine, The Univer-
sity of North Carolina at Chapel Hill; Dr. Sylvia F. Fava, Brooklyn
College of The City University of New York; Dr. Nelson N. Foote,
Hunter College of The City University of New York; Russell C. Ford,
The University of North Carolina at Chapel Hill; Dr. Gorman Gilbert,
The University of North Carolina at Chapel Hill; Dr. David R. Gods-
chalk, The University of North Carolina at Chapel Hill; Dr. Gideon
Golany, The Pennsylvania State University; Professor Philip P. Green,
Jr., The University of North Carolina at Chapel Hill; Dr. George C.
Hemmens, The University of North Carolina at Chapel Hill; Dean
George R. Holcomb, The University of North Carolina at Chapel Hill;
Jonathan B. Howes, The University of North Carolina at Chapel Hill;
Frederick K. Ickes, The University of North Carolina at Chapel Hill;
Dr. Suzanne Keller, Princeton University; Joseph E. Kilpatrick, The
University of North Carolina at Chapel Hill; Professor Alan S. Kra-
vitz, Ramapo College of New Jersey; Dr. Richard M. Langendorf,
University of Miami; Dean Claude E. McKinney, North Carolina State
University; Dr. Robert W. Marans, The University of Michigan; Susan
L. Marker, Bryn Mawr College; Dr. Michael J. Minor, University of
Chicago; Professor Roger Montgomery, University of California,
Berkeley; Daniel W. O'Connell, Harvard University; Dean Kermit C.
Parsons, Cornell University; David R. Paulson, The University of

North Carolina at Chapel Hill; Dr. Francine F. Rabinovitz, University of California, Los Angeles; Dr. Peter H. Rossi, University of Massachusetts; Dr. Arthur B. Shostak, Drexel University; Dr. Michael A. Stegman, The University of North Carolina at Chapel Hill; Dr. Robert Sullivan, Jr., Duke University; Dr. Lawrence Susskind, Massachusetts Institute of Technology; Professor Maxine T. Wallace, Howard University; Dr. William A. Wallace, Carnegie-Mellon University; Kenneth Weeden, The University of North Carolina at Chapel Hill; Professor Warren J. Wicker, The University of North Carolina at Chapel Hill; Dr. Deil S. Wright, The University of North Carolina at Chapel Hill; and Dr. Mary Wylie, The University of Wisconsin—Madison.

Representing the press: Barry Casselman, *Appleseeds* and *Many Corners* newspapers; Thomas Lippman, *The Washington Post*; William B. Richards, *The Washington Post*; and Barry Zigas, *Housing and Development Reporter*.

Foreign observers: Åsel Floderus, The National Swedish Institute for Building Research; and Hans Floderus, Building and Town Planning Department, Avesta, Sweden.

To list all the people who contributed to this study is impossible. Among others, these would include 6485 residents who spent time responding to the household survey interview, 577 professionals who shared their knowledge and opinions about the study communities, and 173 informed individuals who were interviewed in connection with the developer decision studies.

A final note of thanks is due the new community developers and their staffs who were generous in making available their time and expert knowledge to the research team. In reciprocation, this series is offered as an aid in their continuing efforts to realize better communities and a more livable environment.

Shirley F. Weiss and **Raymond J. Burby, III**

The University of North Carolina
at Chapel Hill
December 10, 1975

Author's Note

The reports of most research projects depend on the contributions of many people before reaching fruition, and this volume is no exception. From the initial stages of the New Communities Project in 1972, important contributors on a continuing basis have been Dr. George W. Baker, the National Science Foundation Program Manager for the grant, and my colleagues at the Center for Urban and Regional Studies, Drs. Shirley F. Weiss, Raymond J. Burby, III, Thomas G. Donnelly, and Edward J. Kaiser. Shirley Weiss and Ray Burby, in particular, have been the keystones for the project and the series of volumes that have evolved from it. Together with Tom Donnelly and Barbara Rodgers, they have taken on a major role in the processing of the final manuscript for publication.

Drs. Willard L. Rodgers and Robert W. Marans of the Survey Research Center at The University of Michigan furnished useful advice during the design phase of the quality of life portion of the household interview. Dr. Nelson N. Foote, Ben H. Cunningham, and Dr. Suzanne Keller provided insightful and useful critiques of an earlier draft that have strengthened this volume appreciably. Parts of the chapter on responses to the residential community build on work initiated by Ray Burby. An initial analysis of responses to the dwelling was undertaken by David F. Lewis.

Several others at the Center in Chapel Hill deserve special mention. Mary Ellen McCalla played an integral part in the design of the project's questionnaires and in fieldwork and coding supervision. Inventories of community facilities were conducted in the field in part by

Jerry L. Doctrow, Leo E. Hendricks, and David F. Lewis, with Norman H. Loewenthal having a major role in the coding of the map measurements associated with the inventory data. Mary C. Edeburn proved to have an uncanny ability to translate and expedite data processing requests. The office staff and the production phases of this volume, including the typing of the final manuscript, have been under the supervision of Barbara G. Rodgers.

Robert B. Zehner

Vaucluse, New South Wales
November 30, 1976

Indicators of the
Quality of Life in
New Communities

Chapter 1

Introduction and Summary
of Findings

A popular premise of the new communities movement, at least since Ebenezer Howard's garden cities in England at the turn of the century, has been that residents will find the quality of their lives improved through the new community experience.[a] In essence, new communities are believed to provide and arrange community components to encourage more satisfying encounters with the community and with other residents than would occur in conventional residential communities. Promotional materials for contemporary new communities, for example, include not only descriptions of available (and planned) facilities, design principles, and environmental attractiveness, but also larger visions of creating and enhancing new lifestyles, "the next America," and the like. Implicit is the assumption that factors amenable to manipulation by community planners are, in fact, important components of residents' evaluations of the overall quality of their lives.

Despite the straightforward nature of such a proposition—that characteristics of the environment can have significant effects on the enjoyment of that environment and of life in general—this field of investigation is embedded in a number of conceptual and methodological issues. At the most general level, questions tend to revolve around what elements ought to be included in assessments of life quality. Candidates range from metropolitan crime rates to marital satisfaction to the degree of equanimity obtained through prayer or

[a] See especially the "Author's Introduction," pp. 41–49, and "The path followed up," pp. 128–137, of Ebenezer Howard (1965). (Originally published in 1898.)

meditation. Methodological concerns emerge most clearly once what is to be measured has been decided—crime rates or mental states, for example—and the process of linking concepts to measurements becomes one of continuous reciprocal adjustment.

We do not propose to examine the entire range of problems in research and measurement of the quality of life in this book. To do so would require more than one monograph, and in any case, the task has recently been done well by others.[b] We will, however, relate our efforts to other work in terms of both concept and method and make frequent use of data from other studies when they bear on our own analyses.

THE CONTEXT

The notion of the "quality" of life carries with it a clear connotation of evaluation, of rating, of being better or worse. Worrying about the human condition in these terms has produced reams of analyses about the effect of uses of the environment, of overcrowded central cities and newly minted suburbs, of increasing (or decreasing) affluence on the quality of life, and so on. The concerns are hardly new, but attempts to quantify them are relatively recent. At least three orientations to measuring concepts like "quality of life" deserve mention.

Community-Level Assessments

First, as a supplement to various economic indicators of national well-being like the gross national product (GNP) and the balance of payments, a case has been made for the development of a reliable set of indicators of social well-being. To cite a simple problem, the fact that the GNP and the crime rate can increase simultaneously makes it difficult to argue convincingly that such an economic indicator alone provides an adequate measure of the well-being of the population.

In response to this type of dilemma, a considerable amount of work has been done under the rubric of "social indicators" to develop a broadly applicable series of social welfare measures that could be used to assess the social well-being of a community, state, region, or country.[c] Among the functional areas of the community utilized in

[b]Angus Campbell, Philip E. Converse, and Willard L. Rodgers (1976, Part I, pp. 190–210) include a thorough discussion oriented toward the problems of survey research data gathering. Another useful review is *Social Indicators, 1973* (1973).

[c]See, for example, Otis Dudley Duncan (1969); Michael J. Flax (1972); Terry Nicholas Clark (1973); Joseph A. Ziegler and Charles R. Britton (1975); L. Douglas James *et al.* (1974); and *Social Indicators, 1973* (1973). United Nations

such efforts are public safety (e.g., crime statistics), health (e.g., hospital beds per 1000 persons), education (e.g., annual expenditures per student), and community services (e.g., frequency of garbage collection). Studies that focus on the adequacy of facilities and services in communities sometimes rely primarily on data about the availability or the characteristics of a given facility or service (e.g., the annual expenditures per student in the school system), sometimes on indicators of the performance of the facility or service (e.g., the proportion of students reading at grade level), and often use a combination of characteristic and performance data to make assessments. The data for the various service areas of a community are frequently summarized to provide overall measures of the quality of life or well-being in the community under investigation.[d]

Individual Assessment: I

In contrast to social indicators that generate communitywide measures of well-being, a major body of research has focused on the individual. This research began largely with a concern for mental health, but, much as social indicator studies evolved in response to the inadequacy of gross economic indicators, the study of individual life satisfaction and happiness developed partly in response to the inadequacy of many standard ways of categorizing people (by income, education, and occupation, for example) to determine how "well off" they are—in terms of both mental health and more materialistic well-being.[e] The limitations of simple socioeconomic indicators of individual well-being have been dealt with in two fashions. First, and most important, researchers decided that if they wanted to know how content people were with their lots in life, one of the best ways to find out might be to ask them (rather than relying on "objec-

---

data on literacy, mortality, and the like provide a limited array of similar social welfare measures at the national level of aggregation.

For an excellent critique of social-indicator and quality-of-life research see Walton J. Francis (1973).

[d] One means of summarizing such apparently dissimilar types of data is to rank each community studied on each of the measures collected. In a study of six communities, for example, Community A might rank first in health facilities, sixth in educational expenditures, and third in public safety; Community B might rank second, second, and fourth; and so on. An overall standing could be obtained by averaging each of the communities' ranks on the indicators measured. A similar rationale can be used to compare the situation in a single community at different times.

It is important to recognize, however, that these calculations usually assume implicitly that each of the components measured is of equal importance and that recreation, education, health care, police protection, and so forth should be given an equal weight in assessing the communities or areas being studied.

[e] See Gerald Gurin, Joseph Veroff, and Sheila Feld (1960). For an excellent recent synthesis of work on individual-level assessments, see Nicholas Zill (1974).

tive" measures of well-being). Second, the search for key determinants of individual well-being expanded far beyond concerns for material success into life domains such as marriage, family life, job satisfaction, housing, and the community. One recent study, in fact, included no fewer than 133 possible determinants of satisfaction with various aspects of life (Andrews and Withey 1974).

The decision to investigate peoples' ratings of how well-off they are—of the quality of their lives, as it were—has in turn led to two approaches to defining the main dependent variable for research purposes. The first, best exemplified by the work of Bradburn (1969), has focused on measures of personal "happiness." The second has posed the issue to respondents in terms of how "satisfied" they are with various life domains and with their lives as a whole.[f]

These two approaches to subjective assessments carry somewhat different connotations. Feelings of happiness, for example, appear to imply more of an inward-looking judgment of emotional state and may be more sensitive to short-term fluctuations. In contrast, reports of satisfaction suggest more thoughtful assessments and the weighing of situations in terms of expectations or aspirations. In the present project, the connotations of satisfaction seemed more appropriate to the community facilities and services we wanted residents to assess. As a result, many of the evaluative items discussed in this report were explicitly phrased in terms of satisfaction.[g]

Individual Assessment: II

To a large extent, interest in overall measures of life satisfaction and personal well-being has been the province of academic researchers. The importance of subjective evaluations of many components of people's lives, however, has long been appreciated by sales and marketing organizations. In the case of the new community "prod-

[f]Satisfaction-oriented research has been pursued in considerable detail in recent years at the Institute for Social Research at The University of Michigan, in particular by Campbell, Converse, and Rodgers (1976) and Andrews and Withey (1974). Campbell *et al.* (p. 8) report that happiness and satisfaction measures are often correlated about $r = .50$, a fairly high—but far from perfect—association.

[g]In addition to the emotional versus cognitive distinction that led us to focus on satisfaction items, we simply found it more comfortable to talk in terms of residents' satisfaction with the quality of, say, community health or recreation facilities than their happiness with them. Basically, while *satisfaction* seemed a useful concept for all of a person's life domains, *happiness* seemed apropos primarily for the more personal life domains like marriage and family.

We note also that several previous studies which underlay the present research, to which we hoped to compare our results, also relied on satisfaction items. Chief among these studies were John B. Lansing, Robert W. Marans, and Robert B. Zehner (1970); and Robert W. Marans and Willard Rodgers (1972).

uct," both academics and developers have been interested in the bases of the appeal of such communities and the sources of residents' satisfactions and dissatisfactions once they decided to live in a new community.[h]

A developer might find notions of overall life satisfaction and happiness arcane topics for research, but there is obviously a large overlap with factors that influence the marketability of a community—the quality of the dwellings, the neighborhoods, and the larger community, for example. Despite their common interest in people's reactions to these aspects of the residential environment, however, the academic and the developer can have quite different standards for their interpretation of the data. For a developer, the finding that residents' satisfaction with housing has only limited impact on life satisfaction compared to their satisfaction with marriage or family life would be of less interest than the finding that residents evaluate the housing and facilities in his community more (or less) favorably than people in nearby developments competing in the same housing market. What might appear to be a modest difference between communities to an academic, in other words, might be large enough to enable a developer to differentiate his product successfully from that of the competition.[i] Another difference in the orientation to data is the tendency of researchers to aggregate them and attempt to generalize about phenomena—such as new communities. To a developer intent on a specific market area, aggregated data may have limited relevance. (One way of handling this dilemma is to present data in both aggregated and disaggregated form where possible—the approach we are using in the present New Community Project reports.)

The analyses reported in this volume attempt to be responsive to each of the three major orientations to assessing quality of life that we have outlined. The emphasis, however, is on residents' perceptions of the residential environment and on general measures of life satis-

[h]Although most developers have tested the appeal of their communities with market surveys of varying degrees of sophistication, these data tend not to be made public. An organization that receives significant support from developers, the Urban Land Institute, published *Open Space Communities in the Market Place* (Carl Norcross 1966). Studies by researchers affiliated with academic institutions include *Planning and the Purchase Decision: Why People Buy in Planned Communities* (Carl Werthman, Jerry S. Mandel, and Ted Dienstfrey 1965); *Planned Residential Environments* (Lansing *et al.* 1970); and *Case Studies of Six Planned New Towns in the United States* (James A. Prestridge 1973).

[i]We are indebted to Nelson Foote for emphasizing the developer's viewpoint in his remarks in November 1974 at the New Communities Policy Applications Workshop in Chapel Hill.

faction and the quality of life. A key aspect of these analyses is an attempt to compare the importance of dwelling, immediate neighborhood, and the community with residents' overall satisfaction in domains like health, job, marriage, and family.

We have not attempted to assemble a battery of performance-oriented social indicators to gauge the adequacy of local facilities and services.[j] Instead, inventories of a wide array of facilities and services are summarized at both the neighborhood (32 facilities and services) and community (72 facilities and services) levels to provide objective measures of the range of amenities available in the study communities. A part of the analysis reported in Chapter 3 looks at the relationships between the inventory data and residents' evaluations of their neighborhoods and communities.

We have not tried to resolve the dichotomy between the survey researcher's tendency to aggregate and pursue relatively abstract issues and the developer's interest in disaggregated, community-specific analyses. We do, however, present both aggregated and community-level data wherever possible, and not only consider residents' responses to overall measures of life satisfaction (Chapters 2 and 5) but also look in some detail at ratings of the dwelling, neighborhood, and community (Chapters 3 and 4). In addition, Chapter 6 focuses on the responses of nineteen separate population subgroups to new communities.

Finally, a comparison of new and conventional communities crosscuts many of the analyses. One of the main research objectives that motivated the present project, after all, was to determine the degree to which new and conventional communities differ in their ability to provide residents with a satisfying quality of life. The variety of indicators and the number of distinguishable resident groups (based on income, family lifecycle, race, and so forth) available for analysis made it unlikely that either new or conventional communities would prove to be consistently "better" places to live on all indicators for all groups. Identifying those who benefit most (and least) from new community development becomes, therefore, of central interest in assessing the present and future impact of the new communities movement.

---

[j]Three of the project monographs in this series that focus on functional areas in the study communities make use of some performance data. See *Recreation and Leisure in New Communities* (Raymond J. Burby, III 1976); *Schools in New Communities* (Raymond J. Burby, III and Thomas G. Donnelly 1977); and *Health Care in New Communities* (Norman H. Loewenthal and Raymond J. Burby, III 1976).

THE SAMPLE AND THE DATA

This study focuses on thirteen nonfederally assisted, comprehensively planned new communities. Each was paired with a conventionally developed community nearby which, although it featured less planning, provided housing of similar age, cost, and type. In addition to the nonfederally assisted new communities, two federally assisted communities, which were at a very early stage of development at the time of our sample selection in 1972, were included. They were added to provide baseline data during the early years of such new communities and were also paired with comparable conventional communities.

Because the fifteen conventional communities did not have enough black and low- and moderate-income residents for comparison with the new communities, information was gathered in four additional conventional communities. These included two predominantly black suburban communities and two with subsidized housing. To provide a broader basis for analyses of the responses of elderly persons, the sample included two planned retirement communities.

The locations of the fifteen new communities and 21 comparison communities are shown in Figure 1—1. The thirteen nonfederally assisted new communities include Columbia, Maryland, North Palm Beach, Florida, and Reston, Virginia on the East Coast; Elk Grove Village, Illinois, Forest Park, Ohio, and Park Forest, Illinois in the Midwest; Lake Havasu City, Arizona and Sharpstown, Texas in the Southwest; and Foster City, Irvine, Laguna Niguel, Valencia, and Westlake Village in California.[k] With the exception of Lake Havasu City, which is freestanding, they are all suburban communities, generally located on the fringe of a metropolitan area.

The federally assisted new communities, Jonathan, Minnesota and Park Forest South, Illinois are two of the first three new communities approved for federal assistance. Although selected because they were further along than any of the other developments that had been offered assistance, they were at a much earlier stage of development than the nonfederally assisted communities in our sample. In contrast to the nonfederally assisted communities, whose 1972 populations ranged from 7000 to around 35,000, Jonathan and Park Forest South had populations of only 1500 and 3200, respectively. See Table 1—1. These two communities were also the least advanced in terms of proportion of target population present at the time of our fieldwork.

[k] The procedure used to select this sample of nonfederally assisted new communities is described in Appendix A. Descriptions of the new and conventional communities are provided in Appendix B.

Figure 1–1. New and Comparison Communities

- ● New Community
- ○ Paired Conventional Communities
- ▲ Special Comparison Communities

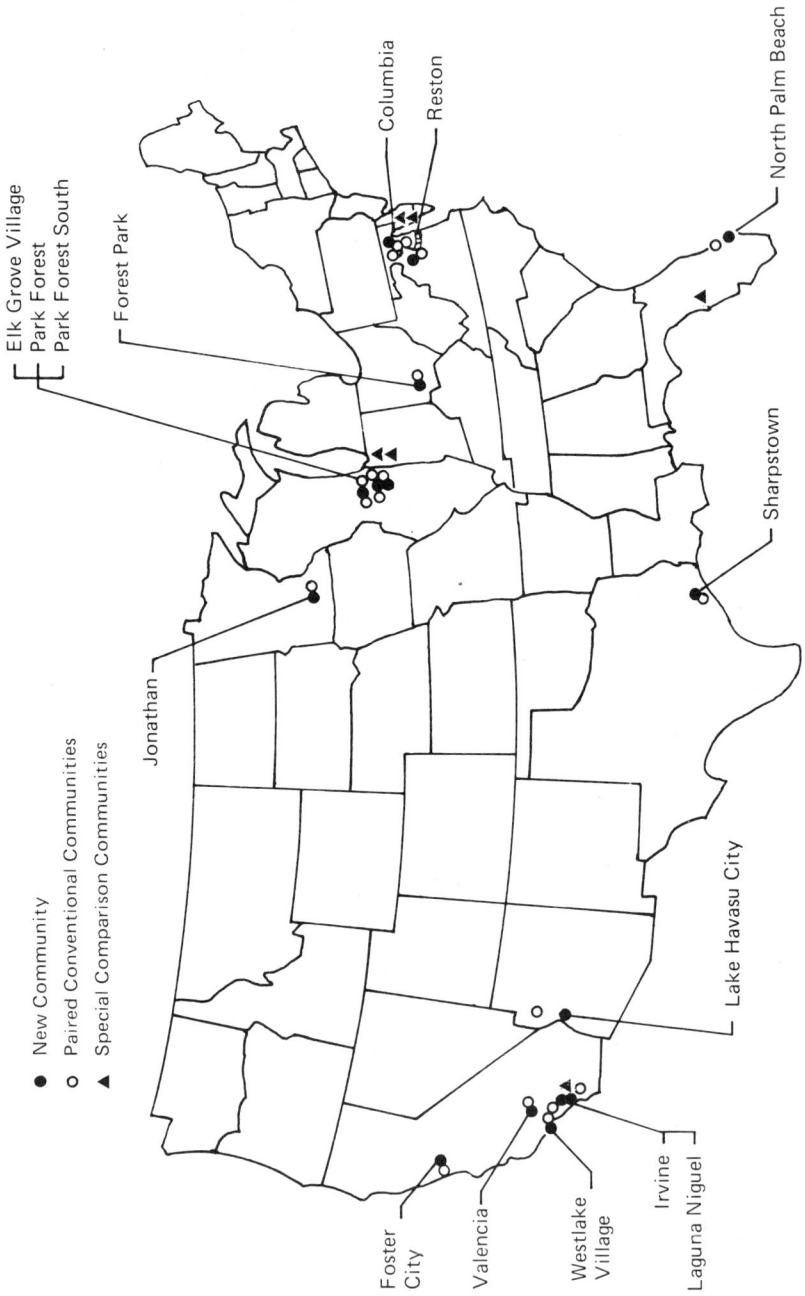

Table 1–1. Year of First Residential Occupancy, Estimated Population, and Median Estimated Family Income for Sample New Communities

Community	Year of First Residential Occupancy	Estimated Population (Fall 1972)	Estimated Target Population	Median Estimated 1972 Family Income (dollars)
Nonfederally assisted				
Park Forest	1948	30,600	35,000	$16,100
Sharpstown[a]	1954	35,000	35,000	15,900
Forest Park	1956	17,000	35,000	16,400
North Palm Beach	1956	12,500	30,000	16,900
Elk Grove Village	1957	22,900	58,500	17,600
Laguna Niguel	1962	8,500	40,000	17,600
Lake Havasu City	1963	8,500	60,000	12,100
Foster City	1964	15,000	36,000	20,200
Reston	1964	20,000	75,000	19,900
Irvine[b]	1966	20,000	338,000	19,000
Valencia	1966	7,000	25,000	19,000
Westlake Village	1966	13,000	50,000	21,600
Columbia	1967	24,000	110,000	17,300
Federally assisted				
Jonathan	1968	1,500	50,000	11,800
Park Forest South	1969	3,200	110,000	16,800

[a] Residential densities in Sharpstown have ended up being greater than initially planned, and its final population will probably exceed the initial target population by 5,000 to 10,000.

[b] Population data refer to the City of Irvine which includes residential areas not developed by The Irvine Company. Only areas developed by The Irvine Company were included in the household interview sample. At the time of our field work these areas had a population of about 12,300.

Both Jonathan and Park Forest South had attained only 3 percent of their target populations compared to a range of 6 percent (Irvine) to more than 85 percent (Park Forest and Sharpstown) among the non-federally assisted communities.

It is not surprising that the first households in the federally assisted communities settled later (1968—1969) than those in the other new communities. Five of the nonfederally assisted areas were initially occupied prior to 1960 (Park Forest, Sharpstown, Forest Park, North Palm Beach, and Elk Grove Village), the others between 1962 (Laguna Niguel) and 1967 (Columbia). From respondent reports of family income, the residents of every community but Lake Havasu City ($12,100) and Jonathan ($11,800) could reasonably be called upper middle class, with median incomes ranging from around $16,000 (Sharpstown, Park Forest) to over $21,000 (Westlake Village).[1]

The households in the sampled communities largely comprised young families with one or more children living at home. See Table 1—2. Overall, in the thirteen nonfederally assisted new communities and their paired conventional communities, roughly half the heads of household were under 40, and almost two-thirds of the households contained three or more persons. A higher proportion of household heads in Columbia and the two federally assisted communities were under 40 (over 70 percent), while households with older heads were found most frequently in two of the communities in the south, Lake Havasu City and North Palm Beach, where at least 40 percent were 55 or older. These were the only two communities where the median household size was two persons or fewer and where there were more likely to be households in which neither head nor spouse was employed. In all of the new communities, between roughly one-fifth and two-fifths of the households included both an employed head and an employed spouse.

In each of the new communities—with one exception—the most common dwelling type was the single-family, detached home on its own lot. In Reston, the exception, more households lived in apartment units than in single-family or townhouses—rowhouses. In four of the nonfederally assisted communities, between 83 and 88 percent

[1]These income data and much of the other information discussed in this book were taken from 90-minute household interviews conducted with a sample of 3,395 new community residents, including special subsamples of blacks and subsidized housing residents, 1,523 paired conventional community residents, and 593 residents of special comparison communities. To complement the household interviews, inventories of community characteristics which focused on the number, accessibility, and characteristics of facilities available to residents, characteristics of their immediate neighborhoods, and housing density were completed in each of the 36 communities. These two data sources—household interviews and community inventories—form the primary bases for the tabulations reported in this book.

of the households lived in detached, single-family dwellings (Elk Grove Village, Laguna Niguel, Valencia, Forest Park). At the other end of the spectrum, besides Reston and Columbia, in the two federally assisted communities fewer than half the occupied units were single-family, detached houses.

Before we review the findings of the study, several limitations of the research methods should be noted. The results of the study have been built largely upon cross-sectional data collected in new and conventional communities during 1973. Although the results of earlier studies and subsequent changes in communities have been taken into account where data are available, considerably more longitudinal analysis and monitoring of new communities over time will be needed to document the long-term effects of large-scale community planning on measures of satisfaction with the dwelling, neighborhood, and community, as well as on global measures of life satisfaction and the quality of life.

It should also be stressed that the communities studied were by no means completed. Some new communities were further developed than others—Park Forest and Sharpstown, for example, had achieved over 85 percent of their initial target populations—but, on average, the new communities were only about one-fifth completed. This book, therefore, deals with developing new communities rather than completed communities. Particular circumstances in individual new and conventional communities will change over time as their populations grow and mature and the provision of a broader array of amenities becomes possible.

Finally, it is appropriate to reiterate that the two federally assisted communities and their paired conventional communities were in the initial stages of development. The findings for them provide an early empirical picture of the results of the federal new communities program and benchmarks for comparison with later studies of these and other federally assisted communities. They should not, however, be used to judge the entire federal new communities program.

SUMMARY OF FINDINGS

A considerable amount of publicity and discussion has accompanied the development of new communities over the past ten years, from the inception of Reston, Virginia and Columbia, Maryland through the rise (and subsequent decline) of a federal new communities program.[m] Several important rationales encouraged new community

[m] For a review of the development of new communities and federal new communities programs in the United States, see Burby and Weiss *et al.* (1976, Chapters 2 and 3).

Table 1-2. Selected Resident Characteristics (percentage distribution of respondents)[a]

	Thirteen New Communities	Thirteen Conventional Communities	Nonfederally Assisted New Communities					
			Columbia	Reston	Irvine	Valencia	Park Forest	Westlake Village
Age of household head								
Under 40	49	53	76	69	53	60	51	34
40–54	33	30	17	24	34	32	30	43
55 or older	18	18	7	7	13	9	19	23
Number of persons in household								
One	9	7	10	9	8	8	7	10
Two	28	26	22	21	31	24	26	32
Three or four	42	44	54	46	46	44	46	38
Five or more	21	23	14	24	16	24	21	20
Employment status of head and spouse								
Only household head employed	57	57	56	68	62	60	56	66
Both head and spouse employed	32	30	39	26	27	34	35	19
Neither employed	10	11	4	5	9	4	6	13
Family income (1972)								
Under $10,000	12	12	16	14	6	6	16	5
$10,000–$14,999	22	26	21	14	19	15	26	15
$15,000–$24,999	47	45	39	40	52	62	45	45
$25,000 or more	19	17	24	32	23	17	14	36
Dwelling unit type[b]								
Single family detached	70	77	48	31	64	86	62	65
Townhouse/rowhouse/ duplex	12	7	20	28	25	7	33	21
Apartment	18	16	32	42	12	7	5	13

[a]Percentage distributions in this and succeeding tables may not add to 100 because of rounding.   [b]Classified by interviewers.

Table 1–2.   continued

	Nonfederally Assisted New Communities (cont'd)							Federally Assisted New Communities	
	Elk Grove Village	Foster City	Laguna Niguel	Lake Havasu City	Sharps-town	Forest Park	North Palm Beach	Jonathan	Park Forest South
Age of household head									
Under 40	53	52	38	31	61	62	25	84	74
40–54	40	38	33	29	28	31	31	11	20
55 or older	7	10	29	40	12	8	45	5	7
Number of persons in household									
One	7	11	7	7	18	5	11	11	5
Two	21	25	37	43	26	17	41	24	27
Three or four	43	45	36	33	41	47	33	46	44
Five or more	30	19	21	18	16	32	14	20	24
Employment status of head and spouse									
Only household head employed	57	61	53	42	59	58	41	58	52
Both head and spouse employed	40	36	26	31	32	38	32	34	42
Neither employed	3	3	21	23	7	4	28	5	5
Family income (1972)									
Under $10,000	8	9	6	33	22	13	16	40	12
$10,000–$14,999	25	16	25	36	23	35	20	25	26
$15,000–$24,999	55	51	48	24	40	45	42	29	50
$24,000 or more	12	24	21	7	16	8	22	6	12
Dwelling unit type[b]									
Single-family detached	83	62	86	72	62	88	57	46	49
Townhouse/rowhouse/ duplex	2	13	12	24	10	5	1	29	14
Apartment	15	26	2	4	28	7	43	26	37

development. Comprehensively planned communities were expected to help organize suburban growth and reduce, at least in the long term, the costs of land development and servicing. It was hoped that they would be pioneers for experimentation and innovation in everything from social services to waste treatment. They were expected to be profitable to their investors, although the investments obviously had to be regarded as long-term commitments. They were also expected to provide better environments for residents than were usually found in traditional suburban developments. This book and the project of which it is a part are a response to this expectation—attempts to determine whether new communities have been more able to provide their residents with a better quality of life than conventional communities.

This assessment was structured to allow comparisons across a sample of new communities and between new communities and conventional communities. In addition, a principle underlying this volume is that one of the best means of evaluating the livability of residential environments is to ask the residents to provide ratings on a wide variety of bases. Our attempt to compile a series of "indicators of the quality of life" has been eclectic, ranging from global questions about life satisfaction to ratings of the maintenance levels of neighborhoods. Beyond highlighting differences between the responses of new and conventional community residents to the battery of rating questions, we pursued a series of multivariate analyses to identify the main determinants of new community residents' satisfaction with their dwellings, neighborhoods, communities, and lives as a whole. One aim of the analyses was to suggest which factors in the environment might be changed by designers to increase levels of resident satisfaction.

Because the data on which this report is based are largely derived from resident perceptions of their communities, they represent only one dimension of assessment. We have not, for example, addressed the issues of the economic viability of such communities (from either a public or a private perspective), their success in encouraging innovation, or their role in a national growth policy. Important as each of these bases for evaluation may be, much of the appeal of new communities has been based on their promise of providing a better quality of life for their residents. It is toward that issue that this study is directed.

Global Measures of the Quality of Life

The first substantive question in the household interview asked respondents to indicate what they thought the quality of their lives depended upon. The most frequently mentioned factor in both new and conventional communities was economic security (cited by 34 percent of the new community respondents), followed by family life, personal strengths (like honesty), and friendship. The quality of the environment was the fifth most frequently mentioned (19 percent) but was not significantly more frequent among new community residents than among people living in conventional communities.

In reply to a question about the effect of moving to their present community, 67 percent of the new community residents reported that the move had improved the quality of their lives, but so did virtually the same percentage of conventional community residents (66 percent). Improvement was reported most often in Elk Grove Village (76 percent) and least often in Sharpstown (58 percent), but there were no significant differences between new communities and comparison communities.

A second global quality of life measure asked respondents to rate satisfaction with their own lives. The proportion of residents who said that they were completely satisfied with their lives was identical in both new and conventional communities, 31 percent. In the new communities, complete satisfaction was reported most often in Foster City (41 percent) and least frequently in Reston (20 percent). In only one instance—the comparison of Foster City with its paired community, West San Mateo—were new community residents significantly more likely to report complete life satisfaction than residents in a paired conventional community.

Multivariate analyses of life satisfaction tended to confirm the findings of previous national studies and the implications of the results just reviewed: aspects of the residential environment (including whether or not an area is planned) have only a limited impact on overall life satisfaction. The most important predictors of the ten life domains studied proved to be satisfactions with one's (1) standard of living, $r = .44$; (2) use of leisure time, $r = .43$; and (3) family life, $r = .42$. The environmental variables entered the multivariate analysis in seventh (dwelling unit), ninth (neighborhood), and tenth (community) place. Given the limited relationship of these measures of environmental satisfaction to the life satisfaction item, the absence of differences between new and conventional community residents on the global measure is less surprising. On the whole, other aspects of life are more important to new community residents, and in retrospect, the hope that new communities would produce a more rewarding life (as measured by these global items) appear to have been both naive and overly optimistic.

The Community

The principal casualties of the inability of new communities to produce new levels of human experience and life satisfaction have probably been those who believed in their utopian promise. A number of developers, policy makers, and researchers, however, would accept the limited contribution of the residential environment to an individual's happiness and life satisfaction and expect rather that the basic virtues of community planning would be reflected primarily in responses to questions about the community and residential environment. To a large extent, our findings affirm this expectation.

For each of three questions focusing on satisfaction with the residential community, new community residents were significantly more favorable than conventional community residents. People living in a new community were more likely to rate it "excellent" (49 percent to 42 percent), to recommend it as a "particularly good" place to move to (81 percent to 74 percent), and to think that it would be a "better place to live" in five years (37 percent to 33 percent). The communities with the highest proportions of "excellent" ratings were Westlake Village (75 percent) and Laguna Niguel (61 percent), but only 21 percent of Park Forest South's residents rated that community excellent.

Residents were also asked to rate various components of their communities, and new community residents provided significantly higher evaluations of recreation facilities, health and medical care facilities, transportation, and their immediate neighborhoods. Extensive inventories of community facilities also indicated that on the average new communities provided a larger variety of recreation and health care facilities. Respondent ratings of other aspects of the communities—schools, for example—showed no significant differences between the nonfederally assisted new communities and the paired communities.

A multivariate analysis to determine which factors contributed most to new community residents' reports of satisfaction with their community indicated that the key factor, by a wide margin, was satisfaction with one's immediate neighborhood. Slightly less important were ratings of the dwelling and of recreation facilities. It is of interest that neither a series of nine personal characteristics nor a group of inventories of eight types of community facilities and services was able to explain much of the variation in satisfaction responses in the multivariate analyses, particularly in comparison with the residents' ratings of community components.

Respondents were asked not only to rate their present community's amenities, at several points in the household interview, but also to compare nineteen attributes of their present situation with those of their former communities. New community residents were significantly more likely to rate their present communities better for overall planning, recreation, health care, ease of getting around, shopping, and opportunities for participation in community life. Conventional community residents were significantly more likely to say that the costs of dwellings were lower and their construction better than in their former communities.

Finally, a distillation of responses from several open-ended questions in the household interview reaffirmed residents' interest in recreation facilities—as an attraction of the communities, a reason for satisfaction with them, and a means of further improving them —and in environmental quality in the community as a whole. The environmental quality issue often took the form of concern about increasing densities, crowding, and growth, which suggests that the necessary relationship between growth and the provision of a full range of amenities has to be communicated to residents at an early point in development to mitigate, if not eliminate, fears about the changes that accompany growth.

Despite concerns about continuing development in some of the communities, most responses to community-related questions indicate that new communities have provided more satisfying environments on several bases than traditionally developed communities. (In all, roughly half the community-related items covered in this book led to significantly higher ratings in new communities.) It is appropriate to note, however, that aggregating the data for all the nonfederally assisted new communities conceals a considerable amount of variation among communities. There was, in fact, more variation across the new communities than between the new and conventional community samples on many of the variables. Nevertheless, the aggregated findings suggest that new community development, on the average, does offer possibilities for more rewarding community environments than are likely to occur in conventionally developed communities.

The Neighborhood and the Dwelling

Analyses of community satisfaction responses indicated that residents' ratings of their immediate neighborhoods and dwellings were primary determinants of satisfaction with the larger community. As has been noted, significantly more new community residents rated their immediate neighborhoods highly.[n] The new community with

[n] Neighborhood was defined for respondents as "the area near here you can see from your front door—that is, the five or six homes nearest to yours around here."

the highest percentage of respondents giving a top score on the neighborhood satisfaction scale was Westlake Village (57 percent) with Laguna Niguel (42 percent) coming next. Three communities shared the lowest proportion (21 percent) of high scores: Park Forest, Sharpstown, and Park Forest South. In addition to the overall ratings, nonfederally assisted new community residents were more likely to say that their neighborhoods were attractive, convenient, and well maintained.

Multivariate analyses of neighborhood satisfaction responses showed that the maintenance level of the immediate area was clearly the dominant determinant of the neighborhood evaluations. Maintenance ratings alone, in fact, explained over half of the variance in a series of ratings of eight neighborhood attributes, although convenience, privacy, and friendliness also added appreciably to the amount of variation explained.

Although tabulations of neighborhood and community factors generated a number of significant differences between the new and conventional community resident responses, comparisons involving dwellings produced a consistent similarity. Among the nonfederally assisted new community respondents, 28 percent were completely satisfied with their housing, but the figure in the paired communities was 29 percent. The highest levels of satisfaction appeared in Laguna Niguel, Foster City, and Westlake Village, where just over half the residents reported complete satisfaction with their dwellings. Satisfaction was lowest in Park Forest, the community with the oldest housing stock, where only 22 percent indicated a comparable level of satisfaction.

Neither age of dwelling unit nor other objective factors proved to be as strongly tied to satisfaction with dwellings as feelings about privacy and space—both indoor and outdoor—afforded by dwellings and their immediate yards and neighborhoods. Also important for housing satisfaction, particularly in higher density areas, were the ratings of how well the neighborhood was maintained.

Probably the most striking findings in regard to dwelling and neighborhood were those relating density to satisfaction. Owners were as satisfied with their housing and their neighborhoods when they lived in apartments or townhouses as when they lived in single-family, detached houses. Renters, on the other hand, associated increasing density with lower levels of satisfaction. The fact that higher density did not decrease owners' satisfaction, however, clearly implies that residential densities can be increased without causing widespread dissatisfaction as long as such increases can be balanced with resident concerns about community growth and as long as they provide appreciable opportunities for ownership.

Resident Groups

Analyses of quality-of-life indicators in this volume conclude with parallel tabulations for nineteen categories of residents in the nonfederally assisted new and conventional community samples. Findings culled from these data confirmed a lack of differences between new and conventional community residents on the global quality of life items. Responses to the two community ratings analyzed (the overall satisfaction and the "recommend as a particularly good place to move to" questions), however, revealed consistent and generally statistically significant differences showing more favorable responses in the new communities.

The most striking of the comparisons occurred among blacks and among residents living in subsidized housing. On the community satisfaction question, 34 percent of the new community black residents rated their community excellent, compared to only 7 percent of the residents of black comparison communities. On the recommendation question, 84 percent of the new community blacks thought that their community would be a particularly good place to move to, but only 37 percent so responded in the comparison communities. Among families in subsidized housing, the highest response on the community satisfaction item in excellent ratings was 32 percent in new communities but 7 percent in the conventional. On the recommendation question, 71 percent in new communities thought their community would be a particularly good place to move to, but only 24 percent in the comparison communities.

Beyond the differences between new and conventional communities, the tabulations revealed a number of contrasts within the new communities. Among the most systematic of these was a positive association between higher income and greater community and overall life satisfaction. Less consistent, however, was the finding that younger persons were more likely than older persons to report that their lives improved on moving to new communities but less likely to report complete satisfaction with their lives as a whole. A similar contrast appeared between men and women. Men were more likely to say that the move improved their life quality, but more women reported being completely satisfied with their lives.

Finally, parallel multivariate analyses for the global quality-of-life items and the community rating question for each of the resident groups showed that there was a great degree of similarity in the main predictors of satisfaction across all nineteen categories of residents. The parallels were strongest in the analyses of community satisfaction responses where the main determinant of satisfaction for each of the groups turned out to be the neighborhood maintenance rating.

Overview

A conclusion whether new communities, as a category of residential development, have been able to provide their residents with a better quality of life is clearly dependent on which indicators of life quality one wishes to emphasize. In this book, four levels of indicators have been included—those having to do with the dwelling, with the immediate neighborhood, with the community, and with overall life satisfaction. At the most circumscribed level, dwelling satisfaction, and the most diffuse level, life satisfaction, the responses of residents in new communities proved to be quite similar to those of people living in conventional communities. In the case of dwelling-related items, the absence of significant differences in satisfaction probably reflects an absence of actual differences. Our sample of paired conventional communities was chosen to maximize comparability in housing stock with the new communities and, in addition, dwellings in a new community and its nearby paired community were often built by the same (or very similar) local builders, faced with identical building regulations, to compete in the same metropolitan market.

At the level of global measures of the quality of life, previous research has shown that factors like dwelling, neighborhood, and community have only limited effects on life satisfaction. The results of this study affirm earlier findings and suggest that, whatever differences there may be between new and conventional communities, these differences are simply not as important for life satisfaction as economic security, health, job, marriage, and family life.

At the neighborhood and the community levels, differences in satisfaction between the more and less planned environments began to emerge. There were sizeable contrasts among the new communities themselves, and community components were not invariably rated more positively in new communities, but both inventories of facilities and resident ratings indicated that, on the average, recreation, health care, and transportation have been provided better for in the new communities. For some groups, most notably blacks and those living in subsidized housing, resident evaluations indicated that vastly higher levels of satisfaction were associated with living in new communities.

In sum, these findings should offer encouragement to proponents of planned residential developments. New communities have not yet fulfilled the utopian aims of some of their more ardent advocates, but this research has shown that the goal of providing a more livable environment than that found in conventional developments has been attained in a number of new communities. The successes of these comprehensively planned environments make clear that this form of residential development, when adapted to local economic conditions, offers considerable promise for continuing improvement in the quality of residential communities.

Chapter 2

Determinants of the Quality
of Life: The Residents' View

Polls and household surveys have posed a variety of questions asking people to define what they feel their happiness and life as a whole most depend upon.[a] Although occasionally influenced by the phrasing of the questions, several types of factors are mentioned with regularity. These include satisfaction with the interpersonal aspects of life—family, marriage, and friendships—and with those of a less social nature—health, employment, and economic security. In the context of this book, it is of interest that aspects of residential communities and environmental quality (other than occasional references to housing) are virtually absent from most lists of responses.

Recent studies of overall life quality, on the other hand, have depended more on the ingenuity and exhaustive efforts of researchers to define dimensions of the quality of life and have tended to include environment-oriented items in their conceptual models and survey instruments.[b] Although this study included a carefully designed set of questions to measure levels of satisfaction with specific life domains,[c] we also wanted to give the respondents an opportunity to

[a]For a collection of items and results, see Hazel F. Erskine (1973, pp. 132–145). Data are cited from surveys from 1946 through 1971.

[b]For example, see Andrews and Withey (1974). Their list of "items used to assess affective responses to specific concerns" includes 133 entries. About one-tenth of the items could be interpreted as having a community services or facilities, residential, or environmental orientation. See also Campbell (1976), especially Chapters 3 and 7, and James R. Murray (1974).

[c]The ten domains included were satisfaction with standard of living, leisure activities, marriage, family life, job, health, housework, dwelling unit, immediate neighborhood, and community. Analyses of these items in relation to a measure of overall life satisfaction appear in Chapter 5.

tell us what they perceived to be the main components of the quality of life. Therefore, at the outset of the household interviews we asked residents to define in their own words what the quality of their lives depended upon. We then asked if moving to their present community had altered the quality of their lives. This possibility was pursued in comparisons rating nineteen of the attributes of the respondents' present and former communities.

WHAT "QUALITY OF LIFE" MEANS TO RESPONDENTS

Although open-ended questions asking people to name the key factors in their evaluation of their life situation have seldom elicited as many environment-oriented responses as responses centering on health, family, and financial security, we thought that if any population were likely to respond to community planning variables, it would be persons who decided to move into a planned new community. Therefore, although the primary rationale for collecting open-ended responses about the "quality of life" was to see which life domains were mentioned most frequently, we also wanted to see if new community residents actually were more sensitive to environmental factors than people living in conventional communities. The first substantive question in the household interview (before any other issues had been raised, in other words) was

> There's quite a bit of talk these days about the overall "quality" of people's lives. What does the phrase "quality of life" mean to you—that is, what would you say are the main things the overall "quality" of your own life depends on?

Responses to the question for new and conventional community residents are summarized in Table 2—1. They show that residents in both environments mentioned virtually the same factors as contributors to the quality of life. Most frequently mentioned in the new communities was economic security (34 percent; 32 percent in the conventional communities). After that, family life, personal strengths (like honesty, courage, intelligence), and friendship were mentioned by over 20 percent of the respondents. Living in an attractive physical environment was the fifth most frequent reason in both types of communities; mentioned by 19 percent and 16 percent, respectively. The adequacy of housing ranked twelfth in both settings and was noted in about 10 percent of the interviews.

Overall, there is little indication that the new and conventional

Table 2—1. Components of the Quality of Life: Responses to an Open-Ended Question[a] *(percentage of respondents)* [b]

| | Nonfederally Assisted Communities | |
| | --- | --- |
Components Mentioned	Thirteen New Communities	Thirteen Conventional Communities
Economic security	34	32
Family life	27	30
Personal strengths and values	23	23
Social relationships (other than family)	21*	16
Physical environment	19	16
Contentment, well-being, happiness	17	16
Job satisfaction	16	19
Leisure and recreation activities	16	13
Health	15	14
Religious values	12	11
Being a good parent	11	12
Housing	9	10
Number of cases	2596	1298

*Difference between new communities and conventional communities is statistically significant at 0.05 level of confidence.

[a] The question was "There's quite a bit of talk these days about the overall "quality"? of people's lives. What does the phrase "quality of life" mean to you—that is, what would you say are the main things the overall "quality" of your own life depends on?"

[b] Percentages in each column will add to over 100 percent because multiple mentions were coded.

community residents in this study held views of the quality of life very different from those of people in previous national studies. More interesting, perhaps, is the finding that residents of less planned conventional communities were almost as likely to note the importance of the environment as were respondents in the new communities.

THE EFFECT OF MOVING TO THE PRESENT COMMUNITY: THE QUALITY OF LIFE

Following the open-ended question on quality of life, respondents were asked:

Compared to the last community you lived in, would you say that for you yourself, moving to this community has improved the quality of your life, has made it worse, or hasn't made much difference?

Virtually the same proportion of new and conventional community respondents said their life had been improved by the move (67 percent and 66 percent, respectively, See Table 2-2). Among the new communities, the favorable responses were most frequent in Elk Grove Village, Westlake Village, and Jonathan, where three of four residents said their lives had improved. At the lower end of the scale, fewer than 60 percent—but still a majority—of the respondents in Forest Park and Sharpstown were as impressed with the consequences of their moves to those communities.

None of the comparisons of new communities with the conventional communities showed differences that quite attained statistical significance. The new communities that fared best on this basis, however, with about 10 percent more "improved" responses than were received in the paired communities, were Columbia and Reston. Respondents in conventional communities were more positive about their communities by the same margin in Kingman, Arizona (paired with Lake Havasu City) and Lansing, Illinois (paired with Park Forest). The highest percentage (81 percent) of people who felt their lives had improved lived in the Agoura–Malibu area that was paired with Westlake Village, California. Evidence of disenchantment with the present community was infrequent in all of the study communities. Among the new community residents, no more than 10 percent (in Lake Havasu City and Park Forest South) reported that the quality of their lives was now worse than in their former community.

We should note that the new communities in this table (and subsequent similar tables) have been listed in the order of their average rank on a continuum of new community planning which is, in essence, a summary social indicator index in its own right. Based on the extent of their adherence to nineteen new-community planning concepts, Columbia, Reston, and Irvine scored highest on this index; North Palm Beach, Forest Park, and Sharpstown scored lowest.[d]

---

[d] The following indicators of adherence to the new community concept were used: (1) architectural controls; (2) bus service; (3) commercial facilities grouped in centers; (4) communications media; (5) ease of access to facilities; (6) environmental protection; (7) housing choice; (8) landscaping of public and common areas; (9) master plan; (10) open space preservation; (11) pedestrian–vehicular separation; (12) self-government; (13) self-sufficiency; (14) income mix; (15) racial mix; (16) underground utilities; (17) unified development by single entrepreneur; (18) preservation or creation of water bodies; and (19) variety of land uses. See Burby, Weiss *et al.* (1976, pp. 41-44, 96-98) for a discussion of the continuum's development.

Table 2–2. Improving the Quality of Life on Moving to the Present Community *(percentage of respondents)*

Community	New Communities			Conventional Communities		
	Percent Saying Quality of Life Is			*Percent Saying Quality of Life Is*		
	Improved	*Same*	*Worse*	*Improved*	*Same*	*Worse*
Nonfederally assisted						
Thirteen new communities	67	28	6			
Thirteen conventional communities				66	27	7
Columbia	67	25	8	58	36	7
Reston	66	26	9	55	34	11
Irvine	71	25	4	63	32	5
Valencia	70	24	6	67	27	6
Park Forest	62	33	6	74	18	8
Westlake Village	75	18	7	81	17	3
Elk Grove Village	76	20	4	72	24	5
Foster City	64	31	5	64	25	11
Laguna Niguel	69	26	5	71	24	5
Lake Havasu City	64	26	10	75	23	2
Sharpstown	58	35	8	62	32	6
Forest Park	59	35	7	63	27	10
North Palm Beach	61	34	5	53	39	8
Federally assisted						
Jonathan	75	24	1	67	27	6
Park Forest South	64	26	10	59	31	11

THE EFFECT OF MOVING TO THE
PRESENT COMMUNITY: NINETEEN
COMMUNITY ATTRIBUTES

In contrast to the broad evaluations of quality of life differences between present and former communities of residence stands a series of comparative ratings of nineteen community attributes summarized in the next four tables. The attributes ranged from the layout and space of dwellings to schools, climate, and the overall planning that went into the community.

For eleven of the nineteen attributes, the differences in ratings between new and conventional communities on these items were literally—and statistically—insignificant. Differences that did emerge generally indicated more favorable ratings in new community areas, the largest, predictably, showed that more new community residents reported that their present communities were better planned (75 percent versus 53 percent, See Table 2−3). Other sizeable contrasts that showed more positive ratings in new communities include the ratings of recreation facilities, ease of getting around in the community, and opportunities for participation in community life. All rated better about 10 percent more often in new communities. By the same margin, conventional community residents were more likely to rate the cost of buying or renting better than in their previous community.

Ratings for each of the nineteen attributes for the fifteen new communities are presented in Table 2−4. The table's columns provide a profile of each community's relative strengths and weaknesses across the nineteen characteristics. The rows, on the other hand, reveal which communities had the most (and least) frequent ratings of "better" in regard to specific community attributes.

In eight of the thirteen nonfederally assisted new communities, the attribute most likely to receive a "better" evaluation was the overall planning of the community, and the attribute least likely to receive "better" evaluations (in ten of thirteen new communities) was the community's cost of living. Residents appeared hard pressed to report that they were better off on that basis whether they lived in new or in conventional communities.

The new communities that fared best are Westlake Village, Elk Grove Village, and Columbia. Westlake residents were the most likely to indicate that they had found better neighborhood appearance, overall community planning, safety from crime, and ease of getting around in the community. Elk Grove Village residents gave the highest proportion of favorable ratings to the layout and space and to the

Table 2–3. Summary of Comparisons of Present Community with Previous Community *(percentage of respondents rating present community better)*

Community Characteristics	Nonfederally Assisted Communities	
	Thirteen New Communities	Thirteen Conventional Communities
Housing		
Construction of the dwelling	45	50*
Cost of buying or renting	37	47*
Layout and space	69	71
Community facilities		
Health and medical facilities	25*	20
Public schools	46	45
Recreation facilities	63*	49
Shopping facilities	41*	36
Physical environment		
Appearance of neighborhood	65	62
Climate	46	46
Nearness to natural environment	61	60
Overall planning of community	75*	53
Social environment		
Good place to raise children	65	61
Participation in community life	59*	47
Safety from crime	49	48
Type of people in the neighborhood	46	42
Work, transportation, and living costs		
Ease of finding a job in community	26	26
Convenience to work	40	40
Ease of getting around community	48*	36
Cost of living in community	18	20

*Difference between new communities and conventional communities is statistically significant at 0.05 level of confidence.

cost of housing, the schools, and the ease of finding a job in the community. Columbia ratings were highest for three attributes: health care, recreation, and the community as a place to raise children.

The most extreme contrasts were found in the desert community of Lake Havasu City which received the most favorable comparative ratings on three bases (climate, nearness to the natural environment, and convenience to work) but was at the bottom of the list on seven other attributes, including health care, schools, shopping, and the

Table 2–4. Comparison of Present Community with Previous Community *(percentage of respondents rating present community better)*

Community Characteristics	Nonfederally Assisted New Communities						
	Columbia	Reston	Irvine	Valencia	Park Forest	Westlake Village	Elk Grove Village
Housing							
Construction of the dwelling	27	43	44	39	40	43	58
Cost of buying or renting	32	21	35	33	48	35	49
Layout and space	69	65	77	72	64	67	84
Community facilities							
Health and medical facilities	47	25	18	13	34	29	40
Public schools	66	53	40	59	54	38	74
Recreation facilities	85	69	70	66	63	77	62
Shopping facilities	55	40	27	19	68	28	52
Physical environment							
Appearance of neighborhood	66	65	71	73	50	79	74
Climate	22	20	64	65	13	77	14
Nearness to natural environment	64	67	73	72	55	76	72
Overall planning of community	87	91	79	84	81	91	81
Social environment							
Good place to raise children	77	62	70	76	62	73	75
Participation in community life	75	71	75	66	67	62	67
Safety from crime	36	35	46	49	46	64	57
Type of people in the neighborhood	54	46	48	56	40	51	49
Work, transportation, and living costs							
Ease of finding a job in community	35	37	26	16	30	19	45
Convenience to work	45	30	38	36	32	35	47
Ease of getting around community	61	53	40	59	52	62	37
Cost of living in community	13	9	13	11	18	18	24

Table 2−4. continued

Community Characteristics	Nonfederally Assisted New Communities (cont'd)						Federally Assisted New Communities	
	Foster City	Laguna Niguel	Lake Havasu City	Sharps-town	Forest Park	North Palm Beach	Jonathan	Park Forest South
Housing								
Construction of the dwelling	38	43	35	45	60	45	48	49
Cost of buying or renting	43	38	13	46	39	29	46	28
Layout and space	61	75	49	61	76	62	69	71
Community facilities								
Health and medical facilities	16	11	5	45	21	25	36	11
Public schools	26	37	25	41	57	26	33	34
Recreation facilities	49	64	64	46	58	63	82	49
Shopping facilities	32	23	6	68	57	49	22	18
Physical environment								
Appearance of neighborhood	60	65	41	55	61	63	72	56
Climate	50	75	82	23	22	56	10	12
Nearness to natural environment	42	74	77	26	59	51	82	59
Overall planning of community	71	65	62	55	71	69	84	70
Social environment								
Good place to raise children	53	63	67	49	68	51	81	60
Participation in community life	51	52	51	36	64	51	73	72
Safety from crime	38	58	56	27	51	48	64	42
Type of people in the neighborhood	34	44	36	42	45	44	53	48
Work, transportation, and living costs								
Ease of finding a job in community	18	11	16	41	31	19	23	15
Convenience to work	49	25	58	39	46	45	33	27
Ease of getting around community	38	35	61	46	45	50	59	22
Cost of living in community	19	15	7	28	20	18	25	12

cost of living. One other community, Sharpstown, ranked last in comparative ratings on six attributes, including recreation facilities and overall community planning.

Compared to the nonfederally assisted communities, Jonathan and Park Forest South did noticeably well in some areas and poorly in others. Jonathan clearly fared much the better. The attributes to which Jonathan residents were particularly likely to give "better" ratings were nearness to the natural environment (82 percent "better" evaluations versus 61 percent for the thirteen nonfederally assisted communities), recreation facilities (82 percent versus 63 percent), and the community as a place to raise children (81 percent versus 65 percent).

Ratings of shopping facilities, schools, and climate in both federally assisted communities were lower than the thirteen-community norms. In addition, Park Forest South ratings of health care, convenience to work, and ease of getting around the community were also low relative to the nonfederally assisted communities. Possibly reflecting the newness and the limited populations of these two communities, their residents were more likely to report better opportunities for participation in community life.

Comparisons between each new community and its paired less planned community revealed a somewhat different pattern of overall community excellence. Data summarizing these comparisons for all fifteen new communities are shown in Tables 2−5 and 2−6. As noted in Chapter 1, each paired conventional community provides housing comparable to that found in the new community and represents a plausible alternative to someone moving into an area. A comparison of a new community with its paired community, in other words, provides a useful measure of its attributes in terms of the housing market in which it operates.

From the rows showing significant differences in Table 2−5, the item most often rated better by new community residents (for thirteen new communities) was the overall planning of the community. Second was recreation (ten times) and third, opportunities for participation in community life (eight times). Of the five broad categories in the table, significant differences were preponderantly in favor of new communities in four cases. In the other area, housing, thirteen of sixteen significant differences indicated more positive ratings in conventional communities.

When the number of attributes on which a paired conventional community was rated significantly more favorably is subtracted from the number of attributes on which the paired new community was rated more favorably (see Table 2−6), the fifteen new communities fall into three rough groupings. Five new communities outshone their paired communities by a net margin of seven to nine. The leading community was Reston (9), followed by Columbia (8), Irvine (8), Jonathan (8), and North Palm Beach (7).

The second group included seven communities with net scores between three and zero. These were, in order, Lake Havasu City, Elk Grove Village, Foster City, Sharpstown, Valencia, Park Forest South, and Laguna Niguel. Finally, three new communities came out with negative net scores: Westlake Village, Park Forest, and Forest Park.

To recapitulate, the thirteen nonfederally assisted communities fared significantly better on six of the nineteen attributes and the conventional communities fared significantly better on two. The areas in which new communities did best were the planning that went into the community, recreation facilities, opportunities for participation in community life, ease of getting around the community, health and medical facilities, and shopping facilities. Conventional communities were more likely to get better ratings for the cost and the construction of housing.

Some of the new communities (Columbia, Reston, and Irvine) were rated quite well both in relation to other new communities and to their paired conventional communities. Westlake Village, on the other hand, received fewer positive ratings on these items than its paired community, Agoura–Malibu (minus 2), even though it fared well in relation to the other fourteen new communties.

Multivariate Analysis of Improvement in the Quality of Life

Besides identifying differences across communities in ratings of the nineteen community attributes in comparison with respondents' former communities, an additional important issue posed by the ratings is which of these factors were most strongly related to residents' overall assessments that the quality of their lives had (or had not) improved after the move to their present communities. The results of a regression analysis addressing this question are shown in Table 2–7.[e]

[e]When there are a number of (independent) variables related to, or believed to be related to, the (dependent) variable whose variation one wants to explain, one technique of cumulating the net effect of variation in the independent variables on the dependent variable is to use stepwise multiple regression analysis. The technique is useful when some of the independent variables are related to one another (e.g., "family income" and "single-family residence") and operates by selecting, at the first step, the independent variable which explains the most variation in the dependent variable; at the second step, the independent variable which explains the greatest amount of the remaining unexplained variation in the dependent variable; and so on. In Table 2–7, the 27 independent variables

Table 2−5. Significant Differences between New and Conventional Communities[a]

Community Characteristics	Nonfederally Assisted New Communities					
	Columbia	Reston	Irvine	Valencia	Park Forest	Westlake Village
Housing						
Construction of the dwelling	−	+	0	−	−	−
Cost of buying or renting	−	0	0	0	0	−
Layout and space	0	0	0	−	−	−
Community facilities						
Health and medical facilities	+	0	0	0	0	+
Public schools	+	+	0	0	0	−
Recreation facilities	+	+	+	+	+	+
Shopping facilities	+	0	0	0	+	0
Physical environment						
Appearance of neighborhood	0	+	0	0	−	0
Climate	+	0	0	0	0	0
Nearness to natural environment	0	+	+	0	0	−
Overall planning of community	+	+	+	+	+	+
Social environment						
Good place to raise children	+	+	+	0	−	−
Participation in community life	+	+	+	0	0	0
Safety from crime	0	0	+	0	−	0
Type of people in neighborhood	+	0	0	0	−	0
Work, transportation, and living costs						
Ease of finding a job in community	0	0	+	0	0	+
Convenience to work	0	0	+	0	0	0
Ease of getting around community	+	+	0	+	+	+
Cost of living in community	0	0	0	0	0	−

+ New community rated "better" significantly more often than conventional community.

0 No significant difference between new community and conventional community.

− Conventional community rated "better" significantly more often than new community.

Table 2−5. continued

	Nonfederally Assisted New Communities (cont'd)								Federally Assisted New Communities	
	Elk Grove Village	*Foster City*	*Laguna Niguel*	*Lake Havasu City*	*Sharpstown*	*Forest Park*	*North Palm Beach*	*Thirteen New Communities*	*Jonathan*	*Park Forest South*
	0	−	0	−	0	0	0	−	0	+
	0	0	0	−	0	0	0	−	0	−
	0	0	0	0	0	0	+	0	0	0
	+	0	−	−	0	0	+	+	+	0
	+	0	0	0	0	0	+	0	0	0
	0	+	0	+	0	−	+	+	+	0
	0	0	0	−	+	0	0	+	0	−
	0	0	0	0	0	0	+	0	+	0
	0	0	0	+	0	0	−	0	0	0
	0	0	0	+	0	0	0	0	+	0
	0	+	+	+	0	+	+	+	+	+
	0	0	0	+	0	0	0	0	+	0
	0	+	+	0	0	0	+	+	+	+
	0	0	0	+	0	0	0	0	+	0
	0	0	0	0	0	0	+	0	0	+
	0	0	0	0	0	−	0	0	0	0
	+	0	−	+	0	−	0	0	−	−
	0	0	0	0	+	0	0	+	0	0
	0	0	0	0	0	0	0	0	+	0

[a] Depending on the number of interviews and the magnitude of the percentages, new and conventional communities had to differ from 8.2 percent to 14.1 percent on an item to be significantly different at the 0.05 level.

Table 2–6. Summary of Significant New Community versus Conventional Community Differences *(derived from Table 2–5)*

New Community	New Community Rated Better Significantly More Often	Conventional Community Rated Better Significantly More Often	Net Rating (Column 1 minus Column 2)
Nonfederally assisted			
Thirteen new communities	6	2	4
Columbia	10	2	8
Reston	9	0	9
Irvine	8	0	8
Valencia	3	2	1
Park Forest	4	6	−2
Westlake Village	5	7	−2
Elk Grove Village	3	0	3
Foster City	3	1	2
Laguna Niguel	2	2	0
Lake Havasu City	7	4	3
Sharpstown	2	0	2
Forest Park	1	3	−2
North Palm Beach	8	1	7
Federally assisted			
Jonathan	9	1	8
Park Forest South	4	3	1

Table 2–7.   Multivariate Analysis of Factors Influencing Resident Ratings of Improvement in Quality of Life[a]

Variables	Simple Correlation Coefficient	Beta	Cumulative R^2	F-Value
I. *Nine socioeconomic and demographic variables[b]*	—	—	.03	7.9
II. *Comparisons with previous community[c]*				
Community as place to raise children	.39	.16	.16	55.8
People living in neighborhood	.37	.17	.22	71.9
Recreation facilities	.28	.10	.24	26.3
Neighborhood appearance	.33	.08	.26	16.1
Construction of home	.22	.05	.26	6.6
Climate	.15	.07	.27	13.8
Convenience to work	.10	.05	.27	6.2
Health care and medical services	.11	.05	.28	5.1
Opportunities for participation in community	.30	.05	.28	5.0
Layout and space of home	.27	.04	.28	4.3

[a]Thirteen nonfederally assisted new communities.

[b]These include respondent's age, sex, education, marital status, family income, dwelling unit value, tenure, length of residence, and the number of children in the household.

[c]These include the comparisons listed in Table 2–5, with the exception of overall planning, which was dropped so as not to detract from the effect of specific facility ratings. Only variables with a significant F-value are included in the table.

The analysis was run in two stepwise stages, the first (not detailed in the table) focused on the impact of nine socioeconomic and demographic variables on the quality of life responses. (See Table 2−7, note *b*.) As has been found in other quality of life analyses (e.g., Marans and Rodgers 1972, Andrews and Withey 1974, and Campbell, Converse, and Rodgers 1976), these personal characteristics were of limited importance and together could explain only 3 percent (R^2 = .03) of the variation in the "did your quality of life improve" item.

In the second stage of the multivariate analysis, the comparative community ratings were added to the equation. The variance explained increased to R^2 = .28. We have included only the comparisons that were significantly related to improving the quality of life in Table 2−7.[f] The ratings most associated with respondent reports of an improved quality of life were those of the community as a place to raise children and of the type of people living in the neighborhood. Recreation facilities and neighborhood appearance were also important, but less so.

Parallel regression analyses that excluded two of the comparative ratings as predictors were also run. These variables—climate and the community as a place to raise children—were deleted because climate is a factor individual developers can do little about and because of the relatively diffuse nature of the "place to raise children" variable. The truncated equation still led to R^2 = .26, almost as high as the result when the two variables were included. With these variables

---

together accounted for 28 percent of the variation in the "improving the quality of life" question in nonfederally assisted new communities.

Beta is the standardized regression coefficient and indicates that for every change of one standard deviation in the independent variable there is a corresponding change of *beta* times the standard deviation of the dependent variable in the dependent variable. The F-values are indications of statistical significance. An F-value of 4.0 or greater indicates a significant relationship in the multivariate context of the 0.05 level or better.

A simple correlation coefficient, *r*, is a measure of the linear association between two variables. Where there is a perfect relationship between variation in one variable and variation in the other variable (for example, the volume of water with the weight of water), the correlation between those variables is 1.00. If there is no relationship between variables (for example, hair color with intelligence), one would expect the correlation between those variables to be 0.00.

The square of a correlation coefficient indicates the proportion of variation in one variable that can be explained by its relation to the other variable. Thus, if two variables are correlated at r = .50, it is possible to say that $(.50)^2$ = .25 or 25 percent of the variance in one variable is explained by variation in the other.

[f] Because of a probe of the comparison of "overall planning" in the present and former community indicated that respondents often were basing their ratings for that item on community facilities, the "overall planning" item was not included in the regressions so that it would not detract from the explanatory power of the specific facility ratings. The correlation of the comparative ratings of overall community planning with improvement in the quality of life was r = .29.

deleted, the type of people in the neighborhood became the most important single variable, followed by recreation facilities. The comparison of recreational facilities in the present and previous community explained roughly three times as much variance in the truncated equation, a finding which suggests that ratings of the perceived improvements in recreation facilities may be providing a partial substitute for the rating of the community as a place to raise children in the regression equation.[g]

SUMMARY

Ratings of improvement in the overall quality of people's lives after moving to a community showed little difference between new and conventional community residents. Given the relative importance of nonenvironmental factors in residents' definitions of the components of life quality, this finding is explicable, if somewhat surprising.

Analyses focusing on specific community attributes, on the other hand, revealed a number of significant contrasts between new and conventional communities, as well as a number of differences in ratings across the new communities in the sample. In comparison with other new communities, Westlake Village and Elk Grove Village fared particularly well. Their residents were the most likely to report improvements .or eight of nineteen community attributes (four in each community) when they made comparisons with their previous communities.

When responses from each new community and its paired conventional community were compared, a considerably different ranking of new communities appeared, Reston, Columbia, Irvine, Jonathan, and North Palm Beach doing best on this basis, and Westlake Village, Park Forest, and Forest Park doing worst.

Finally, a multivariate analysis to determine the best predictors of improvement in the quality of life indicated that the persons most likely to report that the quality of their lives had improved on moving to a new community rated the new community better as a place to raise children, for the types of people in the neighborhood, for recreation facilities, and for neighborhood appearance. Ratings of

[g]The correlation of the comparative ratings of recreation facilities and of ᴢ place to raise children was a modest $r = .27$. A separate correlation analysis, however, showed that the ratings most highly related to the evaluation of the present community as a better place to raise children compared to the previous community were the ratings of nearness to nature and of safety (both $r = .42$), followed by neighborhood appearance and the type of people in the neighborhood (both $r = .37$).

opportunities to participate in community life and of the layout and space of the home were also associated with the overall assessment of changes in life quality as a result of moving. A number of personal characteristics explained little of the variation in responses to the quality-of-life improvement item.

✳ *Chapter 3*

Evaluating the Community

The notion of a new community depends less on the newness of construction than on the idea that such development is significantly different from—and better than—
development in conventional communities. In Chapter 2, we found
that while residents in both new and conventional communities gave
similar responses to broad questions about the quality of their lives,
some differences between the more and less planned environments
began to emerge when specific attributes of the communities were
rated. In this and in Chapter 4, we will try to delineate further the
ways in which the new and conventional communities in our sample
differ by focusing on three levels of the residential environment—the
community, the neighborhood, and the dwelling. This chapter includes data about the provision of facilities and services in the
communities studied, as well as resident assessments of community
components and of the community as a whole. Chapter 4 examines
responses to the more immediate residential setting—the neighborhood and the dwelling. An assessment of the relative importance of
satisfaction with these three levels in comparison with other life
domains is presented in Chapter 5.

SATISFACTION WITH THE COMMUNITY

Besides asking respondents to compare their present and former
communities—the strategy reported in Chapter 2—the household
interview employed a number of other questions designed to elicit
evaluations of the communities. The most explicit of these items

asked respondents to indicate their satisfaction with the community as a whole and indicate the reasons for their ratings. To try to insure that each respondent was considering the same community area, they were asked to think about an area outlined on a map that corresponded to the main boundaries of the community involved. The question used was: "I'd like to ask you how you feel now about this area as a place to live—I mean the area outlined on the map (show map). From your own personal point of view, would you rate this area as an excellent place to live, good, average, below average, or poor?"

Previous studies of American new communities using similar evaluative questions have found high levels of resident satisfaction. Rabinovitz and Lamare (1970, p. 14), for example, reported that 94.4 percent of the residents of Westlake Village were satisfied or very satisfied with their decision to move to that community, and Savitzky (1973, tables, p. 4) reported that 64 percent of the residents of Columbia were very satisfied with that community. One of the few studies to include both new and conventional communities in its design (Lansing *et al.* 1970) found that new town residents were generally more satisfied with their communities than were residents of the less planned communities. Of the residents of Reston and Columbia, 61 and 52 percent, respectively, rated their communities excellent, compared to 36 and 41 percent of the residents in the less planned areas in that study.[a]

Responses to the satisfaction question used in the present study are summarized in Table 3—1. The thirteen nonfederally assisted new communities were rated excellent by 49 percent of the respondents, significantly higher ratings than were found in the conventional communities (42 percent excellent).[b] When excellent and good ratings

[a]The Rabinovitz and Lamare (1970) and Savitzky (1973) studies included all community households in their sampling design. The Lansing *et al.* (1970) study, which used a question virtually identical to the one used in this study, excluded apartment dwellers. When the 1973 data from the present study were adjusted to exclude apartment dwellers, the percentage of excellent ratings among single-family and townhouse residents in Columbia went from 52 percent in 1969 to 47 percent in 1973. In Reston, the excellent ratings went from 61 percent to 62 percent. In Norbeck—Wheaton, a conventional community common to both studies, the number of excellent ratings rose from 41 percent in 1969 to 56 percent in 1973. None of these differences is statistically significant. If excellent and good ratings are combined for single family and townhouse dwellers, the changes become: Columbia, 92 to 88 percent; Reston, 94 to 97 percent; and Norbeck—Weaton, 85 to 92 percent.

[b]These percentages can be compared with the results of a national cross-section surveyed in 1971, in which 38 percent reported that they were completely satisfied with their community as a place to live (Marans and Rodgers 1972, p. 27).

Table 3-1. Satisfaction with the Community as a Place to Live *(percent of respondents)*

Communities	New Communities				Conventional Communities			
	Excellent	Good	Average	Below Average, Poor	Excellent	Good	Average	Below Average, Poor
Nonfederally assisted								
Thirteen New Communities	49	41	9	2				
Thirteen Conventional Communities					42	45	12	2
Columbia	40	42	14	4	44	44	9	3
Reston	55	39	5	2	38	55	5	2
Irvine	52	43	5	0	26	57	15	2
Valencia	57	37	6	1	32	48	18	2
Park Forest	28	55	14	3	27	60	12	1
Westlake Village	75	21	2	1	67	26	8	0
Elk Grove Village	42	49	9	1	46	45	9	1
Foster City	50	36	10	4	44	47	7	2
Laguna Niguel	61	35	3	1	46	47	8	0
Lake Havasu City	31	48	15	7	25	42	32	1
Sharpstown	27	57	16	1	30	58	11	2
Forest Park	32	50	15	3	31	46	18	4
North Palm Beach	59	34	7	a	60	31	9	0
Federally assisted								
Jonathan	41	50	9	a	47	41	13	0
Park Forest South	21	56	20	3	18	45	31	7

a less than 0.5 percent.

are combined, the number of favorable evaluations in new communities rises to an impressive 90 percent. The difference between this level of satisfaction and the 87 percent reported in the conventional communities is still statistically significant, by a smaller margin.

Within both types of communities, there were major contrasts in the percentage of respondents rating their community excellent. Among the nonfederally assisted new communities, Westlake Village received the most excellent ratings (75 percent); Sharpstown received the fewest (27 percent). Despite this range, however, there were few instances where the difference between a new community's rating and that of its paired community were significant. If excellent ratings are compared, for example, there were no significant differences between communities in eleven of the fifteen pairs shown in Table 3—1. The exceptions—all favoring the new community—were Reston, Irvine, Valencia, and Laguna Niguel. If excellent and good ratings are combined, the combined percentages also show four cases where differences between new and conventional community ratings were significant—Irvine, Valencia, Lake Havasu City, and Park Forest South.

REASONS FOR SATISFACTION RATINGS

To explore the reasons underlying evaluations of new and conventional community livability, respondents were asked to elaborate on their ratings. They appear to focus on whatever positive characteristics their communities have to substantiate their generally favorable evaluations of overall community livability. The most frequently given types of response are summarized in Table 3—2. With few exceptions—the mentions of overall planning and of the attractiveness of new communities, and the lack of crowding in the conventional communities—respondents from both settings gave similar reasons for positive evaluations.

The quality of the environment, including lack of crowding, nearness to nature and the outdoors, and the attractiveness of the community, was mentioned most often as a reason for satisfaction. Environmental factors were particularly noteworthy aspects of the appeal of the southern California new communities, which were located on the urban fringe in relatively undeveloped areas. Seventy-six percent of the Laguna Niguel respondents, 63 percent in Irvine, 62 percent in Westlake Village, and 56 percent in Valencia cited various aspects of the environment as reasons for rating these communities as excellent or good places to live.

Close behind the quality of the environment were perceptions that community facilities were conveniently located. Besides general con-

Table 3–2. **Reasons for Community Satisfaction** *(percentage of respondents)*[a]

Reasons for Positive Ratings	New Communities	Conventional Communities
Quality of the environment		
Lack of crowding	16	23*
Nearness to nature and the outdoors	15	16
Attractiveness	15*	11
Convenience of facilities		
Shopping	11	9
Recreation	6	6
Schools	5	3
Health care	1	1
General convenience (nonspecific)	16	15
Quality of facilities		
Schools	8	9
Recreation	5	3
Shopping	4	6
Health care	1	0
General quality of facilities (nonspecific)	2	2
Type of people living in community		
Friendliness	10	10
High social status	8	9
Planning of community	12*	4
Streets and transportation	9	8

[a]Responses add to more than 100 percent because some respondents mentioned more than one reason for rating their communities as excellent or good places to live.

*Difference between new communities and conventional communities is statistically significant at the 0.05 level of confidence.

venience, the convenience of shopping facilities was mentioned most frequently, followed by recreational facilities and schools.

The quality of community facilities and services was also mentioned frequently, but less frequently than their convenience. Respondents were most likely to mention the quality of community schools and, somewhat less often, the quality of recreational facilities and shopping facilities.

The frequency with which convenience and quality of community facilities and services were mentioned varied among the communities. For example, characteristics of the schools were mentioned most often in four new communities—Elk Grove Village, Forest Park, Park Forest, and Sharpstown—which had well-established school facilities.

Shopping facilities were mentioned most frequently in Sharpstown and Park Forest. Both of these communities contain regional shopping centers. Recreational facilities were mentioned most often by Valencia respondents, while health care facilities were mentioned most by Sharpstown respondents.

New community respondents also cited the type of people living in their communities as a reason for their satisfaction. (By type of people, they generally meant friendliness and social status.) Respondents in North Palm Beach, Forest Park, Park Forest, Sharpstown, and Valencia were most likely to cite this reason.

The quality of community planning was mentioned by 12 percent of the new community respondents. As noted in Chapter 2, we ranked communities on the basis of a nineteen-item index of planning criteria. It is not surprising, therefore, that the planning responses summarized in Table 3–2 were most often mentioned by persons who lived in new communities that ranked toward the top of the index. For example, 24 percent of the Valencia respondents, 22 percent in Reston, 21 percent in Irvine, 17 percent in Westlake Village, and 15 percent in Columbia mentioned planning as one of the reasons for rating these communities highly.

A number of other reasons were given for positive overall community evaluations. These included streets and transportation and, less often, convenience to work, safety, social programs and citizen participation, and the quality of police and fire protection.

In sum, although respondents mentioned a variety of reasons for their positive community evaluations, the quality of the environment and convenience of facilities clearly stood out as the key reasons. These two factors received over half of all the mentions of reasons for respondents' ratings and were mentioned by a sizable proportion of the respondents in each of the new communities.

INVENTORIES OF COMMUNITY FACILITIES AND SERVICES

We return to analyses of the determinants of the community satisfaction responses later in this chapter.[c] The main focus there is to

[c]This section draws directly on another volume in this series, *Access, Travel, and Transportation in New Communities* by Robert B. Zehner. See Chapter 2 and Appendix C of that volume.

The facilities inventories are based primarily on intensive visits made by members of the research staff to each of the sample communities in the spring of 1973. Supplemented with information from county planning agencies, municipal governments, and developers, the data collected on these visits were recorded on maps for each of the communities. From that point it was a relatively straight-

determine the relationships of two groups of variables to community satisfaction: the first group is a series of eight objective inventories of different types of facilities and services available in each of the study communities; the second (summarized in the next section of this chapter) is a similar series of subjective resident evaluations of nine types of community facilities and services.

Inventories of 71 types of facilities were made in each of the communities to determine whether or not such facilities existed. The variety of available facilities and services was measured, rather than their performance or the absolute number of facilities available. Summarizing the data in this way allows broad coverage of the amenities a community may provide at the expense of greater depth.[d]

The number of different types of facilities in nonfederally assisted new and conventional communities is shown in Table 3−3. Of the 71 facilities, nearly half (34) were found in virtually the same number of new and conventional communities. The number of new communities offering three-fourths of the remaining facilities (28 of 37), exceeded the number of conventional communities by two or more. Three facilities were located in at least five more new communities than conventional: indoor recreation center (+7),[e] interfaith, nondenominational worship center (+6), and stable or bridle trails (+5).

Of the 71 facilities inventoried, only four (primary school, playground, tennis court, and gas station) were located in all 30 communities. Five facilities (basketball court, baseball diamond, football or soccer field, restaurant, and supermarket) were also available in each of the new communities but missing from one or more of the conventional communities. One type of shopping facility, a convenience

---

forward task to obtain inventories of facilities available to residents in the community.

Information about community facilities that the research staff became aware of after the main data gathering visits has been used to update the initial inventories only to improve their accuracy as of spring 1973. The inventory data reported in this monograph, in other words, are an attempt to portray the range of facilities and services that actually existed in the study communities at the time of the household interview fieldwork. Facilities that were not yet operating—even if they were under construction or a part of a master plan—were not, therefore, credited to a community inventory for this book.

[d] Other volumes in this series which utilize more detailed objective and performance data focus on health (Loewenthal and Burby 1976), education (Burby and Donnelly 1977), and recreation (Burby 1976).

[e] Both new and conventional communities that lacked an indoor recreation center often had a gymnasium available for public use. Of the thirty communities, only two conventional communities had neither a recreation center nor a gymnasium.

Table 3—3. **Communities with 71 Selected Facilities, Spring 1973**

Facility	*Nonfederally Assisted Communities*	
	Thirteen New Communities	*Thirteen Conventional Communities*
Education		
Primary (elementary school)	13	13
Intermediate (junior high school)	8	9
Secondary (high school)	7	9
Tertiary (junior or senior college, university)	5	2
Health care and day care		
Ambulance service	7	6
Day care center	9	5
Dentist	12	9
General practitioner or internist	11	11
Hospital	3	3
Nursery school	11	7
Nursing or convalescent home	1	2
Obstetrician or gynecologist	10	7
Pediatrician	11	9
Private medical clinic	6	4
Psychiatrist	8	6
Public health clinic	0	3
Recreation		
Art—craft—hobby room	10	6
Basketball court	13	12
Baseball diamond	13	12
Bathing beach	4	3
Bike trail	6	5
Boating facility	8	4
Fishing lake	7	5
Football or soccer field	13	12
Golf course	11	10
Gymnasium	8	11
Ice skating facility	3	2
Park with benches	11	11
Picnic area	11	10
Playground for school-aged children	13	13
Recreation center (indoor)	12	5
Stable or bridle trails	6	1
Swimming pool	11	10
Teen recreation center	5	1
Tennis court	13	13
Totlots for preschool children	11	8
Track for running	6	8
Walking paths or trails	10	7

(Continued on facing page)

Table 3-3. continued

Facility	Nonfederally Assisted Communities	
	Thirteen New Communities	Thirteen Conventional Communities
Commercial recreation		
Amusement park	1	0
Bar or tavern	11	9
Billiard parlor	4	4
Bowling alley	3	4
Dinner theater	2	0
Drive-in movie theater	1	4
Health club	4	5
Indoor movie theater	6	6
Motorcycle or drag race track	2	0
Night club	4	7
Outdoor concert hall	2	0
Roller skating rink	0	2
Stage theater	3	0
Commercial		
Drive-in restaurant	7	10
Gas station	13	13
Laundromat	9	11
Motel or hotel	9	7
Restaurant	13	11
Shopping		
Convenience store	12	13
Supermarket	13	12
Neighborhood shopping center (10–19 stores)	10	9
Community shopping center (20–49 stores)	8	9
Regional shopping center (50+ stores)	3	4
Transportation		
Community bus service	8	5
Commuter bus service	2	2
Commuter rail service	1	1
Freeway interchange	10	8
Intercity bus service	9	6
Taxi service	12	12
Public		
County agency or office	3	0
Interfaith, nondenominational worship center	6	0
Library	10	9
Post office	11	12

store, was available in all of the conventional communities and all but one of the new communities.

None of the new communities included all 71 of the facilities and services. Only six had as many as 40. Columbia had the most with 56, followed by Lake Havasu City and Sharpstown with 49 each (See Table 3—4). There was at least as much variation within the new and conventional communities as there was between them, although over-all the new communities averaged more than four more amenities than the conventional communities (39.6 versus 35.1).[f]

Of the fifteen new communities, Columbia, in addition to having the most amenities overall, ranked first in five of the eight categories: recreation, commercial recreation, commercial (tie), education (tie), and transportation (tie). Sharpstown ranked first in three areas: health care, education (tie), and commercial (tie). Lake Havasu City was at the top for public and commercial (tie), and Irvine, the only other community ranking first for at least two categories, did so for education (tie) and transportation (tie).

A comparison of the thirteen nonfederally assisted new communities with the paired communities on the average number of facilities shows only two categories where the new communities averaged at least one more facility per community. These were recreation (14.8 versus 12.5) and health care (6.5 versus 5.3). Of the six other catego-

---

[f]We have not applied any weights to the summarized inventory data. The main reason for this, of course, is that there is no agreed upon set of priorities that could assign a double value, say, to education as opposed to health care or recreation facilities or, within the education category, to a college as opposed to a junior high school. With each of the 71 facilities having equal weight, it is clear that our inventory lends considerable importance to recreation-oriented amenities—35 of the items included fall in the "recreation" or "commercial recreation" categories. The other six categories of facilities are represented by only 36 items in the inventory.

To determine if the unweighted summary data provide distorted profiles of the communities because of the preponderance of recreation amenities in the inventory we (1) calculated for each of the eight categories of facilities the proportion of facilities inventoried that were provided within each of the communities, and (2) calculated an average of those eight proportions for each community. (In effect, these calculations give equal weight to each of the eight facility categories.) Then (3) this average proportion of facilities provided was compared with the unweighted proportion of facilities provided. Differences between the unweighted and average proportion of facilities provided were almost nonexistent. For Columbia, the unweighted proportion of facilities provided was 79 percent (56/71); the eight category average proportion of facilities provided was 80 percent. For Reston the unweighted proportion was 62 percent (44/71); the average proportion was 60 percent. The only community whose mix of facilities led to a noticeable difference (over 6 percent) between the proportions was Jonathan. In that community, the presence of a wide array of recreation facilities and very little else in six of the eight facility categories led to an eight-category average proportion of facilities provided of only 24 percent. The unweighted proportion of facilities provided in Jonathan was 37 percent (26/71).

Table 3-4. Number of Facilities, Spring 1973

Category of Facility (Number Inventoried)	Nonfederally Assisted New Communities (Paired Conventional Communities)						
	Columbia	*Reston*	*Irvine*	*Valencia*	*Park Forest*	*Westlake Village*	*Elk Grove Village*
Education (4)	4 (3)	2 (2)	4 (2)	2 (2)	3 (3)	1 (2)	3 (3)
Health care (12)	9 (3)	8 (7)	5 (6)	1 (0)	8 (7)	7 (3)	10 (7)
Recreation (22)	21 (12)	18 (13)	17 (17)	14 (9)	18 (16)	16 (10)	14 (13)
Commercial recreation (13)	6 (1)	3 (5)	0 (4)	3 (2)	2 (4)	2 (1)	5 (1)
Commercial (5)	5 (2)	3 (3)	3 (4)	3 (3)	4 (5)	4 (4)	5 (5)
Shopping (5)	4 (3)	3 (4)	3 (4)	2 (4)	5 (3)	4 (3)	4 (5)
Transportation (6)	4 (2)	4 (4)	4 (2)	4 (1)	4 (3)	1 (2)	3 (4)
Public (4)	3 (2)	3 (2)	2 (1)	2 (0)	2 (2)	1 (2)	2 (2)
Total (71)	56 (28)	44 (40)	38 (40)	31 (21)	46 (43)	36 (27)	46 (40)

Table 3-4. (continued overleaf . . .)

Table 3–4. continued

Category of Facility (Number Inventoried)	Nonfederally Assisted New Communities (cont'd) (Paired Conventional Communities)					
	Foster City	Laguna Niguel	Lake Havasu City	Sharpstown	Forest Park	North Palm Beach
Education (4)	2 (4)	1 (3)	3 (4)	4 (1)	3 (3)	1 (1)
Health care (12)	2 (11)	7 (3)	9 (10)	11 (5)	6 (5)	6 (5)
Recreation (22)	16 (19)	17 (10)	18 (14)	11 (11)	13 (21)	12 (4)
Commercial recreation (13)	2 (6)	2 (3)	5 (6)	8 (1)	1 (5)	4 (3)
Commercial (5)	3 (5)	3 (5)	5 (5)	5 (4)	3 (5)	5 (2)
Shopping (5)	4 (5)	3 (3)	3 (3)	5 (3)	3 (3)	3 (4)
Transportation (6)	3 (5)	4 (3)	2 (2)	3 (3)	3 (2)	3 (1)
Public (4)	2 (2)	2 (2)	4 (2)	2 (1)	3 (2)	2 (1)
Total (71)	34 (57)	39 (32)	49 (46)	49 (29)	35 (46)	36 (21)

Table 3-4. continued

Category of Facility (Number Inventoried)	Federally Assisted New Communities (Paired Conventional Communities)		Averages	
	Jonathan	Park Forest South	Thirteen Nonfederally Assisted New Communities	Thirteen Conventional Communities
Education (4)	0 (2)	2 (2)	2.3	2.4
Health care (12)	5 (1)	0 (5)	6.5	5.3
Recreation (22)	18 (17)	18 (8)	14.8	12.5
Commercial recreation (13)	0 (3)	2 (2)	3.3	3.0
Commercial (5)	1 (4)	1 (4)	3.9	4.1
Shopping (5)	1 (2)	1 (4)	3.5	3.7
Transportation (6)	0 (1)	4 (1)	3.0	2.6
Public (4)	1 (1)	2 (2)	2.1	1.6
Total (71)	26 (31)	30 (28)	39.6	35.1

ries, three showed small differences in favor of the new communities and three in favor of the conventional communities.

Despite the limitations of the inventories, we expected that they would relate to a community's position on the new community continuum. The correlation between the number of facilities and the continuum index was positive, though modest, at $r = .18$. There was an exceptionally strong positive relationship, however, between the continuum and the number of types of recreation facilities ($r = .71$). The number of transportation ($r = .24$) and education facilities ($r = .14$) was also positively related. Health care ($r = -.15$) and commercial recreation ($r = -.11$) facilities, on the other hand, were negatively related to the new community continuum. The preeminence of recreation is striking and indicates that the variety of recreation facilities available is a far better indicator of a community's "new townness" than any other category or total measure of facilities and services.

RESIDENT EVALUATIONS OF COMMUNITY FACILITIES AND SERVICES

An objective count of the range of facilities in a community provides one indication of its livability. More important, perhaps, are resident evaluations of different components of the community and of the community as a whole which can take into account the quality as well as the variety of facilities available. Items in the household interview rated nine aspects of the communities ranging from the adequacy of recreation facilities to the quality of the school attended by a randomly designated child in the family.

Insofar as the variety of facilities available could affect ratings, the inventory data suggest that new communities might be rated more highly than conventional communities in two areas, recreation and health care. The comparisons of attributes of the present and prior communities included in Chapter 2 showed that in addition to recreation and health care facilities new communities fared significantly better than conventional communities in terms of shopping facilities and the ease of getting around the community. (The latter item has been combined with the rating of convenience to work to provide a composite measure of transportation satisfaction. See Table 3–5, note i.)

Levels of resident satisfaction with nine community components are presented in Table 3–5 together with the items used in the household interview. Entries in the table are not complete distributions but are limited to the percentage of respondents giving the most

Table 3–5. Resident Evaluations of Nine Community Components in New Communities

(percentage of respondents giving most positive ratings)

Component	Columbia	Reston	Irvine	Nonfederally Assisted New Communities					
				Valencia	Park Forest	Westlake Village	Elk Grove Village	Foster City	Laguna Niguel
Dwelling unit[a]	28	28	43	39	22	51	35	52	52
Health care[b]	21	9	11	3	21	47	42	28	26
Homeowners association[c]	10	4	19	22	15	31	—	35	6
Microneighborhood[d]	30	34	36	35	21	57	31	31	42
Recreation facilities[e]	49	49	46	42	27	66	39	28	39
Religious facilities[f]	76	78	69	82	91	91	89	45	72
School attended by child[g]	30	37	48	30	29	32	48	27	41
Shopping facilities[h]	32	23	30	3	43	20	55	31	25
Transportation[i]	32	21	23	23	22	27	24	23	14

Table 3–5. continued

Component	Nonfederally Assisted New Communities (cont'd)				Federally Assisted New Communities		Thirteen Nonfederally Assisted New Communities	Thirteen Conventional Communities
	Lake Havasu City	Sharpstown	Forest Park	North Palm Beach	Jonathan	Park Forest South		
Dwelling unit[a]	45	29	29	42	28	29	40	39
Health care[b]	3	40	13	31	26	12	26	18
Homeowners association[c]	—	—	—	35	10	16	21	28
Microneighborhood[d]	28	21	28	37	29	21	34	30
Recreation facilities[e]	37	15	27	41	55	24	38	26
Religious facilities[f]	92	86	76	88	54	62	80	81
School attended by child[g]	18	26	35	21	28	25	33	36
Shopping facilities[h]	2	54	60	41	8	14	34	32
Transportation[i]	49	28	28	34	26	9	26	22

Table 3–5. continued (Notes)

— Insufficient cases.

[a]Entries in the table represent responses coded 1 to: "Now, overall how do you feel about the (house/apartment) as a place to live? Which number comes closest to how satisfied or dissatisfied you feel?"

Completely Satisfied   1 2 3 4 5 6 7   Completely Dissatisfied

[b]Entries in the table represent responses coded 1 to: "Overall, how good would you say health care facilities and services are for people who live in this community—excellent, good, average, below average, or poor?"

(1) Excellent   (2) Good   (3) Average   (4) Below average   (5) Poor

[c]Entries in the table represent responses coded 1 to: "Based on your experience, how satisfied are you with the overall performance of your association? Which number comes closest to how you feel?"

Completely Satisfied   1 2 3 4 5 6 7   Completely Dissatisfied

[d]Entries in the table represent cases which were coded at the most positive point on the three parts of a twelve-part question that are reproduced here: "Below are some words and phrases which we would like you to use to describe this *neighborhood* as it seems to you. By neighborhood, we mean roughly the area near here which you can see from your front door—that is, the five or six homes nearest to yours around here. For example, if you think the neighborhood is noisy, please put a mark in the circle right next to the word "noisy." If you think it is quiet, please put a mark in the circle right next to the word "quiet." If you think it is somewhere in between, please put a mark where you think it belongs." [Note: the first item of the twelve items of this question asked for a rating on a noisy–quiet dimension.]

Attractive :	___ :	___ :	___ :	___ :	___ :	___ :	___	: Unattractive
Pleasant :	___ :	___ :	___ :	___ :	___ :	___ :	___	: Unpleasant
Very good place to live :	___ :	___ :	___ :	___ :	___ :	___ :	___	: Very poor place to live

[e]Entries in the table represent responses coded 1 to: "All things considered, how good would you say the recreational facilities in this community and its immediate vicinity are for the people who live here—excellent, good, average, below average, or poor?"

(1) Excellent   (2) Good   (3) Average   (4) Below average   (5) Poor

[f]Entries in the table represent cases where 1 was coded in response to: "Can you find the kinds of church and religious activities you want in this community?"

(1) Yes   (3) Don't care about that [missing data]   (5) No

(Table 3–5. notes continued overleaf . . .)

Table 3—5. continued (Notes)

gEntries in the table represent responses coded 1 to the following question (which was asked about the school of a randomly selected child attending school): "All things considered, how would you rate (*name of school*)—do you think it's excellent, good, average, below average, or poor?"

    (1) Excellent   (2) Good   (3) Average   (4) Below average   (5) Poor

hEntries in the table represent responses coded 1 to: "Thinking over everything we've mentioned about shopping facilities, overall, how good would you say they are for people who live in this community—excellent, good, average, below average, or poor?"

    (1) Excellent   (2) Good   (3) Average   (4) Below average   (5) Poor

iEntries in the table represent instances where 1 was coded in response to both of the following items: "Now, I'd like you to compare this community to the one you lived in just before you moved here. For each item on CARD B, please tell me if where you're living now is better, not as good, or about the same as where you lived before."

    Convenience to work; ease of commuting (1) Better   (3) Same   (5) Not as good

    Ease of getting around the community   (1) Better   (3) Same   (5) Not as good

favorable ratings.g For each cell of Table 3—5, we have also calculated whether the ratings for the paired new and conventional communities differ significantly. (See Table 3—6.)

The differences between new and conventional communities summarized in Table 3—6 substantiate earlier impressions that, overall, the thirteen new communities have been able to provide more satisfactory recreation and health care facilities than those found in conventional communities. In addition, the combined ratings indicate that the immediate neighborhood and transportation services also received significantly higher ratings. As noticeable as these differences, however, is the absence of significant differences on ratings of the other five community components. Roughly two-thirds of the entries in Table 3—6 indicate no significant differences between the new and conventional communities. Differences that did appear, however, were not distributed randomly. In the case of recreation facilities, for example, seven nonfederally assisted and both federally assisted new communities received significantly higher ratings than their paired conventional communities. (One conventional community was rated significantly higher.) Similar clusters of significant differences appear in the health care (9 differences) and microneighborhood (7 differences) rows. Westlake Village fared best in comparison with its paired community. Residents gave it significantly higher ratings for health care, the immediate neighborhood, recreation, and religious facilities.

Comparisons among the new communities (see Table 3—5) indicate a considerable range in resident evaluations for most components. Recreation facilities were considered excellent by 66 percent of Westlake Village's respondents, for example, but by only 15 percent of Sharpstown's. Even greater contrasts occurred in the health care and shopping evaluations. Health care facilities and services were rated excellent by 47 percent of Westlake Village's residents but by only 3 percent of Valencia's and Lake Havasu City's. In the case of shopping facilities, the range of excellent ratings dropped from 60 percent in Forest Park to 2 percent in Lake Havasu City and 3 percent in Valencia.

---

gFor complete distributions, see Appendix C. The items used to measure satisfaction in the various component areas used several formats. Four were five-point excellent-to-poor rating scales; two were seven-point completely satisfied–completely dissatisfied items; two were composites of items; and one was a simple dichotomous rating. It would have been very desirable to use strictly comparable question formats throughout the interview, but that desideratum had to be viewed in light of the need to phrase some items to be comparable with other studies and the need to keep the overall interview to less than 75 minutes (it eventually turned out to average about 90 minutes).

Table 3-6.   Differences between New and Conventional Communities in Satisfaction with Nine Community Components[a]

	Nonfederally Assisted New Communities					
Component	*Columbia*	*Reston*	*Irvine*	*Valencia*	*Park Forest*	*Westlake Village*
Dwelling unit	—	0	0	0	—	0
Health care	0	—	—	0	0	+
Homeowners association	0	0	0	0	0	0
Microneighborhood	0	0	0	+	—	+
Recreation facilities	+	+	+	+	0	+
Religious facilities	0	0	—	0	—	+
School attended	0	0	+	—	0	0
Shopping facilities	0	—	0	0	0	0
Transportation	0	0	+	+	0	0
Net difference	*0*	*−1*	*1*	*2*	*−3*	*4*

[a] Depending on the number of interviews and the magnitude of the percentages, new and conventional communities had to differ between about 8.2 percent and 14.1 percent on an item to be significantly different at the 0.05 level.
+ New community given high ratings significantly more often.
0 No significant difference between new and conventional community.
— Conventional community given high ratings significantly more often.

Before proceeding with a multivariate analysis of community satisfaction, we note the extent to which resident evaluations were related to the inventories of facilities and services. There are five types of facilities for which we have both inventory and resident rating data. The highest correlation ($r = .34$) was between the shopping facilities inventory and the shopping facilities rating. The health care correlation was $r = .28$. Recreation ratings correlated positively with noncommercial recreation facilities ($r = .14$) and negatively with commercial recreation facilities ($r = −.09$). The correlation between the education inventory and the ratings of individual schools attended

Table 3–6. continued

	Nonfederally Assisted New Communities (cont'd)						Federally Assisted New Communities		
Elk Grove Village	Foster City	Laguna Niguel	Lake Havasu City	Sharpstown	Forest Park	North Palm Beach	Jonathan	Park Forest South	Thirteen Nonfederally Assisted New Communities
0	0	0	+	0	0	0	0	0	0
+	−	+	0	+	0	+	+	0	+
0	0	0	0	0	0	0	0	0	0
−	0	+	+	0	0	−	0	0	+
0	0	0	+	0	−	+	+	+	+
0	−	0	0	0	0	0	−	0	0
0	0	0	−	+	−	0	0	0	0
0	−	+	0	0	0	+	−	0	0
0	0	−	+	0	0	0	0	−	+
0	*−3*	*2*	*3*	*2*	*−2*	*2*	*0*	*0*	*4*

by randomly designated children was only $r = .01$, while the transportation inventory correlated at $r = -.07$ with its rating. The lower correlations (those for recreation, transportation, and education) indicate that a simple inventory of such facilities has a very limited effect on the ratings. More detailed data on these systems (both quantitative and qualitative) would clearly be needed to identify important determinants of satisfaction.[h]

The correlations between inventory and resident rating data in the case of shopping and health care indicate a more substantial relationship between the variety of facilities available—regardless of other quantitative and qualitative characteristics—and reported satisfaction.

[h]For recreation, see Burby (1976); for education, see Burby and Donnelly (1977); for transportation, see Zehner (1977).

In each of these cases, however, only about 10 percent of the variation in satisfaction responses can be attributed to the inventories.[i]

A MULTIVARIATE ANALYSIS OF COMMUNITY SATISFACTION

Data presented in this chapter include an overall measure of community satisfaction, inventories of eight types of community facilities, and resident evaluations of nine components of their communities. Given these inventories and evaluations, it is possible to determine statistically which factors were most related to respondents' ratings of satisfaction with their communities. (The respondents probably went through a similar process—though less systematically—when they were asked to indicate the main reasons for their overall community ratings.)

Simple correlation coefficients provide one of the most direct ways to gauge the size of the relationships of each of the inventories and resident ratings with the overall satisfaction responses. Among the inventories, only the variety of noncommercial recreation facilities was positively related to community satisfaction responses, and that relationship was small ($r = .06$). The largest relationships between inventories and satisfaction were negative: education facilities with satisfaction, $r = -.21$; public facilities with satisfaction, $r = -.19$. The total number of types of community facilities was related to satisfaction negatively as well, $r = -.14$. In essence, simply providing a wide array of facilities does not produce greater resident satisfaction. To put it another way, the residents most satisfied with their communities must have valued something other than how well stocked they were with facilities. Two possibilities are evident: residents may have ascribed importance to qualities of the various facilities about which we did not collect data; they may have felt that some other aspects

---

[i]Data collected as part of a follow-up study of nonrespondents about ten months after the initial field work lend support to the finding that health care and shopping ratings are sensitive to changes in the number of available facilities. For five of seven rating items included in the follow-up study, there was no significant differences between the initial respondents' evaluations and those of the follow-up respondents. The two exceptions were the ratings of health care and shopping facilities. In most instances, we were able to relate significant improvement in health care evaluations to the opening or commissioning of new hospitals and the improvement in shopping ratings to addition of shopping facilities—especially a major shopping center—in the communities. (The follow-up study used telephone interviews and mail-back questionnaires to obtain data from 757 of the original nonrespondents. See Robert B. Zehner and Mary Ellen McCalla 1974, pp. 5–23.) For extensive health care analyses, see Loewenthal and Burby (1976). For shopping, see Burby, Weiss *et al.* (1976, Chapter 13).

of their residential environment were more important than the facilities we inventoried.

An indication that the latter was at least in part the case appeared in the generally larger correlations of overall satisfaction with the community component evaluations. Each of the ratings was positively correlated with overall satisfaction; i.e., the more satisfied a person was with each of the nine community components, the more satisfied he was with the community as a whole. The largest of these relationships was that of community satisfaction with livability of the immediate neighborhood ($r = .44$), followed by the dwelling ($r = .33$), recreation facilities ($r = .24$), and homeowners associations ($r = .23$). The ratings least related to community satisfaction were those of shopping ($r = .03$) and religious facilities ($r = .07$).

Multivariate analyses of the relationship of these groups of variables to community satisfaction (see Table 3–7) confirmed the importance of the community components, as a group, in comparison with either the facilities inventories or the nine socioeconomic and demographic variables. The last items—including the respondent's age, sex, marital status, education, and income—could account for only 6 percent of the variance in community satisfaction responses.[j] The value of the dwelling unit was the item most related to community satisfaction ($r = .21$) in this group.

The explanatory ability of the facilities inventories ($R^2 = .08$) was not much stronger than that of the group of personal characteristics. The resident ratings of community components, on the other hand, accounted for three to four times as much of the variation in community satisfaction responses ($R^2 = .25$). Further, when combined with the resident ratings, the other groups of variables were able to add very little to this explanatory power. These ratings alone, in fact, accounted for almost 90 percent (.25/.28) of the variance explained.[k]

The relative importance of each of the nine resident ratings for

[j] A parallel analysis by Marans and Rodgers reported in Campbell, Converse, and Rodgers (1976, pp. 225–231) found that personal characteristics explained only 7 percent of the community satisfaction responses in a national sample.

[k] In the study reported in Campbell, Converse, and Rodgers (1976), resident assessments of six community attributes explained 18 percent of the variance in community satisfaction, and a combination of resident assessments and personal characteristics explained 21 percent of the variance. A study of satisfaction with English housing developments also found that socioeconomic characteristics were "not related" to satisfaction. These factors were correlated at less than $r = .20$ with satisfaction. In those analyses the key predictors were the appearance and the maintenance level of the area and dwelling satisfaction. These three factors accounted for close to 90 percent (.46/.52) of the variance in satisfaction ratings (Reynolds *et al.* 1972).

Table 3–7.   Variance in Community Satisfaction Explained Using Socio-economic/Demographic, Inventory and Resident Evaluation Variables, in Nonfederally Assisted New Communities

Variable Group	R^2
A. Nine socioeconomic and demographic characteristics[a]	.06
B. Eight facility inventories[b]	.08
C. Nine resident evaluations of community components	.25
Combinations of Variable Groups	
A + B	.10
A + C	.26
B + C	.27
A + B + C	.28

[a] These include the respondent's age, sex, education, marital status, family income, dwelling unit value, tenure, length of residence, and the number of children in the household.

[b] See Table 3–3 for listing of the inventories and their components.

explaining community satisfaction responses is the focus of Table 3–8. By a considerable margin, the evaluation most tied to the overall community rating was that of the respondents' microneighborhoods, defined in the interview as "the area near here which you can see from your front door—that is, the five or six homes nearest to yours around here." Following the immediate neighborhood in importance were the ratings of the dwelling unit and of community recreation facilities. The ratings of shopping and religious facilities had the least effect on overall satisfaction.[1]

One of the main implications of these results is that if a developer wishes to encourage residents' satisfaction with the community, a focus on the immediate residential environment is likely to pay sig-

[1]The leading predictor of community satisfaction in the Campbell, Converse, and Rodgers (1976) analyses was satisfaction with schools. Other studies (Goldsmith and Munsterman (1967), Durand and Eckart (1973) have ascribed importance to the socioeconomic characteristics of residents vis à vis the socioeconomic character of the surrounding neighborhood or community (usually operationalized as one or more census tracts). Durand and Eckart, however, found "little support for arguments to pursue the social rank homogeneity of dwelling areas in order to maximize community satisfaction" (p. 84.) Dillman and Dobash (1972) documented a modest negative relationship (gamma = −.15) between the population size of communities and people's levels of community satisfaction.

Table 3–8. Multivariate Analysis of Community Satisfaction in Nonfederally Assisted New Communities

Variables	Simple Correlation Coefficient	Beta	Cumulative R^2	F-Value
I. Nine socioeconomic and demographic variables[a]	—	—	.06	15.9
II. Eight facility inventories[b]	—	—	.10	18.3
III. Resident evaluations of				
Microneighborhood	.44	.29	.24	178.3
Recreation facilities	.24	.09	.25	20.3
Dwelling unit	.33	.11	.27	29.9
School	.14	.07	.27	12.4
Health care facilities and services	.16	.06	.28	6.9
Transportation	.08	.05	.28	9.0
Homeowners association	.23	.06	.28	9.5
Shopping facilities	.03	.03	.28	1.5
Religious facilities	.07	.02	.28	1.0

[a] These include the respondent's age, sex, education, marital status, family income, dwelling unit value, tenure, length of residence, and the number of children in the household.
[b] See Table 3–3 for listing of the inventories and their components.

nificantly greater dividends than attention to health care, shopping, education, or other facilities in the larger community. That is not to say that the quality of these other facilities cannot help attract residents to the community and do not contribute to community satisfaction. The effect of satisfaction with these aspects of a community—with the possible exception of recreation facilities—is simply very limited in comparison with ratings of the immediate neighborhood and the dwelling.

ADDED PERSPECTIVES ON
THE COMMUNITY

In addition to direct questions about community satisfaction and evaluations of community components, the household interview included several other items that could provide insight into the advantages and disadvantages of living in the communities. The first of these centered on decisions to move and the reasons cited by prospective movers for leaving. We also asked residents if they would recommend their present community to a close friend or relative who was planning to move. Finally, in case the variety of satisfaction questions failed to elicit reports of difficulties residents encountered in their communities, they were also asked what they thought were the main issues and problems facing the community, what the community would be like in five years, and what could be done to improve it.

Moving Intentions, Reasons for Moving, and
Recommendations to Prospective Residents

Moving intentions were slightly higher in new communities than in the conventional (see Table 3—9). That difference disappears, however, once differences in tenure and age of household heads are taken into consideration. This lack of difference in the rate of prospective mobility also obtained when each new community was compared with its paired conventional community. The only exceptions were the Park Forest–Lansing pair, where 23 percent more Park Forest residents were probable movers in the next two to three years, and the Sharpstown–Southwest Houston pair, where 16 percent more Sharpstown residents planned to move.

Determining actual rates of mobility would require recontacting sampled addresses to find out if residents' expectations proved accurate. Based on previous analyses of moving intentions, however, it is possible to estimate that between 70 percent and 80 percent of the households who say that they are going to move actually do so. On the other hand, 20 percent to 30 percent of those who think they will stay in their dwellings have been subsequently found to move over a two- to three-year period. If one assumes the 80 percent and 30 percent figures (with uncertain residents given a probability of .50), then 44 percent of the new community residents and 42 percent of those in conventional communities are likely to move in the next two to three years. An assumption of lower mobility (70 percent, 50 percent, and 20 percent) leads to 36 percent and 34 percent, respectively. Neither method of estimation yields a significant difference between the new and conventional communities.[m]

Households who intended to move were not representative of the new community population as a whole. Renters, apartment dwellers, younger households, those living in less well maintained dwellings, and those who had moved in more recently were more likely to be planning to move than other residents. These findings are consistent with other research on residential mobility. (See references in note *m*.)

The relationship between dwelling type and plans to move is caused by tenure, which is associated with dwelling type as well as with plans to move. Renters were four to five times more likely to be planning to move within two or three years, regardless of whether they were renting a single-family detached house or an apartment and regardless of the age of the head of the household.

The reasons given for moving differed somewhat by community type. New community residents were more likely to cite job-related reasons for moving (28 percent versus 24 percent for prospective movers in conventional communities). People in conventional communities were more likely to cite problems with the quality of the physicial environment (17 percent versus 12 percent for people in new communities). In both settings, the main impetus for moving involved housing, primarily because of a desire for more living space and for ownership.

A comparison across communities of the prospective mobility responses showed that the communities with the highest proportions of renters (see Appendix B, Table B—1) were the communities with

[m] Both the new and conventional community findings on prospective mobility are comparable to the findings of metropolitan mobility research conducted since the 1950s. The two- to three-year prospective mobility rate of 44 percent among the new community households (certain plus uncertain movers) is bracketed by the 48 percent five-year prospective mobility rate found by Lansing and Mueller, with Barth (1964) and Lansing (1966) in two national metropolitan area samples in 1963 and 1965; and the average of 24 percent in one-year prospective mobility rates found by Rossi (1955), Van Arsdol, Sabagh, and Butler (1968), Butler *et al.* (1969), Varady (1973), and Zehner and Chapin, with Howell (1974).

Table 3-9. Moving Intentions, Reasons for Moving, and Recommendations to Others about Moving *(percentage of respondents)*

Responses		Columbia	Reston	Irvine	Valencia	Park Forest	Westlake Village	Elk Grove Village
					Nonfederally Assisted New Communities			
A.	Likelihood of moving in next two to three years							
	Certain to move	28	31	10	16	23[a]	14	15
	Uncertain	28	36	23	25	37[a]	23	26
	Plan to stay	45	33	65	59	40[b]	62	58
B.	Reasons for moving							
	Changes in family size or composition	7	4	9	8	5	11	4
	Job changes, transfer, or other job related reasons	28	39	25	43	28[a]	41	29
	Aspects of housing	28	38[b]	39	25	31	30	44
	Problems with community facilities	1	1	6	0	6	5	0
	Problems with the quality of the physical environment	12	6	5	7	14[b]	5	10[b]
	Other reasons	24	13	16	18	16	8	13
C.	Recommendation to close friend or relative							
	Community is A particularly good place to move to	80[c]	92[c]	85[c]	90[c]	70	91[c]	82
	About like other communities	12	4	12	6	21	5	15
	Could probably do better elsewhere	9	4	4	4	10	4	3

[a] Percentage in new community is significantly higher than that in paired conventional community at 0.05 level of confidence.

[b] Percentage in conventional community is significantly higher than that in paired new community at 0.05 level of confidence.

Table 3-9. continued

	Nonfederally Assisted New Communities (cont'd)					Federally Assisted New Communities			
Foster City	Laguna Niguel	Lake Havasu City	Sharpstown	Forest Park	North Palm Beach	Jonathan	Park Forest South	Thirteen Nonfederally Assisted New Communities	Thirteen Conventional Communities
19	9	21	22[a]	19	13	31	20	17	14
27	19	27	30	26	14	27	27	25	24
54	71	52	46[b]	55	73	41	52	58	62[b]
3	5	6	6	3	0[b]	4	1	5	5
29[a]	8[b]	11[b]	21	34[a]	12	24	35	28[a]	24
32	27	60[a]	37	18[b]	46	32	32	34	33
4	5	2	5	0	4	3	1	3	3
18	24	10	9	23	14	18	15	12	17[b]
15	31	13	23	23	20	19	17	18	17
84[c]	84	65	70	64	88	84[c]	66[c]	81[c]	74
7	10	15	18	20	8	9	25	11	19
9	6	20	12	16	4	7	9	8	7

[c]Responses in new community are significantly more positive than those in the paired conventional community.

the highest proportion of certain or possible movers. Specifically, the leading rental communities were Reston and Jonathan (48 percent renting), Columbia (43 percent renting), and Sharpstown (38 percent renting). The leading communities on the proportions of residents who were certain or possible movers were Reston (67 percent), Jonathan (59 percent), Columbia (55 percent), and Sharpstown (54 percent).[n]

Sizable differences across communities on reasons for moving were infrequent, the two leading reasons for moving in twelve of the fifteen communities being job- or housing-related issues. Job changes, which might be more likely to require leaving a community, were cited most frequently in Valencia (43 percent of the probable movers) and least often in Laguna Niguel (8 percent). Problems with housing were noted most often in Lake Havasu City (60 percent) and least often in Forest Park (18 percent).

The final panel in Table 3–9 summarizes responses to another summary evaluation of the community. In this case the question was phrased in terms of residents' willingness to recommend the community as a place to live: "If a close relative or friend asked you if they should consider moving to this community, would you tell them that this would be a particularly good community to move to, that it's pretty much like other communities around here, or that they could probably do better somewhere else?"

Respondents in new communities were significantly more likely to recommend their community than were paired conventional community respondents in eight of the fifteen community pairings and for the nonfederally assisted communities overall. Community enthusiasm was highest in Reston, Westlake Village, and Valencia where at least 90 percent of the respondents said they would recommend their community. At the other end of the spectrum, the proportion of positive recommendations was around 65 percent in Park Forest South, Lake Havasu City, and Forest Park.

Community Problems

In early visits to the study communities at the time the household interview was being developed, it was not surprising to find that the issues people felt were important differed considerably from community to community. To try to capture some of this variety, we asked

[n] It is important to note, however, that when respondents were asked if they planned to move from "this place" in the next two or three years, that question followed a series of dwelling unit questions. There is little doubt, in other words, that some of the prospective mobility being tapped here will be intracommunity moving from rental apartments to owned single-family or townhouse homes.

Table 3–10. Community Problems Most Frequently Mentioned
(percentage of respondents) [a]

Community Problems	Thirteen Nonfederally Assisted New Communities	Thirteen Conventional Communities
Quality of the environment		
Increasing density, crowding, growth	20	24[b]
Ugliness, poor maintenance	5	3
Lack of natural open space	3	11[b]
Schools		
More schools needed	14[b]	8
Poor quality of existing schools	5	6
Recreation facilities		
More facilities needed, existing facilities are inconvenient	6	5
Poor quality of existing facilities	3	2
Lack of facilities for children	3	4
Cost of living (including taxes)	11	9
Police, fire, and other public services	11	12
Transportation and street maintenance	10	17[b]
Teenagers (primarily drug use)	9	9
Developer and local officials	9	8
Poor planning, plans not followed	7	8
Safety from crime	6	8

[a] Responses add to more than 100 percent because some respondents mentioned more than one community problem.
[b] Difference between new communities and conventional communities is statistically significant at 0.05 level of confidence.

respondents (roughly three-fourths of the way through the interview): "In your opinion, what are the most important issues or problems facing the *community as a whole* at the present time? Anything else?" (Emphasis appeared in the interview.)

Responses for the nonfederally assisted new communities appear in Table 3–10. Concerns about the quality of the environment were foremost in residents' minds. In particular, about one-fifth of the new community respondents mentioned increasing density and growth as an important problem. Although the density of respondents' immediate neighborhoods was not statistically associated with evaluations of new community livability, increasing density in the community as a whole and its effects on the environment were obviously viewed by many respondents as a threat to their communities' livability.

Difficulties with school construction and educational programs were also reflected in respondents' assessments of community problems. The need for a greater number of schools was the second most frequently mentioned problem. A lower proportion of respondents were concerned about the quality of community schools.

Other issues included concerns about community recreational facilities, the cost of living and taxes, police protection and safety from crime, fire protection, transportation and street maintenance, teenagers and drug use, and the behavior of the developer and local officials. With some exceptions, including significantly greater concern with the lack of natural open space and with transportation and street maintenance, conventional community residents perceived about the same array of problems as new community residents.

The types of problems residents mentioned varied from one new community to another. For example, although increasing density and crowding were mentioned as problems by 10 percent or more of the respondents in eleven of the fifteen new communities, they were cited by a quarter or more of those living in Laguna Niguel (51 percent), North Palm Beach (33 percent), Reston (26 percent), and Irvine (25 percent). With the exception of North Palm Beach, the lack of crowding and nearness to the outdoors were the most common reasons respondents gave for rating these communities as excellent or good places to live. Obviously, many residents felt these aspects of their communities' livability were threatened by the increasing proportion of townhouses and rental apartments being built.

Concern for the provision of schools was greatest in new communities where the pace of school construction had fallen behind initial expectations. Almost a third of the Reston and Foster City respondents mentioned the need for more schools as a major community problem. The need for additional schools was also noted by more than 10 percent of the respondents in Forest Park, Irvine, Laguna Niguel, North Palm Beach, Park Forest South, Valencia, and Westlake Village.

A variety of other public facilities and services were viewed as major problems in some new communities. The need for more recreational facilities was mentioned by 10 percent or more of the respondents in eight of fifteen new communities. Limited shopping facilities were viewed as problems in Lake Havasu City and Valencia. Although the lack of health care facilities was the most frequently mentioned community problem facing Lake Havasu City, it was probably alleviated by the subsequent construction of two community hospitals. Other community services, including police protection, fire protection, and garbage collection were a major concern of North Palm Beach respondents (mentioned by 40 percent) and were also viewed as problems in Elk Grove Village, Lake Havasu City, and Sharpstown.

Although Columbia and Park Forest South were the only new communities where more than 10 percent of the respondents were concerned with excessive developer control, in Reston and in Jonathan more than 10 percent of the respondents cited the developer's deviation from the community master plan as a major issue. Free-standing Lake Havasu City, where residents had to rely on employment opportunities located within the community, was the only new community where more than 10 percent of the respondents mentioned the lack of employment opportunities as a problem. Park Forest and Forest Park, where black inmigration had increased markedly since 1970, were the only new communities where more than 10 percent of the respondents were concerned with the character of race relations. Finally, the young, highly educated population of Columbia indicated the greatest concern with the status of social service programs and citizen participation.

Five Years From Now

The fact that new community residents reported many of the same types of problems that arose in conventional communities is not too surprising since, with the exception of Park Forest, each of the study communities was undergoing development and was at an intermediate stage of that process. Nevertheless the existence of more extensive community planning and the centralized direction of development might be expected to give new communities an edge in resolving problem situations and evolving into more desirable places to live than less planned conventional suburbs. To see whether the residents shared this belief, respondents were asked whether in five years they thought their communities would be better places to live, about the same, or not as good.

A majority of the respondents in each new community said that their community would be as good or better in five years. Least optimistic were Laguna Niguel residents where only 55 percent thought things would be as good or better. In Lake Havasu City and Elk Grove Village, on the other hand, 89 percent said things would be just as good or be better by 1978.

Focusing on the most positive prognoses (see Table 3—11) shows that new community residents were slightly but significantly more likely than residents in conventional communities to think that their

Table 3–11. Percentage of Residents Who Think Their Community Will Be a Better Place to Live in Five Years

Community	New Community	Conventional Community
Nonfederally assisted		
Thirteen new communities	37[a]	
Thirteen conventional communities		33
Columbia	43[a]	20
Reston	27[a]	14
Irvine	46	40
Valencia	58[a]	34
Park Forest	10	17
Westlake Village	36	48
Elk Grove Village	33[a]	50
Foster City	64[a]	23
Laguna Niguel	33	23
Lake Havasu City	69	61
Sharpstown	20	22
Forest Park	29	28
North Palm Beach	21	18
Federally assisted		
Jonathan	55	50
Park Forest South	55	52

[a]Statistically significant difference at the 0.05 level of confidence.

communities would be better places to live in five years (37 percent versus 33 percent). There was greater variation in optimism about the future among the new communities than there was between new and conventional communities. Of those in Lake Havasu City, 69 percent expected things to be better in five years, but only 10 percent of the residents in Park Forest saw the future that positively.

Not surprisingly, there was some association between the stage of community development and residents' optimism. Residents of older new communities, such as Park Forest, Sharpstown, Forest Park, and North Palm Beach, were generally less likely to think their communities would be better places to live in five years. In four new communities—Laguna Niguel, Park Forest, Reston, and Sharpstown—a higher proportion of the respondents thought that their community would be a worse place to live in five years than thought that it would be better.

The question asking residents for five-year prognoses was followed by a request for the residents' suggestions about what could be done to make the community a better place to live. The most frequently mentioned type of improvement was the provision of more and better community facilities. Recreational facilities—mentioned by 20 percent of the nonfederally assisted community respondents—topped the list. In addition, respondents in a number of communities thought that the addition of more shopping facilities and more schools would improve community livability.

The concern about increasing population and density (Table 3–10) was reflected in suggestions for improving community livability. For example, almost a fifth of the respondents in the nonfederally assisted communities thought that continued growth of their communities should be controlled and that higher density development (townhouses and apartments) should be limited. This strong sentiment for limited growth, if translated into more restrictive zoning requirements, could be disastrous for the financial viability of many new community ventures. It also presents new community residents with a hard choice, though few residents may realize that they cannot have the best of both worlds. The provision of improved community facilities and services depends, in part, on the accumulation of an adequate supporting population. New community residents want the facilities and services, but many do not want the increased population density that is a necessary prerequisite for their provision. One approach to this problem would be to inform residents about a new community's anticipated population and the location of future high density development, or to remove control of population density from local government.

Increasing density, therefore, also has implications for new community marketing. Because new communities are often located at or beyond the developing urban fringe during the initial years of development, developers have used the undeveloped character of their communities' surroundings as an aid in marketing. In fact, just over a quarter of the new community respondents as a whole chose their communities, in part, because of the nearness to the outdoors and the natural environment. Over half of the respondents move to Lake Havasu City, Laguna Niguel, and Westlake Village because of the proximity of the natural environment, and between 25 and 50 percent chose Reston, Irvine, Valencia, and Columbia for this reason. Since they moved to a new community because of its natural surroundings, it is understandable that residents would seek to preserve this feature by limiting population growth. Developers might diminish residents' adverse reactions to continued development by publicizing the pace and intensity of future development and by making clear the association between population growth and improved facilities and services.

SUMMARY

In an effort to provide a broad-based assessment of the communities, this chapter has considered an assortment of evaluative measures— from inventories of community facilities to an interview item that dealt with recommending the community to close friends and relatives. Despite the diversity of the measures, the findings tended to cluster around a limited number of themes. For each of the three communitywide resident ratings, for example, new community residents produced significantly more positive responses than did people living in conventional communities.° The differences were modest but consistent:

	Thirteen New Communities	Thirteen Conventional Communities
Rating of community as "excellent"	49%	42%
Would recommend as a "particularly good place to live"	81%	74%
Think community will be "better place to live" in five years	37%	33%

At the level of specific facilities and services, the results were mixed, much as they were when nineteen attributes of the present and the former communities were compared in Chapter 2. On the basis of both facility inventories and resident evaluations, recreation and health care facilities fared noticeably better in new communities than in the paired conventional communities. Residents' ratings were also significantly higher in new communities for the immediate neigh-

---

°Predictably, the broad satisfaction measures we have considered in this and the previous chapter were correlated. (If they had not been, their validity as measures might be questioned.) The responses were not strongly associated with the position of the respondents' communities on the new community continuum. The simple intercorrelations (rs) were:

	A	B	C	D	E
A. Overall community satisfaction					
B. Overall improvement in quality of life after move to new community	.28				
C. Likely to move in two to three years	−.22	−.19			
D. Would recommend community to close friend or relative	.47	.30	−.21		
E. Community will be better in five years	.17	.09	−.12	.19	
F. New community continuum	.06	.06	.08	.10	.09

borhood and for transportation services. Ratings of other community components (e.g., schools and shopping), however, showed no differences of any significance between the more and less planned settings.

A multivariate analysis for nonfederally assisted new community residents was done to determine which components of a community contributed most to overall satisfaction. Neither a series of nine personal characteristics nor the eight inventories of types of community facilities proved to explain much of the variation in satisfaction responses.[P] Much more important were resident ratings of nine aspects of the community. The key factor turned out to be the ratings of residents' immediate neighborhoods. Important, but less so, were ratings of the dwelling and of recreation facilities. (Analyses of responses to the dwelling and neighborhood are discussed in Chapter 4.)

The adequacy of recreation facilities was mentioned by respondents in other contexts as well. Roughly 10 percent of the new community residents said that the convenience and quality of recreation facilities were important reasons for rating their communities favorably. On the other hand, in eight of the fifteen new communities from 11 percent to 18 percent of the respondents felt that the adequacy of recreation facilities was a problem, and one-fifth of all new community residents said that an improvement in recreation facilities would be a good way to make their communities better places to live.

Another aspect of communities that was brought out in several contexts was a generalized concern about the quality of the physical environment. In response to the probe of the overall community ratings, the most frequently mentioned reasons for evaluating a community highly had to do with the attractiveness of the surroundings, a sense of nearness to nature, and an absence of crowding. Parallel concerns about the pressures of increasing growth on environmental quality arose when people were asked to identify the important issues or problems their communities faced and when they were asked to suggest ways (limit growth or limit high density development) to improve their communities.

The extent to which developers can continue to provide a range of community facilities and services *and* preserve open space and the

---

[P]In addition to using the inventory data to summarize the availability of facilities, access information on the distance to the nearest of fifteen types of facilities and to twelve types of facilities most often used were also collected. See Zehner (1977, Chapter 2). Preliminary analyses indicated that these distance measures of access had little affect on satisfaction (Zehner, Burby, and Weiss 1974), and we chose to focus on the more inclusive facilities inventories in this book. An earlier study has also documented a weak relationship between road distance access measures and satisfaction in an inner suburban working class community (Zehner and Chapin 1974, Chapter 5).

quality of the natural environment *and* manage to attain a sufficient pace of development to remain in business remains to be seen. Residents clearly need to be more aware, however, of the relationship between plans for present and future development and the provision of facilities and services.

The improvements people reported on moving to their present communities, the reasons they cited for community satisfaction, the issues they raised as community problems, and the results of multivariate analyses of their overall community ratings suggest that four factors are key elements of community livability. These include satisfaction with: (1) the immediate neighborhood, (2) the dwelling unit, (3) the availability of community recreational facilities, and (4) the proximity of the natural environment. In general, new communities have met these conditions for a livable environment. An overwhelming proportion of the residents rated each new community as an excellent or good place to live.

✳ *Chapter 4*

The Neighborhood
and the Dwelling

The address on a letter defines an individual's residence within a series of increasingly specific contexts—country, state, community, street, and dwelling. From a resident's point of view, by far the most important of these contexts are likely to be those closest to home—the immediate neighborhood and the dwelling. These are the places, after all, where most persons—even commuters—have day-to-day experiences. These are the settings where children are raised, where interaction with neighbors occurs, where homeowners often have a significant investment, and where people spend most of their leisure hours.[a] Analyses reported in the previous chapter, in fact, affirmed the importance for residents of these settings in comparison with other aspects of the wider community including schools, health care, and transportation.

This chapter parallels Chapter 3 in that we will focus attention on both overall satisfaction measures and ratings of neighborhoods and dwelling units. In addition, to control for the effects of the density of development, a number of tabulations and multivariate analyses of satisfaction look separately at residents of single-family detached houses, townhouses, and apartments. Chapter 5 then returns to the consideration of overall quality of life and the impact of residential environment—dwelling, neighborhood, and community—on life satisfaction in relation to other life domains.

[a]Hammer and Chapin (1972, pp. 98–99), for example, using time budget data for the Washington, D.C. metropolitan area, found that residents spent from 64 percent (Sunday) to 83 percent (Monday and Wednesday) of their leisure hours at home. Chapin (1974, p. 101) also reported that on average people spend from 63 percent (weekdays) to 74 percent (Sunday) of *all* their time at home.

THE MICRONEIGHBORHOOD

Asking residents about neighborhoods raises the problem of definition. To some people, the neighborhood may take in an area of several square miles in an urban setting and include a population of thousands of households; to others the neighborhood might consist of their house and front yard and little else.[b] To reduce, if not eliminate, the ambiguities that result if one asks about "neighborhood" in a general sense, we decided to include a definition in the interview to try to focus the respondents' attention on the immediate area around their homes, an area for which they ought to be able to provide the most informed evaluations. The wording used to delineate the neighborhood was "roughly the area near here which you can see from your front door—that is, the five or six homes nearest to yours around here."

In the context of this definition, respondents were asked to rate a series of aspects of their neighborhood on five-point, semantic differential items. Responses to the three most general items (attractive−unattractive, pleasant−unpleasant, very good place to live−very poor place to live) were summed to create a simple neighborhood satisfaction scale. The proportions of most favorable ratings occurring in each new community for the scale, the scale components, and eight other attributes of the immediate neighborhood are summarized in Table 4−1.[c]

As was noted in Chapter 3, the nonfederally assisted new communities as a group were significantly more likely to have respondents with high neighborhood satisfaction scale scores, although the margin of difference between new and conventional communities was a modest 4 percent. By similar margins, the thirteen nonfederally assisted new communities received significantly better evaluations of neighborhood attractiveness, convenience, and maintenance level. Most comparisons of neighborhood attribute and scale component ratings in new and paired conventional communities, however, did not reveal significant differences. For two new communities—Columbia and Forest Park—no ratings were significantly different, and in four other instances—Reston, Foster City, Sharpstown, and Jonathan—only one statistically significant difference was found. Two new commu-

---

[b]Marans (1975, p. 13) reported considerable variation in the areas chosen by respondents to describe their neighborhoods. Roughly 28 percent chose definitions of a microneighborhood of "five or six dwellings" or "the immediate block." About one-fifth of the respondents said "a 2−5 block area" was appropriate, and a similar proportion opted for "a square mile."

[c]Complete distributions of responses to these items, by community, are included in Appendix C, Table C−2.

nities, however, fared consistently better than their comparison areas: Laguna Niguel (paired with Dana Point) and Lake Havasu City (paired with Kingman) each received significantly more highly favorable ratings on seven of the eleven neighborhood attributes and scale components tabulated.

These two new communities also fared well in comparison with the other thirteen new communities studied, and each had the highest proportion of favorable ratings for three of the eleven questionnaire items included in Table 4—1. Laguna Niguel was rated quiet, friendly, and a very good place to live more often than the other new communities, and Lake Havasu City, reflecting its desert setting, was twice as likely as most of the other communities to have its neighborhoods rated uncrowded. It also led the evaluations of privacy and neighborhood homogeneity.

Neighborhood Amenities Inventory

An inventory of 32 facilities and services available to residents within one-half mile of their homes was collected to parallel, in a less extensive fashion, that done in the community scale.[d] (See Zehner 1977, Chapter 2, for a detailed summary of the neighborhood inventory data.) Overall, residents in the nonfederally assisted new communities averaged 4.7 amenities within one-half mile of their homes, compared to 3.6 amenities in the conventional communities. The leading new community, Columbia, provided an average of 7.6 facilities and services within the half-mile radius of each household surveyed.

On the basis of the proportion of residents having a facility within the larger neighborhood area, new communities proved to be noticeably more likely to provide bus stops (21 percent more residents had them nearby) and biking or hiking paths (19 percent more). Conventional community residents were particularly more likely to have a gas station within a half-mile radius by a 16 percent margin.[e]

[d]The amenities inventoried included primary school, intermediate school, secondary school, general practitioner or internist, nursery school or day care center, public health facility, biking or hiking path, golf course, ice skating rink, picnic area, playground for children under 12, roller skating rink, swimming facility, teen recreation center, tennis court, convenience store, supermarket, neighborhood or community shopping center, regional shopping center, bar or tavern, billiard parlor, bowling alley, gas station, laundromat, movie theater, restaurant, bus stop, church, community center, library, and post office.

[e]The household interview included an item which asked residents to nominate three facilities they "would most prefer to have . . . within one-half mile of here" from a list of 23 facilities. Only four facilities were mentioned by one-fifth or more of the new community respondents. These were a library (31 percent), a supermarket (30 percent), a quiet place to walk and sit outdoors (27 percent), and an outdoor swimming pool (24 percent). Responses for the 23 facilities for each of the new communities are presented in Appendix C, Table C—5.

Table 4-1. Resident Ratings of Microneighborhoods
(percentage of respondents giving most favorable ratings)

Rating		Columbia	Reston	Irvine	Valencia	Park Forest	Westlake Village	Elk Grove Village
						Nonfederally Assisted New Communities		
A.	*Microneighborhood satisfaction scale* [c]							
	Highest rating	30	34	36	35[a]	21[b]	57[a]	31[b]
B.	*Satisfaction scale components* [d]							
	Microneighborhood is							
	Attractive	39	47	47	55[a]	31	68[a]	44
	Pleasant	57	60	62	55	46	73	51
	Very good place to live	51	58	64[a]	62	45	75	55
C.	*Neighborhood attributes* [d]							
	Microneighborhood (is/has)							
	Convenient	57	42[b]	48	44[a]	58	52[a]	53
	Enough privacy	44	41	52	52	41[b]	57	46[b]
	Friendly	45	40	43	45	42	49	40
	People like me	17	13	18	20	16[b]	29[a]	28
	Quiet	39	35	43[a]	41	38	46[b]	39
	Safe	34	48	58[a]	37	47	62	53
	Uncrowded	36	27	34[a]	38	37	39[b]	31[b]
	Well kept up	51	44	53	59[a]	41[b]	69[a]	56

[a] New community given high ratings significantly more often than paired conventional community at the 0.05 level of confidence.

[b] Paired conventional community given high ratings significantly more often than new community at the 0.05 level of confidence.

[c] The summary neighborhood satisfaction scale is based on the three items included in panel B of this table. See also Table 3-5, note d. For more detailed distributions for each new community, see Appendix C, Table C-1.

[d] The percentages tabulated here represent the proportions who selected the most positive point on five-point semantic differential items. See Appendix D, page 219 (self-administered section, question 34). For complete distributions for each new community, see Appendix C, Table C-2.

It was surprising to find that the range of neighborhood facilities was not strongly related to any of the rating variables in Table 4-1.

Table 4–1. continued

	Nonfederally Assisted New Communities (cont'd.)					Federally Assisted New Communities			
Foster City	*Laguna Niguel*	*Lake Havasu City*	*Sharpstown*	*Forest Park*	*North Palm Beach*	*Jonathan*	*Park Forest South*	*Thirteen Nonfederally Assisted New Communities*	*Thirteen Conventional Communities*
31	42[a]	28[a]	21	28	37[b]	29	21	34[a]	30
46	51[a]	38[a]	34	38	48[b]	42	40[a]	47[a]	42
53	66	64	48	54	56	60	54	57	56
57	76[a]	48	44	49	64[b]	52	41	59	57
57	46[a]	47	62	65	61	45	29[b]	54[a]	50
55	62	64[a]	46	45	54[b]	39	43	51	50
42	54[a]	53[a]	33	43	52	52[a]	42	45	42
16	29[a]	33[a]	17	21	27[b]	20	20	22	24
34[b]	62[a]	58[a]	36	34	43	39	41	42	41
49	67	59	32[a]	49	59	70	55	51	51
33	47	73[a]	30	32	30[b]	39	26	36	38
55	48[a]	47[a]	41	42	48[b]	50	46	51[a]	47

For the nonfederally assisted new community sample, the largest correlation was between the number of nearby facilities and neighborhood quietness ($r = -.10$) followed by that with the convenience rating ($r = .07$). The correlation with the neighborhood satisfaction scale was virtually nonexistent, $r = .02$.

Neighborhood Ratings and Density

All of the new communities provided townhouses or apartments as well as single-family, detached houses. (See Table 1–2.) In Columbia, Reston, North Palm Beach, and the two federally assisted new communities, fewer than half the dwelling units were detached single-family homes in 1973. In four other new communities—Irvine, Westlake Village, Foster City, and Sharpstown—between 50 and 60 percent of the houses were single-family, detached dwellings. Higher proportions of lower density development, over 80 percent of the dwellings being single family, typified Valencia, Laguna Niguel, and Forest Park. Overall, in the thirteen nonfederally assisted new communities, 70 percent of the respondents lived in single-family, detached houses, 12 percent in townhouses, and 18 percent in apartments.

Not unexpectedly, homeownership was not equally common in the three housing categories. In the nonfederally assisted new communities, over 97 percent of those living in detached single-family dwellings owned their homes compared to 58 percent of those living in townhouses and 18 percent of those living in apartments. (See Appendix B, Table B−1.) Since satisfaction responses seemed likely to be associated with tenure,[f] Table 4−2 is focused on differences in response to the immediate neighborhood that was related to density while controlling for tenure. Two categories of accommodation, rented single-family, detached houses and owned apartments, are omitted because of their limited incidence in the sample.

A number of significant differences emerged when new and conventional communities were compared, almost all in favor of the nonfederally assisted new communities. Higher levels of satisfaction were noticeably more frequent among the rental households. Much more interesting was the absence of significant differences in satisfaction between homeowners living in single-family, detached houses and those living in townhouses. Overall neighborhood satisfaction and ratings of seven of the eight neighborhood attributes, including those of noise level, privacy, and crowdedness, were actually slightly more positive in the townhouse areas. Marans and Mandell (1972) found that feelings of being crowded were not completely explained by objective density measures and, as in the case of their research, our data indicate that high resident satisfaction levels are not precluded by raising dwelling densities to those found in townhouse development.[g]

Within the rental households, there was only one attribute where a comparison of townhouse and apartment responses indicated a signif-

[f] The correlation of tenure and the neighborhood satisfaction scale turned out to be a modest $r = .15$.

[g] Lansing *et al.* (1970) did not control for tenure, but their data suggest that density has only marginal effects on satisfaction responses up to about 12.5 dwellings per acre. Satisfaction levels above that density dropped significantly (pp. 106–111).

Table 4–2. Resident Ratings of Microneighborhoods in Nonfederally Assisted New Communities

(percentage of respondents giving most favorable ratings)

Rating	Ownership		Rental	
	Single Family Detached	Townhouse	Townhouse	Apartment
A. Microneighborhood satisfaction scale				
Highest rating	35[a]	45	29	26
B. Satisfaction scale components				
Microneighborhood is				
Attractive	47[a]	55	44	39[a]
Pleasant	59	68	53[a]	45
Very good place to live	62	67	49	43[a]
C. Neighborhood attributes				
Microneighborhood (is/has)				
Convenient	54[a]	60	50	53[b]
Enough privacy	53	58	48[a]	43
Friendly	47	53[a] *	36	31[a]
People like me	23	29[a] *	16	16
Quiet	42	48	40[a]	35[a]
Safe	52	55 *	39	42[a]
Uncrowded	39	41	36[a]	24[a] *
Well kept up	52[a]	52	50[a]	46[a]

*Difference between adjacent columns significant at the 0.05 level of confidence.

[a] New community given high ratings significantly more often than paired conventional community at the 0.05 level of confidence.

[b] Paired conventional community given high ratings significantly more often than new community at the 0.05 level of confidence.

icant difference. In this case, townhouse residents were more likely to say that their neighborhoods were uncrowded. With that exception, however, it appears that within the groups of households renting their dwellings, the density of the neighborhood had few major effects on satisfaction levels.

A comparison of rental versus ownership households was possible only at the medium-density, townhouse level. In that instance, all eight neighborhood attributes were rated higher by those who owned their homes. Three of the contrasts—for friendliness, homogeneity, and safety—were significant. Clearly, people in neighborhoods typified by home ownership are likely to feel more comfortable about their neighbors than people in less settled rental areas, a point made by Michelson (1970, Chapter 8), Gans (1968, Part III), Keller (1968) and others.

Given the relationship between tenure and satisfaction, it is appropriate to note that the lowest levels of satisfaction were recorded in the apartment neighborhoods. Since denser areas tend to have larger rental populations (who report less satisfaction), in other words, one would expect to find—in the aggregate—lower levels of satisfaction in denser neighborhoods. An implication of this, therefore, is that until homeownership is as prevalent in denser neighborhoods as it is in less dense neighborhoods, resident satisfaction is likely to be lower. Other factors (like the neighborhood attributes listed in Table 4–2), however, are more highly related to neighborhood satisfaction than tenure, and unless an environment is also congruent with a household's perceived needs, ownership alone is unlikely to create highly satisfied residents. It is unlikely, for example, that many large families would find apartment house living as satisfying as lower density living even if they were able to own their dwelling.[h]

Multivariate Analyses of Microneighborhood Satisfaction

The neighborhood satisfaction multivariate analyses follow those done for community satisfaction in Chapter 3. We attempt to gauge the separate and combined explanatory power of socioeconomic and demographic characteristics, objective measures of the neighborhood (listed in note *b* of Table 4–3), and resident ratings of attributes of the immediate neighborhood. To determine if different groups of factors were important in different types of neighborhood (single-

[h]The notion of the desirability of "intersystem congruence" is pursued in detail by Michelson (1970). A particularly persuasive argument for the appropriateness of lower density living for families can be found in Stretton (1974). See also Halkett (1976) and Gans (1966).

Table 4–3. Variance in Neighborhood Satisfaction Explained Using Socioeconomic/Demographic, Objective and Resident Rating Variables in Nonfederally Assisted New Communities

| | R^2 | | | |
| | Type of Neighborhood | | | |
	Single Family Detached	Townhouse	Apartment	Overall
I. Variable group				
A. Nine socioeconomic and demographic characteristics[a]	.08	.10	.11	.09
B. Thirteen objective neighborhood measures[b]	.05	.06	.16	.05
C. Eight resident ratings of micro-neighborhood attributes[c]	.53	.56	.65	.56
II. Combinations of variable groups				
A + B	.10	.13	.21	.11
A + C	.55	.59	.67	.58
B + C	.55	.60	.67	.57
A + B + C	.56	.62	.69	.58

[a] These include the respondent's age, sex, education, marital status, family income, dwelling unit value, tenure, length of residence, and the number of children in the household.

[b] These include whether the utilities were underground, there was a sidewalk adjacent to the dwelling, there was a curb and gutter in front of the dwelling, the street was a dead end or a through street, the microneighborhood bordered on water or on a golf course or on open space, there was foundation planting in front of the dwelling. Also included were measures of the density (dwellings per acre) of the immediate neighborhood, interviewer ratings of the condition of buildings, of lawns and gardens, and of the street servicing the microneighborhood, and a variable summarizing the availability of 32 types of facilities and services within one-half mile of the microneighborhood. (The 32 item inventory was a less extensive version of the community-wide inventory noted in Chapter 3. For further detail, see Zehner [1977, Chapter 2 and Appendix C.])

[c] These include the attributes in panel C of Table 4–2.

family detached, townhouse, apartment), parallel runs were made for residents living in each of the three housing categories as well as for the overall nonfederally assisted new community sample.[i]

The results of these runs, summarized in Table 4–3, show that the variable groups have similar impacts in different types of neighborhood. In each instance, the attribute ratings alone could explain over 90 percent of all the variance explained by the three variable groups combined. Total explained variance ranged from $R^2 = .56$ (single-family detached) to $R^2 = .69$ (apartment).[j] Variance explained was highest for the apartment dwellers at each point in the table, the largest proportional difference coming in relation to the explanatory power of the objective measures. Objective neighborhood measures explained roughly three times as much variation in satisfaction in apartment areas as in the other settings. The key objective predictors of neighborhood satisfaction among those living in apartments were the interviewer ratings of the maintenance level of the buildings and the grounds ($r = .27$ and $r = .28$, respectively). In the other types of settings, the most important objective predictor of satisfaction was whether or not utilities were underground ($r = .15$ for both single-family, detached and townhouse neighborhoods).

Table 4–4 focuses on the relative importance of the resident ratings of eight microneighborhood characteristics. The most important single predictor was the rating of the maintenance level of the neighborhood, which alone accounted for over half (.30/.56) of the variance explained by all eight of the ratings combined. (This was also

[i]Tenure was not introduced as a key control variable as in Table 4–2, but was included among the socioeconomic and demographic characteristics in the first group of variables used.

[j]A proportion of the variance explained by the attribute rating variables is undoubtedly caused by the fact that the attribute ratings and the components of the dependent variable, the neighborhood satisfaction scale, were not distributed in different parts of the questionnaire but were collected in the context of a single multi-item question in the interview. The problem inherent in such formats is that a person might respond to a series of items favorably even though, had he been asked one or more of the items in a different situation—say in a casual chat with a neighbor—he might have offered a less favorable response. The presence of response sets can lead to inflated intercorrelations among attitude factors and, in the present analysis, between the suggested determinants of satisfaction and the satisfaction scale.

Two previous studies that used items and formats directly comparable to those of the present study found that response set effects had little effect on the relative importance of the items but that the R^2s were reduced by up to half (Zehner, 1970, pp. 151–152; Zehner and Chapin, 1974, pp. 112–113). If a comparable effect operated in the data reported here, the attribute ratings would remain the most important variable group although their eminence would be proportionally reduced.

Table 4—4. Multivariate Analysis of Microneighborhood Satisfaction
in Nonfederally Assisted Communities

Resident Ratings of Microneighborhood Attributes	Simple Correlation Coefficient	Beta	Cumulative R^2	F-Value
Neighborhood (is/has):				
Well kept up	.55	.31	.30	453.8
Convenient	.41	.18	.39	156.8
Enough privacy	.44	.15	.45	91.9
Friendly	.44	.17	.50	134.5
Safe	.41	.13	.52	77.7
People like me	.42	,14	.54	92.6
Uncrowded	.33	.09	.55	36.9
Quiet	.38	.09	.56	35.6

the preeminent predictor for each of the neighborhood types.)[k] Following maintenance level in importance was a group of five factors, all of which were correlated with the satisfaction scale at about $r = .40$. These included the ratings of convenience, privacy, safety, and two measures of the social setting, friendliness and the extent to which the respondent's neighbors were perceived as similar to the respondent.

In sum, although satisfaction or dissatisfaction with each of the eight attributes noted in Table 4—4 was clearly related to satisfaction or dissatisfaction with the neighborhood as a whole, by far the most important of the factors was how well kept up the immediate area was rated. This finding parallels that of earlier researchers in both planned and less planned environments (see Lansing *et al.* 1970, pp. 102—134) and Zehner and Chapin 1974, Chapter 5) and serves to emphasize the likelihood that, to the extent that a developer is able to design residential areas for ease of maintenance or provide for their upkeep through neighborhood association covenants, the planner–developer will be able to have a significant impact on resident reports of neighborhood satisfaction.

THE DWELLING UNIT

Satisfaction with the dwelling was one of the main determinants of satisfaction with the larger community in the nonfederally assisted

[k]The next variables to enter the equation for residents of single-family, detached housing were ratings of privacy and of friendliness; for townhouse areas, of safety and of convenience; for apartment neighborhoods, of convenience and of homogeneity of neighbors.

8

Table 4–5. Resident Ratings of Dwelling Characteristics
(percentage of respondents)

Rating	Columbia	Reston	Irvine	Valencia	Park Forest	Westlake Village	Elk Grove Village
				Nonfederally Assisted New Communities			
A. *Dwelling unit satisfaction*							
Completely satisfied[c]	28[b]	28	43	39	22[b]	51	35
B. *Attributes*[d]							
Indoor space[e]							
About right/more than needed	74[b]	70	79	82	70	87	67
Outdoor space[f]							
About right/more than needed	81	82	83	79	85	86	88
Outdoor privacy[g]							
Yes	42	54	77	69	42[b]	71	58
Home as investment[h]							
Compared to other places considered, this one will be better	72	77	77	71	41[b]	77	68[b]

[a] New community given rating significantly more often than paired conventional community at the 0.05 level of confidence.

[b] Paired conventional community given rating significantly more often than new community at the 0.05 level of confidence.

[c] For complete distributions for the new communities, see Appendix C, Table C–1.

[d] For complete distributions for the new communities, see Appendix C, Table C–3.

[e] The question was: "Do you have more space indoors in this (house/apartment) than you and your family need, too little space, or about the right amount?"

[f] The question was: "How do you feel about the amount of outdoor space near your home which members of your family can use for their different activities— do you have more space than you need, too little space, or about the right amount?"

[g] The question was: "Do you have a place where you can be outside and feel that you really have privacy from your neighbors if you want it?"

Table 4–5. continued

	Nonfederally Assisted New Communities (cont'd.)					*Federally Assisted New Communities*			
Foster City	*Laguna Niguel*	*Lake Havasu City*	*Sharpstown*	*Forest Park*	*North Palm Beach*	*Jonathan*	*Park Forest South*	*Thirteen Nonfederally Assisted New Communities*	*Thirteen Conventional Communities*
52	52	45[a]	29	29	42	28	29	40	39
77	81	76	67[b]	76	77	71	75	76	77
78	89	88	67[b]	71	84	86	78	81	79
61	77[a]	58	59	35	50[b]	48	37	59	60
88[a]	78	55	54	56	75	64	63[a]	70	73

[h] The question was: "Compared to other homes you considered at the time you were buying, do you think that this home will be a better financial investment, a worse financial investment, or about the same?" Asked only of homeowners; for N's see Appendix C, Table C–3.

new communities. In Chapter 5 it will prove to be more strongly related to overall life satisfaction than either community or neighborhood evaluations. Unfortunately, since the research as a whole was more concerned with the neighborhood and community scale of development, there were relatively few items in the household interview that were directed to resident evaluations of dwelling characteristics. These included items about indoor and outdoor space, privacy, and the investment potential of the home. See Table 4–5. As with the responses to the summary dwelling satisfaction question introduced in Chapter 3, there were only a scattering of significant differences between individual new and conventional communities and none between the aggregated communities. Individual new communities whose dwellings and dwelling attributes were rated comparatively well on the five items tabulated here were overall dwelling satisfaction—Foster City and Laguna Niguel (52 percent completely satisfied), indoor space—Westlake Village (87 percent with the right amount or more than enough), outdoor space—Laguna Niguel (89 percent with the right amount or more than enough), outdoor privacy—Irvine and Laguna Niguel (77 percent with private outdoor space), and investment potential—Foster City (88 percent reporting better than other places considered).

New community homeowners' satisfaction steadily increased with the value of the units. The breaking point in complete satisfaction occurred in the $35,000 to $44,999 price range. A lower than average proportion of respondents who owned homes valued at less than $35,000 and a higher than average proportion of those with homes valued at $45,000 or more were completely satisfied with their dwellings. Except for houses and apartments renting for less than $150 a month, whose tenants were less likely to be satisfied with their dwellings, the amount of rent paid per month was not associated with greater satisfaction with the dwelling unit.

The physical size of dwelling units had little effect on housing satisfaction. However, when dwelling unit space was combined with household size, space did make a difference. For example, complete satisfaction with single-family, detached homes increased from 18 percent of the respondents living in homes with less than one room per person to 59 percent of those living in units with three or more rooms per person. A similar relationship was also true for other types of ownership housing units and for rental units.

Dwelling Ratings and Density

Favorable responses to the dwelling unit items among new community homeowners were as frequent among residents of detached single-family homes as those of townhouses. See Table 4—6. Among the rental households, however, townhouse residents were significantly more likely than apartment dwellers to say that they had enough indoor space (73 percent versus 60 percent) and enough outdoor privacy (51 percent versus 27 percent). In concordance with the microneighborhood tabulations, a comparison of owner and rental townhouse respondents showed noticeably more positive evaluations

Table 4–6. Resident Ratings of Dwelling Characteristics in Nonfederally Assisted Communities *(percentage of respondents)*

Rating	Ownership		Rental	
	Single Family Detached	Townhouse	Townhouse	Apartment
A. *Dwelling unit satisfaction*				
Completely satisfied	44	43 *	24	23[a]
B. *Attributes*				
Indoor space				
About right or more than needed	79	77 *	73 *	60
Outdoor space				
About right or more than needed	82	86 *	67 *	75[a]
Outdoor privacy				
Yes	65	73 *	51 *	27[b]
Investment				
Better	70	71	NA	NA

*Difference between adjacent columns significant at the 0.05 level of confidence.

[a] New community given high ratings significantly more often than paired conventional community at the 0.05 level of confidence.

[b] Paired conventional community given high ratings significantly more often than new community at the 0.05 level of confidence.

among the owners. Although inventory data failed to identify characteristics which clearly distinguished owner and rental townhouse areas other than a greater incidence of underground utilities in the owner settings, it is apparent that satisfaction with the availability and privacy of outdoor space near the dwelling were the bases for sizeable differences in the ratings of dwellings. Had data on characteristics of space associated with dwelling units been collected, we might have been able to detect other ways in which owner and rental townhouse areas differed objectively, but it is also possible that the reasons for higher satisfaction with outdoor space among owners were related more to the greater freedom owners felt to make use of the available space.[1]

Multivariate Analyses of Dwelling Unit Satisfaction

Multivariate analyses of satisfaction with the dwelling unit differ slightly from those reported elsewhere in this volume in that tenure and dwelling unit value were included among the objective characteristics of the dwelling rather than among the socioeconomic and demographic characteristics. In addition, because of the dearth of items focused explicitly on the dwelling (and because the dwelling and immediate neighborhood are closely related in any case), we have augmented the few dwelling unit items in the data set with the objective measures of neighborhood characteristics and the resident ratings of microneighborhood attributes used earlier in this chapter.

The amount of variance in dwelling evaluations explained by the three groups of predictors is summarized in Table 4-7. The dominant variable group, both overall and for each type of housing, was the group that included the resident ratings of dwelling and neighborhood characteristics. These variables accounted for at least 85 percent of the total variance explained by the combinations of groups of variables for each category of dwelling.

The second most effective predictors were the seventeen objective measures. In single-family, detached areas, the factor most strongly related to satisfaction was the value of the dwelling ($r = .27$, higher value associated with higher satisfaction) followed by the age of the

---

[1]Homeownership was associated with greater dwelling satisfaction when controls for race, family income, education, and family life cycle were added as well. Though not included in Table 4-6 because of the limited number of cases, it is striking that 44 percent of the apartment owners were completely satisfied with their dwellings (precisely parallel to the figures for single-family and townhouse owners) and that 20 percent of the single-family detached renters were completely satisfied with their dwellings (precisely parallel to the figures for townhouse and apartment renters). In the overall nonfederally assisted new community sample, tenure and dwelling satisfaction were correlated $r = .22$.

Table 4–7. Variance in Dwelling Unit Satisfaction Explained Using Socioeconomic/Demographic, Objective, and Resident Rating Variables in Nonfederally Assisted New Communities

	R^2			
	Dwelling Type			
	Single Family Detached	Townhouse	Apartment	Overall
I. *Variable Group*				
A. Seven socioeconomic and demographic characteristics[a]	.05	.04	.11	.05
B. Seventeen objective dwelling and neighborhood characteristics[b]	.10	.10	.16	.11
C. Twelve resident ratings of dwelling and microneighborhood attributes[c]	.29	.40	.35	.32
II. *Combinations of Variable Groups*				
A + B	.13	.13	.21	.14
A + C	.30	.42	.37	.33
B + C	.32	.44	.39	.34
A + B + C	.32	.45	.41	.35

[a]These include the respondent's age, sex, marital status, education, family income, length of residence, and the number of children in the household.

[b]In addition to the objective measures listed in Table 4–3, these include the number of rooms (excluding bathrooms) in dwelling, the age of the dwelling, dwelling unit value, and tenure.

[c]These include the items in panel B of Table 4–5 and those in panel C of Table 4–1.

dwelling ($r = .18$, newer dwelling related to higher satisfaction). For townhouse residents, the leading objective predictors were tenure ($r = .18$) and the interviewer's rating of the condition of the building ($r = .18$). Apartment residents' ratings of satisfaction were correlated most strongly with the interviewer's rating of the building's condition ($r = .28$) and tenure ($r = .24$).

On the basis of simple correlation coefficients, the four resident ratings most strongly associated with overall housing satisfaction in new communities were the measures of privacy in the immediate neighborhood ($r = .35$), the adequacy of space inside the dwelling ($r = .33$), the availability of private outdoor space ($r = .32$), and the maintenance rating of the microneighborhood ($r = .31$). See Table 4–8. Seven of the eight remaining ratings were modestly correlated (between .21 and .25) with dwelling satisfaction as well, but they added only about 4 percent to the variance explained by the first four ratings.

The main predictors of dwelling satisfaction for residents of single-family, detached homes paralleled those of the overall sample exactly.[m] For townhouse residents, on the other hand, the most important factors proved to be whether there was private outdoor space near the dwelling ($r = .38$), the amount of outdoor space ($r = .36$), the amount of indoor space ($r = .34$), and maintenance level of the immediate neighborhood ($r = .32$). Apartment residents' ratings of housing satisfaction were correlated most highly with neighborhood maintenance ($r = .44$), followed by neighborhood privacy ($r = .36$), the amount of indoor space ($r = .35$), and the existence of outdoor privacy ($r = .31$).

To a designer of dwellings and their immediate surroundings, it is obviously quite important to know that, whatever types of dwellings people live in, there are common concerns with the adequacy of indoor and outdoor space that provides a sense of privacy. The availability of outdoor privacy, in fact, was more strongly related to housing satisfaction than the amount of outdoor space. Also important for satisfaction with one's housing was the maintenance level of the immediate neighborhood. How well the neighborhood was kept up increased in importance in tandem with dwelling unit density and was clearly the main determinant of dwelling satisfaction for residents of apartments.

SUMMARY

Two essential building blocks of a residential community are the homes and the neighborhoods. Analyses reported in Chapter 3 indi-

[m] The correlation coefficients were .33, .30, .28, and .27.

Table 4–8. Multivariate Analysis of Dwelling Unit Satisfaction in Nonfederally Assisted New Communities

Resident Ratings of Dwelling Unit and Microneighborhood Attributes	Simple Correlation Coefficient	Beta	Cumulative R^2	F-Value
Dwelling unit neighborhood (is/has):				
Enough privacy (neighborhood)	.35	.11	.12	22.6
Indoor space (dwelling unit)	.33	.23	.20	137.1
Well kept up (neighborhood)	.31	.14	.24	41.0
Outdoor privacy (dwelling unit)	.32	.17	.28	63.4
Better investment (dwelling unit)	.21	.11	.29	29.7
Friendly (neighborhood)	.24	.08	.30	14.9
Outdoor space (dwelling unit)	.24	.08	.31	14.2
Uncrowded (neighborhood)	.25	.06	.31	7.3
Safe (neighborhood)	.23	.04	.32	4.2
Quiet (neighborhood)	.24	.05	.32	5.0
Convenient (neighborhood)	.16	.04	.32	3.4
People like me (neighborhood)	.22	.04	.32	3.1

cated, in fact, that from the residents' point of view the quality of the immediate neighborhood and of the dwelling were more important for their feelings of satisfaction with the community than several other key community components, including schools, transportation, shopping, and health care facilities. In this chapter, in addition to further comparisons of new and conventional communities, the aim has been to explore the factors that contribute to satisfaction with the dwelling and the neighborhood.

At the scale of the neighborhood, which was defined as "the area near here which you can see from your front door," comparisons of ratings in new communities and paired conventional communities revealed many more similarities than differences. Residents of non-federally assisted new communities did give significantly higher ratings (if only by margins of four or five percentage points) to their neighborhoods overall and to the maintenance level, attractiveness, and convenience of these areas.

In the case of dwelling unit evaluation, on the other hand, there were no differences in the aggregate between the new and conventional communities and only a scattering of significant differences between specific new and paired conventional communities. From the resident responses, it is clear that new community claims of providing higher quality residential environments than conventional communities are largely inapplicable to an integral part of these environments, the dwellings themselves. That this should be the case is not surprising. Most new community developers sell land to or enter contracts with large-scale homebuilders who build comparable homes at several locations in a metropolitan area. Only at the level of the neighborhood and the community did differences in resident ratings between the new and conventional communities begin to emerge.

Some of the most interesting findings presented in this chapter concern the absence of differences in dwelling and neighborhood satisfaction associated with dwelling density when controls were made for tenure. Homeowners, for example, were as satisfied with their dwellings and their neighborhoods when they lived in medium density townhouses or in lower density, detached, single-family homes. In the case of renters, a few differences between residents' ratings of apartments and townhouses and their microneighborhoods did emerge, townhouse ratings, especially in the availability of adequate outdoor private space, faring better than apartments.

Homeownership was consistently related to higher levels of both housing and neighborhood satisfaction, this finding indicates that one means of increasing aggregate levels of resident satisfaction in a community is to increase the proportion of ownership units. The fact that homeowners were as satisfied with their environments at medium densities as at lower densities further suggests that residential densities can be increased in communities typified by detached, single-family housing without sacrificing dwelling and neighborhood satisfaction levels, but only if the more dense housing provides significant opportunities for homeownership as well as rental accommodation. From the concerns of residents about the growth of their communities and residential densities mentioned in Chapter 3, however, it is apparent that increasing densities—even if accompanied by greater opportunities for ownership—may be difficult if they are attempted after a low density character has been established in a community.

The final part of the neighborhood and dwelling analyses consisted of multivariate attempts to identify the key determinants of satisfaction with these levels of the residential environment. At the neighborhood level, by far the most important predictor of resident satisfaction was their rating of the maintenance level of the immediate neighborhood.[n] Maintenance was also one of the main determinants of dwelling satisfaction, increasing in importance with increasing density. It was the primary predictor of housing satisfaction among apartment dwellers. Other factors of importance at the neighborhood level included ratings of neighbor friendliness and homogeneity, safety, convenience, and privacy. In the dwelling unit analyses, ratings of outdoor privacy and indoor space were important determinants of satisfaction, the rating of privacy in the immediate neighborhood being the most important factor for the nonfederally assisted new community sample.

Although the multivariate analyses support the notion that satisfaction with dwellings and neighborhoods is, in fact, dependent on a number of variables, two types of factors recurred more often than the others. These were ratings of privacy and of maintenance, the factor with the most significant impact overall. Both of these variables appear amenable to manipulation by environmental designers, and it is apparent that improvements in these areas—particularly improvements that result in higher evaluations of maintenance—will result in higher resident ratings of neighborhoods and dwellings.

---

[n] Maintenance was also highly related to whether or not residents felt that their neighborhoods had a "good reputation" ($r = .40$). Slightly more strongly associated with reputation ratings in the nonfederally assisted new communities was the rating of neighborhood safety ($r = .41$). The relation between maintenance and reputation ratings was stronger than that between safety and reputation for townhouse and apartment residents. In single-family areas, the safety rating was somewhat more important.

❋ Chapter 5

Satisfaction with Life

A 1969 study that included two new communities, Columbia, Maryland and Reston, Virginia in its sample asked respondents to evaluate their lives and found that 18 percent of the respondents felt their lives were "completely satisfying," 74 percent said their lives were "pretty satisfying," and 8 percent reported that their lives were "not very" or "not at all" satisfying (Lansing *et al.* 1970, pp. 58–60). In comparison with earlier national data (using the same item), the new community residents reported somewhat lower levels of life satisfaction, but the authors found no evidence that the degree of community planning was significantly related (either positively or negatively) to life satisfaction.

In the present study, to gather data that would be comparable to a 1971 national cross-sectional sample (Campbell, Converse, and Rodgers 1976), respondents were asked the following questions toward the end of the 90-minute interview:

We have talked about various parts of your life; now I want to ask you about your life as a whole. How satisfied are you with your life as a whole these days? (HAND CARD) Which number on the card comes closest to how you feel?

Completely Satisfied 1 2 3 4 5 6 7 Completely Dissatisfied

The 1971 national cross-section responses to the same question among persons with family incomes of $17,000 and up (the category most comparable to the present sample) indicated that 25.7 percent of the respondents were completely satisfied with their lives

101

(response 1); 63.4 percent were satisfied (responses 2 and 3), and 10.8 percent were neutral or dissatisfied (responses 4 through 7).[a]

The distribution of responses among both residents of the nonfederally assisted new communities and those of the paired conventional communities in this study was virtually identical, but it also showed greater life satisfaction than the national data. To be specific, 31 percent of the new community residents were completely satisfied with their lives, 57 percent were satisfied, and 12 percent were neutral or dissatisfied. See Table 5-1.

The highest proportions of completely satisfied people lived in Foster City (41 percent), followed closely by Westlake Village (39 percent). In only two cases was there a significant difference in reports of complete satisfaction between new and conventional communities. The Foster City residents were significantly more satisfied with their lives than those living in West San Mateo, and the Park Forest residents were significantly less satisfied than those living in Lansing.

LIFE DOMAINS

In addition to the overall evaluation of life satisfaction, the household survey included items to obtain respondent ratings of each of ten life domains. The selection of domains for inclusion in the interview was based primarily on a desire to be able to assess the relative importance of environmental factors compared to health, family, marriage, and other factors that are usually related closely to life satisfaction.[b] Of the ten life domains for which we have measures of satisfaction (see Table 5-2), three are clearly ratings of aspects of the residential environment: the dwelling, the immediate neighborhood, and the community. The other domain items include satisfaction with standard of living, use of leisure time, health, family life, marriage, job, and housework.[c]

[a] The national data are taken from the 1971 quality of life study conducted by the Survey Research Center at the University of Michigan (Campbell, Converse, and Rodgers 1976). The percentages here are based on material provided by Dr. Willard Rodgers of the Survey Research Center.

[b] See Marans and Rodgers (1972, pp. 102–104) for one report of the relative importance of environmental variables.

[c] Willard Rodgers of the Survey Research Center provided advice on the areas to be included during the domain selection stage of this project (Summer 1972) drawn from his work on the 1971 Quality of Life Study. For items that are comparable with the questions used in this research, the percentages of people in the 1971 study with incomes of $17,000 or more who said they were "completely satisfied" were: standard of living (51.1 percent), leisure time (36.6 percent), health (55.7 percent), job (39.6 percent), and dwelling unit (36.3 percent). Satisfaction in the national sample was higher than in the new community sample for standard of living, leisure, and health. It was somewhat higher in the new communities for job and dwelling unit.

Table 5–1. Satisfaction with Life as a Whole *(percentage distributions of respondents)*

Communities	New Communities			Conventional Communities		
	Completely Satisfied	*Satisfied*	*Neutral or Dissatisfied*	*Completely Satisfied*	*Satisfied*	*Neutral or Dissatisfied*
Nonfederally assisted						
Thirteen new communities	31	57	12			
Thirteen conventional communities				31	55	13
Columbia	21	56	23	30	46	24
Reston	20	65	16	22	61	17
Irvine	28	61	11	34	50	16
Valencia	25	62	13	24	59	17
Park Forest	27	58	16	43	44	13
Westlake Village	39	52	9	35	58	8
Elk Grove Village	31	58	11	39	53	8
Foster City	41	48	11	25	64	11
Laguna Niguel	36	57	7	36	53	12
Lake Havasu City	38	48	14	36	58	6
Sharpstown	23	64	13	24	58	18
Forest Park	33	50	17	35	53	12
North Palm Beach	28	63	9	31	51	9
Federally assisted						
Jonathan	31	54	15	23	63	14
Park Forest South	27	58	15	27	50	24

Table 5–2. Satisfaction with Ten Life Domains *(percent of respondents giving most positive responses)*

Life Domains	Nonfederally Assisted New Communities								
	Columbia	Reston	Irvine	Valencia	Park Forest	Westlake Village	Elk Grove Village	Foster City	Laguna Niguel
Standard of living[a]	29	32	32	35	20	43	36	47	46
Use of leisure time[b]	21	22	24	24	29	38	25	42	35
Health[c]	47	46	54	43	44	56	49	55	54
Family life[d]	44	47	53	51	54	61	54	54	60
Marriage[e]	54	55	64	66	59	67	64	61	66
Job[f]	33	31	45	24	44	59	41	61	47
Housework[g]	22	23	30	25	34	33	28	32	31
Dwelling unit[h]	28	28	43	39	22	51	35	52	52
Neighborhood[i]	30	34	36	35	21	57	31	31	42
Community[j]	40	55	52	57	28	75	42	50	61

↑ continued below ↑

Table 5-2. continued

Life Domains	Nonfederally Assisted New Communities (cont'd.)				Federally Assisted New Communities		Thirteen Nonfederally Assisted New Communities	Thirteen Conventional Communities
	Lake Havasu City	*Sharpstown*	*Forest Park*	*North Palm Beach*	*Jonathan*	*Park Forest South*		
Standard of living[a]	42	33	29	46	29	27	38	36
Use of leisure time[b]	41	27	29	36	17	24	31	29
Health[c]	55	49	48	51	52	49	50	45
Family life[d]	60	53	60	61	60	49	56	57
Marriage[e]	74	64	63	65	67	61	64	66
Job[f]	47	34	40	46	41	36	43	41
Housework[g]	33	37	34	29	25	24	31	31
Dwelling unit[h]	45	29	29	42	28	29	40	39
Neighborhood[i]	28	21	28	37	29	21	34	30
Community[j]	31	27	32	59	41	21	49	42

Table 5-2. continued

aEntries in the table represent responses coded 1 for the following question: "The things people have—housing, car, furniture, recreation, and the like—make up their standard of living. Some people are satisfied with their standard of living, others feel it is not as high as they would like. How satisfied are you with your standard of living?"

Completely Satisfied   1   2   3   4   5   6   7   Completely Dissatisfied

bEntries in the table represent responses coded 1 for the following question: "Overall, how satisfied are you with the ways you spend your spare time? Which number comes closest to how you feel?"

Completely Satisfied   1   2   3   4   5   6   7   Completely Dissatisfied

cEntries in the table represent responses coded 1 for the following question: "Now we have some questions about your health and health care. Of course, most people get sick now and then, but overall, how satisfied are you with your own health? Here is a card I'd like you to use to answer this question."

Completely Satisfied   1   2   3   4   5   6   7   Completely Dissatisfied

dEntries in the table represent responses coded 1 for the following question: "All things considered, I am very satisfied with my family life—the time I spend and the things I do with members of my family."

(1) Agree Strongly   (2) Agree Somewhat   (3) Disagree Somewhat   (4) Disagree Strongly

eEntries in the table represent responses coded 1 for the following question: "All things considered, how satisfied are you with your marriage? Which number comes closest to how you feel?"

Completely Satisfied   1   2   3   4   5   6   7   Completely Dissatisfied

fEntries in the table represent responses coded 1 to whichever of the following questions referred to the respondent: "(1) All things considered how satisfied is (HEAD) with (his/her) main job? Which number comes closest to how satisfied or dissatisfied (HEAD) feels?"

Completely Satisfied   1   2   3   4   5   6   7   Completely Dissatisfied

"(2) All things considered, how satisfied is (SPOUSE) with (SPOUSE'S) main job? Which number comes closest to how satisfied or dissatisfied (SPOUSE) feels?"

Completely Satisfied   1   2   3   4   5   6   7   Completely Dissatisfied

Table 5-2. continued

gEntries in the table represent responses coded 1 for the following question: "As often as not, I actually enjoy cooking, cleaning, and doing other chores around the house."

    (1) Agree Strongly   (2) Agree Somewhat   (3) Disagree Somewhat   (4) Disagree Strongly

hEntries in the table represent responses coded 1 for the following question: "Now, overall how do you feel about the (house/apartment) as a place to live? Which number comes closest to how satisfied or dissatisfied you feel?"

    Completely Satisfied   1 2 3 4 5 6 7   Completely Dissatisfied

iEntries in the table represent persons whose responses were coded 1 to the three parts of the following question that are reproduced here: "Below are some words and phrases which we would like you to use to describe this *neighborhood* as it seems to you. By neighborhood we mean roughly the area near here which you can see from your front door—that is, the five or six homes nearest to yours around here."

            Attractive : $\underline{1}$: $\underline{2}$: $\underline{3}$: $\underline{4}$: $\underline{5}$: Unattractive

            Pleasant : $\underline{1}$: $\underline{2}$: $\underline{3}$: $\underline{4}$: $\underline{5}$: Unpleasant

   Very good place to live : $\underline{1}$: $\underline{2}$: $\underline{3}$: $\underline{4}$: $\underline{5}$: Very poor place to live

jEntries in the table represent responses coded 1 for the following question: "I'd like to ask you how you feel now about this area as a place to live—I mean the area outlined on the map. From your own personal point of view, would you rate this area as an excellent place to live, good, average, below average, or poor?"

    (1) Excellent   (2) Good   (3) Average   (4) Below average   (5) Poor

The percentages of respondents giving the most favorable responses to each of the items are shown in the table for each of the new communities. (See Appendix C, Table C-4 for complete distributions.) Differences between the aggregated thirteen nonfederally assisted new communities and the thirteen conventional communities are modest. For most of the domains listed, however, there is a sizeable range in favorable replies across the new communities sampled. Two of the new communities rate particularly well in that their residents each proved to be the most satisfied with four domains. These were also the communities where residents responded most positively to the overall life satisfaction item. Foster City respondents were most satisfied with their standard of living, use of leisure time, job, and (tied with Laguna Niguel) dwelling unit. Westlake Village residents gave the most favorable reactions to their health, family life, neighborhood, and community. The most positive responses for the other two domains were found in Lake Havasu City (marriage) and Sharpstown (housework).

In the case of the three residential environment ratings, the least positive dwelling unit ratings occurred in Park Forest. The immediate neighborhood and the community both received the fewest positive evaluations in Sharpstown. The only new community with several ratings at the bottom of the rankings was Columbia where residents were least likely to express high levels of satisfaction with their use of leisure time, family life, marriage, and housework. Columbia ranked fourteenth in positive responses to the "life as a whole" evaluation.

With the exception of dwelling, neighborhood, and community satisfaction, we have not pursued detailed analyses to identify the correlates of satisfaction in the ten life domain areas. Among the strengths ascribed to new communities, however, are expectations for higher leisure satisfaction and greater satisfaction with family life. None of the residents of the fifteen new communities were significantly more satisfied with either their leisure or their family lives than residents in the paired communities, but in the aggregate there was a significant difference in favor of new communities on the family life item. Satisfaction with family life tended to decrease with greater adherence to the new community concept. For example, fewer than half the Columbia and Reston respondents indicated that they were highly satisfied with their family lives, while in Laguna Niguel, Lake Havasu City, Forest Park, and North Palm Beach, which ranked toward the bottom of the new community continuum, three-fifths of the respondents were satisfied.

The proportion of respondents satisfied with their family lives tended to be higher in communities where the median education of respondents was lower, where a higher proportion of respondents reported that they could find the church and religious activities they desired within their community, and where a higher proportion of respondents rated neighborhood safety and compatibility highly.

The availability of leisure facilities was associated with lower satisfaction with family life. For example, satisfaction with family life tended to be lower in communities where a higher proportion of respondents were aware of nearby child play areas and rated them highly, where a relatively large number of recreational opportunities, particularly for tennis and swimming, were available, and where a higher proportion of respondents were aware of a bus stop within a ten-minute walk of home. Thus, the mere presence of facilities was not enough to insure a satisfying family life.

Satisfaction with leisure time was not highly associated with either the new community continuum or the extent of available recreation facilities. Columbia and Reston, for example, which ranked first and second (tie) in the number of recreation facilities in the community inventory and second and third in the resident evaluations of recreation facilities, ranked thirteenth and fourteenth on leisure satisfaction. In contrast, Foster City ranked first in satisfaction with leisure, but was ninth (tie) on the inventory and eleventh in resident evaluations of recreation facilities. It is apparent that simply providing an array of facilities in a community will not, of itself, generate satisfaction with the way people spend their leisure time.

Table 5-3 shows the instances where new and conventional community responses differed significantly for the ten domains. The table demonstrates very few significant differences. In the aggregate, however, new community residents were significantly more satisfied with their health, immediate neighborhoods, and communities. Conventional community residents were more satisfied with none of the domains included in the analysis. Of the new communities, Lake Havasu City and Valencia both had a net advantage over their paired communities in three domains. In each instance, these domains included the standard of living and the neighborhood. Valencia residents also rated their community more highly than residents of Bouquet Canyon. Lake Havasu City residents were also more satisfied than Kingman residents with their health and their dwellings, but less satisfied with their family lives.

MULTIVARIATE ANALYSIS OF LIFE SATISFACTION

Determining which aspects of people's lives have the greatest impact on life satisfaction has been a concern of a number of recent studies, three of which used national data bases. Marans and Rodgers (1972),

Table 5–3.   Significant Differences in Satisfaction with Life Domains

Life Domains	Nonfederally Assisted New Communities													Federally Assisted New Communities		Thirteen Nonfederally Assisted New Communities
	Columbia	Reston	Irvine	Valencia	Park Forest	Westlake Village	Elk Grove Village	Foster City	Laguna Niguel	Lake Havasu City	Sharpstown	Forest Park	North Palm Beach	Jonathan	Park Forest South	
Standard of living	0	0	0	+	−	0	0	0	0	+	0	0	0	0	0	0
Use of leisure time	0	0	−	0	−	0	0	0	0	0	0	0	0	0	0	0
Health	0	0	0	0	0	0	0	+	0	+	0	0	+	0	0	+
Family life	0	0	0	0	0	0	0	0	0	−	0	0	0	0	0	0
Marriage	0	0	0	0	0	0	0	0	0	0	0	0	0	0	0	0
Job	0	0	0	0	0	0	0	+	0	0	0	0	0	0	0	0
Housework	0	0	0	0	0	0	0	0	0	0	0	0	0	0	0	0
Dwelling unit	−	0	0	0	−	0	−	0	0	+	0	0	0	0	0	0
Neighborhood	0	+	0	+	−	+	−	0	+	+	0	0	−	0	0	+
Community	0	+	+	+	0	0	0	0	+	0	0	0	0	0	0	+

+ = New community residents significantly *more* satisfied than conventional community residents at 0.05 level of confidence.

0 = No significant difference between new and conventional community residents.

− = New community residents significantly *less* satisfied than conventional community residents at 0.05 level of confidence.

for example, found that satisfaction with leisure activities and with family life were the most important predictors of life satisfaction. Andrews and Withey (1973) reported that, in addition to a measure of personal efficacy, key factors were satisfaction with family life, leisure, economic security, and housing. Murray's (1974, Table 9) results indicated that satisfaction with leisure and with one's financial status were the most strongly related to life satisfaction of the variables he tested.[d] The mixture of domain satisfactions used as predictors differed across these studies, but their results are comparable enough to lend credence to the importance, in particular, of leisure, economic security, and family life for overall life evaluations. Satisfaction with housing and other aspects of the residential environment, which were included in each of these studies, proved to be significantly related to life satisfaction but to have a relatively limited effect in comparison with the leisure, economic security, and family life domains.

The stepwise regression analysis summarized in Table 5—4 reaffirms the limited importance of satisfaction with the dwelling, neighborhood, and community as predictors of overall life satisfaction among new community residents. These variables ranked seventh (dwelling unit), ninth (neighborhood), and tenth (community) among the ten domains included in the calculations. The initial step of the analysis, which included nine personal characteristics as predictors, was able to explain relatively little of the variance (R^2 = .05). When the life domains were added, the variance explained increased to R^2 = .44. (The life domains alone could account for 43 percent of the variance.)[e] The predominant factors turned out to be satisfaction with one's standard of living and satisfaction with the way leisure time was spent. On the basis of bivariate correlations, other factors of importance were satisfaction with family life, (r = .42) followed by marital satisfaction (r = .36) and job satisfaction (r = .35).

[d]Other recent studies in this area include work reported by the Environmental Protection Agency (1973), Easterlin (1973, pp. 3–10), and Clemente and Sauer (1976, pp. 621–631). The E.P.A. volume includes several attempts to identify key life components, one of which (p. II–195) places "health," "status," and "affluence" at the top of the list. Easterlin presents a distillation of a number of studies and concludes that affluence and economic security are tied to happiness but that as incomes rise, aspirations (and happiness thresholds) rise as well. Clemente and Sauer included only one measure of satisfaction with a life domain, "perceived health," and found that it was more strongly related to life satisfaction than most demographic variables.

[e]Andrews and Withey (1973, p. 37) found that the twelve domain variables they used were able to explain 52 percent of the variance. Six demographic variables alone accounted for 8 percent of the variance. The domain variables and the demographic variables together could explain 53 percent of the variance.

Table 5–4. Multivariate Analysis of Life Satisfaction for Nonfederally Assisted New Community Residents

Variables	Simple Correlation Coefficient	Beta	Cumulative R^2	F-Value
I. Nine socioeconomic and demographic variables[a]	—	—	.05	14.9
II. Satisfaction with ten life domains				
Standard of living	.44	.21	.22	146.6
Use of leisure time	.43	.18	.31	107.3
Marriage	.36	.15	.36	77.7
Job	.35	.16	.39	97.8
Family life	.42	.15	.41	67.8
Health	.28	.12	.42	56.5
Dwelling unit	.33	.11	.44	32.0
Housework	.14	.04	.44	6.7
Neighborhood	.23	.03	.44	2.7
Community	.17	.01	.44	0.1

[a]Includes the respondents' age, sex, education, marital status, family income, dwelling unit value, tenure, length of residence, and the number of children in household.

SUMMARY

Analyses in previous national studies of the quality of life have generally shown that satisfaction with different aspects of the residential environment—the house, the neighborhood, and the community—have only a minimal effect on measures of overall life satisfaction in comparison with domains like economic well-being, satisfying family life, and leisure satisfaction. Our data confirm the importance of nonenvironmental evaluations among new community residents and show, as was presaged by the number of "economic security" responses to the "what does the quality of your life depend on" question (Chapter 2), that satisfaction with one's standard of living was the life domain most closely related to the overall satisfaction measure. Next most important was satisfaction with the use of leisure time. We also found, however, that satisfaction with leisure time was not tied to the number of recreation facilities in the community. The availability of recreation facilities proved to be unrelated to satisfaction with one's family life as well.

Predictably, the new communities that fared particularly well compared to other new communities in regard to several of the ratings of specific life domains—Foster City and Westlake Village—were also the communities with the highest proportions of residents completely satisfied with their lives. Residents of Columbia, on the other hand, who tended to be less satisfied with more of the domains than people in other communities, were the second least satisfied residents in the new community sample. The lowest levels of overall life satisfaction were reported in Reston.

Although new community residents in this study were slightly more satisfied with their lives than a reasonably comparable group of respondents (income = $17,000 and up) in a national study done in 1971, it is interesting that the satisfaction of Columbia and Reston residents in 1973 was slightly below the 1971 national averages, a finding that paralleled earlier research on these communities (Lansing *et al.* 1970, pp. 58–60).

Finally, there were few cases where new community and conventional community responses to the overall and individual domain measures of life quality showed significant differences. In only two instances, for example, were the percentages of completely satisfied residents significantly different on the overall life satisfaction measure. Foster City residents' responses were significantly more positive, and Park Forest residents' responses were significantly less positive. Of 150 opportunities for significant differences in the paired community comparisons, only 24 (16 percent) attained significance. About three-fifths of those favored new communities.

Chapter 6

Indicators of the Quality
of Life for Resident Groups

To this point, most of the analyses reported have focused on comparisons of new and conventional community residents using aggregated data. The households in the study communities are a diverse lot, however, and although it has been possible to control the effect of personal and household characteristics statistically in multivariate analyses, we have not tried to detail the relationships of personal and household variables to the satisfaction measures included in the study. In this chapter, the data will be disaggregated to allow a review of the responses of nineteen classifications of new community residents to four satisfaction items touched upon in earlier chapters.

The interview items to be considered include (1) the effect of moving on the quality of life, (2) overall life satisfaction, (3) satisfaction with the community, and (4) whether or not respondents would recommend their community to relatives and friends as a particularly good place to live. The nineteen categories of residents are derived from seven ways of classifying the respondents based on (1) sex, (2) marital status, (3) age, (4) family income, (5) dwelling type, (6) race, and (7) whether the household lived in subsidized housing.

The chapter concludes with summaries of multivariate analyses of three of the satisfaction measures—the effect of the move on the quality of life, overall life satisfaction, and community satisfaction— for each of the nineteen categories of new community residents.

TWO GLOBAL MEASURES OF
QUALITY OF LIFE

For the first two items (effect of the move on quality of life and over-all life satisfaction) there was only one significant difference between the responses of residents living in new communities and those living in conventional communities. See Table 6–1. The only exception to the pervading absence of large differences occurred for subsidized housing residents. They were significantly more likely to report that the move to the community had improved their lives if they were living in a new community rather than a comparison community (68 percent versus 49 percent).

Differences between resident categories within the new and conventional community settings, though easier to identify, do not invariably show consistent differences across the first items in the table. (Unless otherwise noted, the text from this point will focus on new community residents.) For example, while men were more likely to report that their lives improved on moving to a new community, women were more likely to say they were completely satisfied with their lives as a whole. The absence of consistent differences in the relationships of sex to these satisfaction measures is not too surprising. Previous research on sex and life satisfaction has generally found little or no significant difference in the responses of men and women.[a] It is interesting to note that men and, in particular, women in the new communities reported higher overall life satisfaction levels than those reported in Campbell *et al.* (1976, p. 396) in their national study. Of the new community men, 27 percent were "completely satisfied" with their lives compared to 21 percent in the national study, and 35 percent of the women compared to 22 percent in the national sample.

Marital status, unlike sex, did produce consistent differences on the quality of life items. Studies of life satisfaction have invariably found the married persons report higher life satisfaction levels than the unmarried,[b] and new and conventional community residents are

[a] Research based on national samples that has found little or no difference between men's and women's happiness or life satisfaction include Alston and Dudley (1973), Alston, Lowe, and Wrigley (1974), Spreitzer and Snyder (1974), Clemente and Sauer (1976), and Campbell, Converse, and Rodgers (1976, pp. 396, 423). Parallel results were noted by Bradburn and Caplovitz (1965, p. 9) in their study of four Illinois communities. Spreitzer and Snyder (1974) found that although aggregated data showed no sex differences, men tended to be happier than women over the age of 65 and women tended to be happier than men at younger ages. Campbell *et al.* (1976, Chapter 12) devote considerable analyses to the joint (and differentiating) effects of sex and family life cycle on satisfaction.

[b] See Bradburn and Caplovitz (1965, p. 13), Robinson and Shaver (1969,

no exception. Married respondents were also more likely to see improvement in their lives after their move to a new community than the nonmarried.

Differences related to age were among the largest contrasts shown in Table 6—1, but the direction of the differences varied by the question. Thus, younger respondents (under 50) were significantly more likely to perceive improvement in life quality after a move but were significantly less likely to report satisfaction with their lives as a whole. The finding that the ages of new community residents were positively related to life satisfaction parallels those of some earlier national studies.[c] Several previous studies have *not* come to similar conclusions, however, and a number of reports have found the opposite or conflicting results.[d] A comparison of the responses of planned retirement community residents revealed no differences on the improved life quality question, but did indicate that significantly higher proportions of retirement community residents were completely satisfied with their lives as a whole (61 percent).

Of the two quality of life questions tabulated, family income turned out to be systematically related only to satisfaction with life as a whole (under $10,000, 25 percent completely satisfied; $25,000 and over, 39 percent completely satisfied). As with the relationship of marital status to satisfaction, the association of income level and satisfaction is consistently and strongly supported by prior research.[e]

---

p. 18), Palmore and Luikart (1972), Clemente and Sauer (1976), and Campbell *et al.* (1976, p. 36).

[c] Campbell *et al.* (1976, p. 37) found a strong relationship between age and satisfaction. The strength of the relationship, however, was tied to very positive responses of people over 65. Under 65 there was actually little consistent relationship of age with satisfaction. Clemente and Sauer (1976) report a small positive correlation between age and satisfaction, $r = .07$. Alston *et al.* (1974) found little relationship between age and happiness for whites but a clear positive relationship for blacks. Spreitzer and Snyder (1973) found a strong positive relationship between age and happiness for men and a weak negative relationship for women.

[d] See Bradburn and Caplovitz (1965, p. 9), Alston and Dudley (1973), Palmore and Luikart (1972), and Robinson and Shaver (1969, p. 20).

[e] See Alston *et al.* (1974), Spreitzer and Snyder (1974), Palmore and Luikart (1972), Bradburn and Caplovitz (1965), Robinson and Shaver (1969, p. 22), Easterlin (1973), Clemente and Sauer (1976) and Campbell *et al.* (1976). Campbell *et al.* (1976) also note, on the basis of trends in satisfaction responses from 1957 to 1972 (four national studies), "the income—happiness relationship has changed quite dramatically between 1957, when a clear positive relationship existed for all cohorts, and 1971, when this relationship had considerably weakened among young respondents but remained intact among older respondents (p. 29)." They also note that while the relationship between income and satisfaction is strong for those lacking a college degree, for those with one or more degrees income and life satisfaction are only weakly related (p. 56).

Table 6-1. Two Quality of Life Measures for Nineteen Resident Groups (percentage of respondents)

Resident Group	Moving to Community Improved Quality of Life		Completely Satisfied with Life as a Whole		Number of Cases	
	NC	CC	NC	CC	NC	CC
Sex of respondent						
Male	69	71	27	29	1143	554
Female	64	63	35	33	1447	735
Marital status of respondents						
Married	69	68	33	33	2162	1093
Not married[a]	56	57	22	24	424	194
Age of respondent						
Under 35	69	72	26	32	1012	528
35-49	69	66	33	29	938	463
50-64	59	56	35	31	462	194
65 and over	60	53	40	37	153	95
Family income						
Under $10,000	62	60	26	28	283	145
$10,000-$14,999	65	72	25	32	533	294
$15,000-$24,999	70	69	32	32	1140	527
$25,000 and up	65	62	39	32	472	214
Dwelling type						
Single-family detached	69	70	32	32	1809	992
Townhouse or rowhouse	64	58	32	34	310	88
Apartment	58	53	25	28	455	205

Race[b]						
Black	70	66	28	28	290	197
Nonblack	64	—	25	—	1040	—
Subsidized[c]						
Subsidized housing	68	49	23	21	271	187
Nonsubsidized	66	—	29	—	974	—

NC = New Communities   CC = Conventional Communities

[a] Includes single, widowed, divorced, separated.

[b] Includes only the five new communities which had sufficient black populations to analyze (Columbia, Reston, Forest Park, Park Forest, and Park Forest South). Comparison community data refer to the black suburban communities in Seat Pleasant, Maryland and Markham, Illinois. See Appendix A.

[c] Includes only the five new communities which had occupied subsidized housing at the time of the fieldwork (Columbia, Reston, Forest Park, Lake Havasu City, and Jonathan). Comparison community data refer to subsidized housing respondents in Laurel, Maryland and Chicago Heights, Illinois.

Table 6—1 also focuses on the relationship of dwelling type to reported satisfaction levels. Differences in housing and neighborhood satisfaction were treated in some detail in Chapter 4. Here, density proved to be inversely related to satisfaction, the gap between apartment and townhouse living being larger than that between townhouse and single-family living. The relationship proved to be strongest for the effect of the move on quality of life, followed in strength by the overall life satisfaction responses.

The final panels in the table focus on black and subsidized housing residents living in the new communities where sufficient numbers of these resident groups were available for analysis. The conventional community data are based on interviews in special suburban comparison areas—two black communities and two subsidized housing areas.[f] No significant differences arose on improved life quality or overall life satisfaction in regard to race, either between blacks and nonblacks within the new communities or between blacks in new communities and blacks in the comparison communities.

Because we originally expected to find sizeable contrasts between blacks in new communities and those in the comparison communities (just as we expected to find differences between the aggregated new and conventional community samples), it is surprising to find a lack of significant difference between blacks and nonblacks in the new community setting. Almost without exception, other studies have found blacks to be appreciably less happy or satisfied than whites, not only on an aggregated basis, but also when controls are included for demographic and socioeconomic differences.[g] Alston *et al.* (1974) tabulated four happiness and satisfaction measures (happiness, health, work, finance) for thirteen categories of respondent (based on sex, age, education, income, and occupation) for whites and blacks. For 49 of the 52 possible comparisons, happiness and satisfaction were lower for blacks.[h] The new community results, in other words, indi-

[f]The selection of black and subsidized housing subsamples and the special comparison communities are described in Appendix A.

[g]A particularly thorough discussion is provided by Bracy (1976) in Campbell *et al.* (1976). Other studies documented lower happiness or satisfaction among blacks include Clemente and Sauer (1976), Spreitzer and Snyder (1974), and Robinson and Shaver (1969, pp. 23—26). The latter authors cite one (not yet published) study by Converse and Robinson in which no significant differences in satisfaction between the races appeared.

[h]While the consistency of the Alston *et al.* (1974) findings is clearly significant, some of the differences were not large. A check of their data, using standard errors for percentages to gauge the statistical significance of individual comparisons (see the discussion of using standard errors of percentages under the heading of sampling error in Appendix A), showed that roughly 40 percent of the differences they observed were significant at the .05 level. In none of the cases were blacks significantly more happy or satisfied than whites.

cate much closer levels of life satisfaction for blacks and whites than have been reported in other research on the topic.

Finally, in contrast to the absence of significant differences involving blacks, residents in subsidized housing in new communities were more likely to report an improved quality of life on moving to the new community setting vis à vis moving to the comparison communities. As with the blacks, their responses on the quality of life items did not differ significantly from those of nonsubsidized new community residents.

In sum, despite initial expectations that new community settings would provide an appreciably more satisfying overall quality of life than conventional communities, the findings of this section—as well as those of earlier chapters—have not demonstrated that new communities lead to higher satisfactions on global measures of quality of life. Several results are in line with previous quality of life studies, in that we found the more satisfied new community residents to be married and to have higher incomes. Living in lower density housing was also associated with higher life satisfaction. The results of tabulations involving breakdowns by sex and by age were mixed. (Previous research that has looked at age has also produced mixed results. Most prior studies have found little or no difference between the sexes in life satisfaction.) Men and people under 50 were more likely to say that moving to a new community had improved the quality of their lives. New community women and older respondents were more likely to report complete satisfaction with their lives as a whole.

A comparison of the overall life satisfaction responses of black and nonblack residents in new communities revealed no significant differences. Since previous studies have consistently documented lower satisfaction levels in the black population, a finding of no differences supports the proposition that new community environments may provide an environment where blacks find a measure of equality in both a psychic and a materialistic sense.

TWO MEASURES OF COMMUNITY EVALUATION

In marked contrast to the results of the overall quality of life evaluations, responses to the rating of the community as a place to live and to the community recommendation item revealed a number of significant differences between new communities and conventional communities but fewer major contrasts within the new community setting. See Table 6-2.

In fifteen of the seventeen comparisons, residents of new communities responded to the community satisfaction item with much more

Table 6-2. Two Community Evaluations for Nineteen Resident Groups (percentage of respondents)

Resident Group	Rate Community as Excellent Place to Live		Would Recommend Community as a Particularly Good Place to Live		Number of Cases	
	NC	CC	NC	CC	NC	CC
Sex of respondent						
Male	50	43	81	74	1143	554
Female	48	41	81	75	1447	735
Marital status of respondents						
Married	49	43	81	76	2162	1093
Not married[a]	46	35	80	66	424	194
Age of respondent						
Under 35	42	40	80	73	1012	528
35–49	52	39	81	74	938	463
50–64	57	48	83	78	462	194
65 and over	52	60	84	78	153	95
Family income						
Under $10,000	32	38	75	68	283	145
$10,000–$14,999	42	41	78	77	533	294
$15,000–$24,999	50	42	83	73	1140	527
$25,000 and up	61	46	84	76	472	214
Dwelling type						
Single-family detached	50	43	81	77	1809	992
Townhouse or rowhouse	53	45	83	73	310	88
Apartment	41	35	79	66	455	205

Race[b]

Black	34	7	84	37	290	197
Nonblack	35	—	72	—	1040	—

Subsidized[c]

Subsidized housing	32	7	71	24	271	187
Nonsubsidized	41	—	78	—	974	—

NC = New Communities   CC = Conventional Communities

[a] Includes single, widowed, divorced, separated.

[b] Includes only the five new communities which had sufficient black populations to analyze (Columbia, Reston, Forest Park, Park Forest, and Park Forest South). Comparison community data refer to the black suburban communities in Seat Pleasant, Maryland and Markham, Illinois. See Appendix A.

[c] Includes only the five new communities which had occupied subsidized housing at the time of the fieldwork (Columbia, Reston, Forest Park, Lake Havasu City, and Jonathan). Comparison community data refer to subsidized housing respondents in Laurel, Maryland and Chicago Heights, Illinois.

positive community evaluations. Differences were significant for ten of the resident groupings, all in favor of the new communities.[i] Within the new communities, community satisfaction was lower for those under 35, those with incomes under $10,000, those living in apartments, and those living in subsidized housing. The three largest differences associated with the community satisfaction question—by a wide margin—were those comparing the new community residents with those of black, subsidized, and retirement communities. In the first two cases, new community residents were four to five times more likely to give their communities a high rating as a place to live— 35 percent versus 7 percent for blacks, 32 percent versus 7 percent for residents of subsidized housing. Three-fourths of the retirement community residents, on the other hand, rated their communities excellent, a proportion well above that for any age group in either new or conventional communities.

The second satisfaction indicator in Table 6—2 asked respondents if they would recommend their community to a close relative or friend as a particularly good place to live. This question generated the most consistent responses of the indicators tabulated. In all seventeen resident groups, new community respondents were more likely to indicate that their community would be a particularly good choice. Eleven of these comparisons are statistically significant and, as with the community satisfaction item, the greatest differences involved blacks (84 percent versus 37 percent) and residents of subsidized housing (71 percent versus 24 percent).[j] Also as before, residents of the retirement communities provided the most favorable responses of all (over 92 percent would recommend their communities), significantly above the proportions in the basic sample.

Within the new community setting there was a noticeable consensus among residents as far as recommending their communities to friends or relatives. Only two variables led to significant differences, race and subsidized residence. In these instances, blacks and nonsubsidized residents were more likely to recommend their communities.

The principal finding from comparisons of a number of categories of new and conventional community residents on their responses to two community evaluation questions was a consistently more favorable response in the new communities. These differences were

---

[i]The significant comparisons were for men, women, married, not married, blacks, subsidized housing residents, people in single-family homes, respondents 35–49 years old, and persons in families with incomes of $15,000–$24,999, and $25,000 and over.

[j]The significant comparisons parallel those found for the community satisfaction question, with the addition of the under 35 age group and apartment dwellers and the subtraction of the $25,000 income and up respondents.

strongest for the blacks and the residents of subsidized housing. Although not included in the data tabulated here, residence in planned retirement communities also turned out to be associated with significantly greater community satisfaction for respondents over the age of 64 than either new or conventional community residence.

MULTIVARIATE ANALYSES OF THE EFFECT OF THE MOVE TO THE PRESENT COMMUNITY ON QUALITY OF LIFE

To determine the extent to which different community attributes affected nineteen resident group's evaluations of the move to their present community on the quality of their lives, parallel regressions were run for each of the resident classifications. The results of these runs, summarized in Table 6–3, indicate a striking similarity across the analysis groups. In all cases, the predictive power of personal characteristics was minimal with R^2s ranging from .01 to .05. Total R^2s when eighteen community attribute ratings were included, were almost as similar. Fifteen of the nineteen R^2s were close to or at .30; three were higher (about .40), and one was lower (about .20). This combination of personal characteristics and attribute ratings did least well in predicting reports of an improved quality of life for persons living in apartments (R^2 = .18), and did best for townhouse residents (R^2 = .40) and respondents age 65 or over (R^2 = .39).

Four factors dominate the listings of key predictors for the nineteen resident groups. Most frequently included among the first three community attributes to enter the regression equations were the ratings of the type of people in the neighborhood (in the first three fifteen of nineteen times), the community as a place to raise children (fourteen of nineteen), recreation facilities (eleven of nineteen), and neighborhood appearance (nine of nineteen).[k] In only two instances was one of these ratings not the most important. For respondents age 50–64, the prime determinant was their rating of opportunities for participation in community life. For persons age 65 or older, the

---

[k] The stepwise regression procedure operates by including, first, the "predictor" variable with the largest bivariate correlation with the dependent variable. The second (and succeeding) variable to be included is that which explains the most of the remaining variation in the dependent variable. A variable included at the second step, in other words, may not necessarily be the predictor with the second highest bivariate correlation with the dependent variable, particularly if the variable with the second highest r is highly correlated with the first ranking predictor.

Table 6–3. Multivariate Analyses of Factors Influencing Ratings of Improving the Quality of Life in Nonfederally Assisted New Communities[a]

Resident Group	Cumulative R^2		First Three Rating Variables Entering Equation (r =)
	Personal Characteristics	*Personal Plus Eighteen Ratings*	
Sex of respondent			
Male	.02	.27	place to raise children (.38)
Female	.04	.30	people in neighborhood (.39)
Marital status of respondent			
Married	.02	.28	place to raise children (.40)
Not married[b]	.03	.34	people in neighborhood (.38)
Age of respondent			
Under 35	.05	.29	place to raise children (.38)
35–49	.03	.33	place to raise children (.46)
50–64	.04	.27	opportunity for participation (.36)
65 and over	.03	.39	layout and space of home (.42)
Family income			
Under $10,000	.03	.29	place to raise children (.34)
$10,000–$14,999	.04	.28	people in neighborhood (.35)
$15,000–$24,999	.03	.30	place to raise children (.41)
$25,000 and up	.01	.38	place to raise children (.45)
Dwelling type			
Single-family detached	.04	.32	place to raise children (.43)
Townhouse or rowhouse	.04	.40	recreation facilities (.44)
Apartment	.01	.18	people in neighborhood (.27)
Race[c]			
Black	.04	.30	place to raise children (.40)
Nonblack	.03	.28	place to raise children (.41)
Subsidized[d]			
Subsidized	.03	.29	people in neighborhood (.38)
Nonsubsidized	.03	.31	place to raise children (.41)

[a]Personal characteristic variables are those enumerated in Table 2–7, note a. Regressions for a given group—males, for example—did not include the corresponding personal characteristic—sex as a predictor variable. For ratings, see Table 2–7, note b.

[b]Includes single, widowed, divorced, separated.

Table 6—3. continued

First Three Rating Variables
Entering Equation (r =   ) (cont'd.)

neighborhood appearance (.34) place to raise children (.39)	recreation facilities (.30) recreation facilities (.26)
people in neighborhood (.36) recreation facilities (.30)	neighborhood appearance (.35) convenience to work (.21)
people in neighborhood (.38) people in neighborhood (.41) people in neighborhood (.30) recreation facilities (.29)	recreation facilities (.27) recreation facilities (.30) climate (.20) cost of living (.12)
recreation facilities (.29) place to raise children (.34) people in neighborhood (.38) neighborhood appearance (.44)	convenience to work (.22) neighborhood appearance (.32) recreation facilities (.29) people in neighborhood (.40)
people in neighborhood (.39)	neighborhood appearance (.36)
place to raise children (.39) neighborhood appearance (.26)	people in neighborhood (.37) layout and space of home (.22)
neighborhood appearance (.38) people in neighborhood (.36)	opportunity for participation (.34) neighborhood appearance (.36)
neighborhood appearance (.38) people in neighborhood (.35)	recreation facilities (.22) recreation facilities (.33)

[c]Includes only the five new communities which had sufficient black populations to analyze (Columbia, Reston, Forest Park, Park Forest, and Park Forest South).
[d]Includes only the five new communities which had occupied subsidized housing at the time of the fieldwork (Columbia, Reston, Forest Park, Lake Havasu City, and Jonathan).

most important rating was that of the layout and space of dwelling unit.

Ratings of two of the factors that seem most amenable to influence by planners and developers, recreation facilities and neighborhood appearance, are seldom one of the first two factors to enter the equations summarized here. The lone exception comes in the case of townhouse dwellers whose responses to the recreation facilities rating proved to be most associated with improvement in the quality of their lives as a consequence of the move to a new community.

MULTIVARIATE ANALYSES OF SATISFACTION WITH LIFE AS A WHOLE

Andrews and Withey (1974) reported analyses using predictors distilled from over 100 items and scales which indicate that the upper limit of predictability in multivariate life satisfaction analyses may be an explanation of 50 to 60 percent of the variance. In the analyses summarized in Table 6−4, the ten life domains together with eight personal characteristics led to R^2s of, roughly from .45 to .50, a level of explanation not too far below that obtained in the far more comprehensive Survey Research Center study.

Personal characteristics, though having a greater effect on responses concerning life satisfaction than on responses concerning the degree of improvement resulting from the move, remained minor contributors to the explained variance in all the resident groupings. The largest R^2 (.11) caused solely by the predictive power of personal characteristics came in the regression for persons 65 years of age or older. In that instance, the characteristic with the greatest impact was the presence of children in the household; the fewer the children, the higher the satisfaction reported.

Four domain satisfaction measures were regularly among the leading predictors. The rating of one's standard of living appears in Table 6−4 for fifteen of the nineteen groups. Satisfaction with the use of leisure time occurs in thirteen of nineteen, satisfaction with family life, eleven of nineteen, and satisfaction with job, nine of nineteen. For six of the groups, marital satisfaction was among the first three domain variables to enter the predictive equation. Neither neighborhood nor community satisfaction was influential enough in any of the resident groups to be included among the key domains. Dwelling unit satisfaction entered the regressions third for the lower income and black subpopulations.

The leading domain for fifteen of the nineteen groups was either satisfaction with the standard of living or with the use of leisure time. Marital satisfaction proved most important for those under 35, family life for those with incomes under $10,000 and for those in subsidized housing, and job satisfaction for townhouse residents.

Satisfaction with one's health appears only once in Table 6—4 as the third variable to enter the equation for the older (65 years and over) residents. Regression analyses with different predictor variables reported by two other studies have found self-assessed health to be the most important predictor of happiness or satisfaction among older people (Spreitzer and Snyder 1974, Palmore and Luikart 1972). Spreitzer and Snyder (1974) found that satisfaction with one's financial status was the primary predictor for young (under 65) respondents in their study.

The importance of the standard of living evaluation in the regression analyses reported here corresponds to its position as the most frequent mention in the responses to the open-ended quality of life question with which we began this report. The second most frequent mention to the open-ended question had to do with family life, and this also concurs with the frequent appearance of family life as an important variable in the multivariate analyses. The importance of leisure satisfaction in the multivariate analyses in this and the preceding chapter, on the other hand, does not follow as closely from the open ended responses where it ranked eighth among life quality components volunteered by respondents.

MULTIVARIATE ANALYSES
OF COMMUNITY SATISFACTION

The most striking aspect of the results presented in Table 6—5 is the fact that the evaluation of the immediate neighborhood was the most important predictor of community satisfaction for every one of the nineteen resident groups. Beyond that, ratings of recreation facilities was the leading community component appearing as the second variable eight times and as the third variable six more times. Satisfaction with the dwelling unit, which appeared for ten of the nineteen resident groups analyzed, was the next most frequent component to appear. Three of the six other community component evaluations are listed in the table: school, homeowners association, and health care. Health care emerged as the second factor (after the neighborhood) for the age 50—64 and the age 65 plus groups.

As has been the case in the earlier summaries, personal charac-

Table 6–4.   Summary of Multivariate Analyses of Life Satisfaction for Selected Resident Groups in Nonfederally Assisted New Communities[a]

Resident Group	Cumulative R^2		First Three Domain Variables Entering Equation ($r =$)		
	Personal Charac- teristics	Personal Plus Ten Domains			
Sex of respondent					
Male	.04	.42	standard of living (.44)	job satisfaction (.40)	family life (.37)
Female	.06	.46	use of leisure time (.45)	standard of living (.44)	marriage (.40)
Marital status of respondent					
Married	.03	.42	standard of living (.44)	family life (.41)	use of leisure time (.42)
Not married[b]	.03	.48	use of leisure time (.48)	standard of living (.46)	job satisfaction (.39)
Age of respondent					
Under 35	.05	.44	marriage (.44)	use of leisure time (.39)	standard of living (.40)
35–49	.07	.50	standard of living (.52)	family life (.46)	use of leisure time (.47)
50–64	.08	.39	standard of living (.44)	use of leisure time (.38)	job satisfaction (.33)
65 and over	.11	.50	use of leisure time (.48)	family life (.41)	health (.42)
Family income					
Under $10,000	.07	.47	family life (.49)	job satisfaction (.37)	dwelling unit (.34)
$10,000–$14,999	.03	.49	standard of living (.50)	use of leisure time (.45)	marriage (.33)
$15,000–$24,999	.03	.43	standard of living (.46)	family life (.44)	job satisfaction (.34)
$25,000 and up	.05	.45	use of leisure time (.44)	marriage (.43)	job satisfaction (.33)

Dwelling type					
Single-family detached	.04	.43	use of leisure time (.43)	standard of living (.44)	marriage (.37)
Townhouse or rowhouse	.09	.52	job satisfaction (.49)	use of leisure time (.46)	family life (.40)
Apartment	.06	.50	standard of living (.54)	family life (.48)	job satisfaction (.32)
Race[c]					
Black	.09	.47	standard of living (.52)	family life (.42)	dwelling unit (.46)
Nonblack	.06	.45	use of leisure time (.46)	standard of living (.46)	family life (.44)
Subsidized[d]					
Subsidized	.04	.52	family life (.48)	standard of living (.42)	marriage (.43)
Nonsubsidized	.05	.41	use of leisure time (.40)	standard of living (.40)	job satisfaction (.35)

[a] Personal characteristic variables are those enumerated in Table 2–7, note b. Regressions for a given group—males, for example—did not include the corresponding personal characteristic as a predictor variable. Domain variables are those listed in Table 5–2.

[b] Includes single, widowed, divorced, separated.

[c] Includes only the five new communities which had sufficient black populations to analyze (Columbia, Reston, Forest Park, Park Forest, and Park Forest South).

[d] Includes only the five new communities which had occupied subsidized housing at the time of the fieldwork (Columbia, Reston, Forest Park, Lake Havasu City, and Jonathan).

Table 6-5. Summary of Multivariate Analyses of Community Satisfaction for Selected Resident Groups in Nonfederally Assisted New Communities[a]

Resident Group	Cumulative R² Personal Characteristics	Cumulative R² Personal Plus Nine Components	First Three Component Variables Entering Equation (r =)		
Sex of respondent					
Male	.06	.30	neighborhood (.47)	homeowners association (.31)	recreation facilities (.25)
Female	.06	.25	neighborhood (.42)	recreation facilities (.24)	dwelling unit (.30)
Marital status of respondent					
Married	.05	.24	neighborhood (.41)	recreation facilities (.25)	dwelling unit (.30)
Not married[b]	.12	.40	neighborhood (.57)	dwelling unit (.44)	health care (.20)
Age of respondent					
Under 35	.07	.29	neighborhood (.46)	recreation facilities (.24)	dwelling unit (.33)
35-49	.06	.28	neighborhood (.43)	homeowners association (.35)	dwelling unit (.34)
50-64	.04	.25	neighborhood (.35)	health care (.27)	recreation facilities (.29)
65 and over	.09	.39	neighborhood (.44)	health care (.32)	recreation facilities (.25)
Family income					
Under $10,000	.10	.29	neighborhood (.42)	recreation facilities (.34)	health care (.19)
$10,000-$14,999	.05	.22	neighborhood (.37)	homeowners association (.27)	recreation facilities (.20)
$15,000-$24,999	.03	.27	neighborhood (.44)	recreation facilities (.25)	dwelling unit (.29)
$25,000 and over	.04	.31	neighborhood (.51)	school (.19)	dwelling unit (.39)

Dwelling type				
Single-family detached	.05	neighborhood (.42)	homeowners association (.27)	recreation facilities (.23)
Townhouse or rowhouse	.12	neighborhood (.46)	dwelling unit (.35)	school (.24)
Apartment	.10	neighborhood (.48)	recreation facilities (.27)	dwelling unit (.35)
Race[c]				
Black	.16	neighborhood (.45)	school (.38)	recreation facilities (.45)
Nonblack	.07	neighborhood (.46)	recreation facilities (.28)	dwelling unit (.36)
Subsidized[d]				
Subsidized	.06	neighborhood (.32)	homeowners association (.31)	school (.26)
Nonsubsidized	.07	neighborhood (.42)	recreation facilities (.33)	health care (.27)

[a] Personal characteristics are those listed in Table 2–7, note b. Regressions for a given group—males, for example—did not include the corresponding personal characteristic as a predictor variable. Community component variables are those listed in Table 3–5.

[b] Includes single, widowed, divorced, separated.

[c] Includes only the five new communities which had a sufficient black population to analyze (Columbia, Reston, Forest Park, Park Forest, Park Forest South).

[d] Includes only the five new communities which had occupied subsidized housing at the time of the fieldwork (Columbia, Reston, Forest Park, Lake Havasu City, and Jonathan).

teristics proved to have a limited ability to explain community satisfaction. R^2s for personal characteristics, alone, ranged from .03 to .16 (for blacks). The key characteristic associated with black satisfaction reports was family income. Total R^2s, for the regressions which included the component ratings, ranged from .22 to .41.[1] The combination of characteristics and ratings explained proportions of variance for blacks (R^2 = .41) and those who were not married (R^2 = .40) and explained the least variance for those with family incomes of \$10,000–\$14,999 (R^2 = .22) and the married respondents (R^2 = .24).

SUMMARY

The dilemma faced by researchers and policy makers who hope to assess new communities "from the residents' point of view" is captured in the initial sections of this final chapter.[m] In essence, the expectation or hope that new communities would provide a better quality of life for residents than conventional communities in terms of general happiness or life satisfaction has not been fulfilled.[n] As we saw in Chapters 2 and 5, a few new communities have done somewhat better than others, but, as yet, new communities as a group have not achieved their utopian promise.

On the other hand, at the more modest scale of the community, there is little question that new communities have been able to generate more highly satisfied residents than conventional communities.

[1]To parallel the regressions reported earlier in this chapter, the regressions summarized here do not include the community inventory variables as predictors (cf. Tables 3–7, 3–8).

[m]It bears repeating that "the residents' point of view" is only one orientation to evaluating the development of new communities. Important bases for assessing the net impact of new communities which we have not addressed include: the long range economic and administrative costs to local, county, and state governments of opting for new community versus less coordinated suburban development; the ecological impact of a major new community on surrounding communities and habitats; and the application of new community location as an instrument of national urban growth and social policies. For example, though not tied to the evaluation of specific communities, the Real Estate Research Corporation's (1974) *The Costs of Sprawl: Detailed Cost Analysis* provides a broad ranging analysis of the relative costs of planned versus unplanned development at various densities. See also *Evaluation of the New Community Program* prepared by the Office of Program Analysis and Evaluation, Office of Policy Development and Research, U.S. Department of Housing and Urban Development (1975).

[n]Max Neutze, an Australian urban economist, has observed that Americans seem particularly concerned that their new communities should be *better* than existing development. In his experience, British and Australians would judge a new town to be a success if it were simply *as good as* existing development (personal communication, February 1975).

For fifteen of seventeen new community resident groups that could be compared with similar groups in conventional communities, the new community residents were more likely to give their community an "excellent" rating. On the second community-level rating item, all seventeen categories of new community residents were more likely than conventional community residents to tell friends or relatives that their communities would be "particularly good" places to which to move.

An indication of which resident groups have been best served by present new community development can also be gleaned by looking at satisfaction levels across all of the resident classifications for new communities. Although rankings varied from item to item, the groups that tended to report the highest satisfaction levels were the more affluent (incomes of $25,000 or more), the older persons, and the blacks. Groups consistently on the lower end of the ratings in comparison with other new community residents were the apartment dwellers, the nonmarried, and the subsidized housing residents. Of special interest, however, was the finding that blacks and persons living in government subsidized housing—thus parts of the population that have not, historically, had equal access to the housing market—reported levels of community satisfaction that were vastly higher than blacks and subsidized housing residents not living in a new community setting.

A major indication of why new communities fare better at the community satisfaction level than the life satisfaction level appeared in the multivariate analyses. The main predictors of community satisfaction for the resident groups were ratings of the immediate neighborhood and recreation facilities, factors on which a community developer could reasonably hope to have a positive impact. The major determinants of life satisfaction, however, were residents' satisfaction with their overall standards of living, their marriages, their family lives, and their use of leisure time. Of these variables, only satisfaction with leisure time would appear amenable to the direct influence of a developer although, as was noted in Chapter 5, leisure satisfaction was not strongly related to the variety of recreation facilities provided in a community.

In sum, the benefits of new community design are most evident up to the community level of analysis. Beyond that, in the context of global concepts of life satisfaction, aspects of the residential community are able to have only limited effects on life satisfaction measures in comparison with peoples' ratings of their families, marriages, and overall standards of living. Although the rhetoric of developers, journalists, policy makers, and researchers has often encouraged the vision of new communities as utopian answers to many of the problems of twentieth century America, that appears to be too heavy a load for the present new communities movement to carry. What they have been able to do, however, is provide neighborhood and community environments that are, in fact, more satisfying places to live than contemporary, conventional communities, particularly for blacks and subsidized housing residents, an accomplishment that should be taken into account in evaluations of the future prospects for the new communities movement.

※

Appendixes

✳ *Appendix A*

Sampling and Data Collection Procedures

The data reported in this study were collected in a sample of 36 new and conventional communities in the United States. Three data collection procedures were used. These included a household survey, surveys of developers and professional personnel involved in the provision of community facilities and services, and field inventories and map measurements. This appendix describes the methods used in selecting new and conventional communities for the study and in conducting the various surveys and field measurements.

SELECTION OF SAMPLE COMMUNITIES

The 36 communities studied included fifteen new communities, fifteen paired conventional communities, two retirement communities, two conventional suburban communities with predominantly black residential areas, and two conventional suburban communities with subsidized housing for low- and moderate-income residents.

Selection of the New Communities
The sample of new communities was selected in stages. First, 63 new communities and large-scale developments were identified from a list prepared by the New Communities Division of the Department of Housing and Urban Development (1969). The communities on the HUD list were screened against two sets of criteria. First, the communities were evaluated in terms of their conformity to five criteria basic to the new community concept:

1. *Unified ownership*—community development under the direction of a single entrepreneur or development company to assure unified and coordinated management of development.
2. *Planning*—development programmed in accordance with an overall master plan.
3. *Size*—2,000 or more acres planned for an eventual population of 20,000 or more people to allow for social diversity and to support a variety of urban functions.
4. *Self-sufficiency*—provision for a variety of urban functions through the reservation of land for residential, commercial, industrial, public, and institutional uses.
5. *Housing choice*—provision of a variety of housing choices, including, at a minimum, opportunities for owning and renting and for single-family and apartment lifestyles.

The application of these criteria to the communities on the HUD list significantly narrowed the number of projects eligible for inclusion in the study. Large-scale land development projects that were excluded from the study at this stage included special purpose communities, such as resort and retirement projects; suburban planned unit developments, which could not meet the size and self-sufficiency criteria; and new towns-in-town, which could not meet the size criterion.

Three additional criteria were applied to meet the specific needs of the overall new communities study. These included:

6. *Location*—communities located outside of the contiguous 48 states were eliminated in order to limit data collection costs.
7. *Age*—communities that ceased all active development prior to 1960 were eliminated in order to simplify recall problems in case studies of development decisions.
8. *Population*—communities with less than 5,000 residents on January 1, 1972 were eliminated to assure that communities had enough homes, facilities, and services in place to provide an adequate basis for evaluation.

The two screening processes eliminated 36 of the 63 communities on the HUD list.

From the 27 remaining new communities, thirteen privately developed communities were selected for intensive study. Five new communities were selected because they contained unique features of particular interest to the research team:

1. Columbia, Md.—100 percent sample of stratum: communities with 10 percent or more nonwhite population on January 1, 1972.

2. Irvine, Calif.—100 percent sample of stratum: regional cities with projected populations over 150,000.
3. Lake Havasu City, Ariz.—100 percent sample of stratum: free-standing new communities.
4. Park Forest, Ill.—100 percent sample of stratum: recognized outstanding completed post World War II new community.
5. Reston, Va.—100 percent sample of stratum: recognized outstanding design.

A simple random sample of eight additional communities was then selected from the 22 communities remaining in the sample frame. These included:[a]

6. Elk Grove Village, Ill.
7. Forest Park, Oh.
8. Foster City, Calif.
9. Laguna Niguel, Calif.
10. North Palm Beach, Fla.
11. Sharpstown, Tex.
12. Valencia, Calif.
13. Westlake Village, Calif.

The privately developed new communities selected for study allow adequate coverage of the range of variation in the characteristics of nonfederally assisted new communities now under development in the United States. There is no evidence that the inclusion of a greater number of new communities would have yielded greater variation in community characteristics.

Finally, although both Jonathan, Minn., and Park Forest South, Ill., had fewer than 5000 residents as of January 1, 1972, these two communities were selected to assure the inclusion in the study of new communities participating in the federal new communities program. At the time the sample was drawn, the universe of federally assisted new communities included Flower Mound, Tex., Jonathan, Minn., Maumelle, Ark., Park Forest South, Ill., Riverton, N.Y., and St. Charles Communities, Md. Most of these were in the very initial stages of development. Only Jonathan and Park Forest South had

[a] After these eight communities were selected, the fourteen communities remaining in the new community sampling frame were (1) Clear Lake City, Tex., (2) Coral Springs, Fla., (3) Diamond Bar, Calif., (4) Janss/Conejo (Thousand Oaks), Calif., (5) Lehigh Acres, Fla., (6) Litchfield Park, Ariz., (7) Miami Lakes, Fla., (8) Mission Viejo, Calif., (9) Montbello, Col., (10) Montgomery Village, Md., (11) Northglenn, Col., (12) Palm Beach Gardens, Fla., (13) Pikes Peak Park, Col., and (14) Rancho Bernardo, Calif.

enough occupied housing for a baseline evaluation. Because at least two federally assisted new communities were required to avoid the problem of generalizing from a unique case, both were included in the sample.

Selection of the Paired Conventional Communities

For each of the sample new communities, a less planned, conventionally developed area was delineated to serve as a control and basis of comparison. The new communities and paired conventional communities were otherwise matched in terms of the age of housing, range of housing costs, and location within the metropolitan area. In some cases it was necessary to delineate a set of contiguous subdivisions as a comparison area in order to match more nearly the range of housing costs in the paired new community. An effort was also made to match on the mix of housing types; however, this could not be done consistently because the range of housing types available in new communities was not found regularly in other suburban settings. Where older, established communities were listed as comparison communities, only the tracts or neighborhoods within these communities that matched the new community as to age and price range of housing were included in the universe from which the household sample was selected. However, respondents in such areas were asked about the whole community rather than only the subselected tracts where they lived in household survey questions that referred to the community as a whole.

The paired conventional communities were chosen on the basis of information gathered during site visits to the market areas of the sample new communities and from consultations with county and municipal planning agencies and local real estate firms, analyses of census tract data, and visual inspection of all areas that met the matching criteria. The sample new communities and their paired conventional communities include:

New Community	*Paired Conventional Community*
1. Columbia, Md.	Norbeck–Wheaton, Md.
2. Elk Grove Village, Ill.	Schaumburg, Ill.
3. Forest Park, Oh.	Sharonville, Oh.
4. Foster City, Calif.	West San Mateo, Calif.
5. Irvine, Calif.	Fountain Valley, Calif.
6. Jonathan, Minn.	Chanhassen, Minn.
7. Laguna Niguel, Calif.	Dana Point–Capistrano Valley, Calif.

8.	Lake Havasu City, Ariz.	Kingman, Ariz.
9.	North Palm Beach, Fla.	Tequesta, Fla.
10.	Park Forest, Ill.	Lansing, Ill.
11.	Park Forest South, Ill.	Richton Park, Ill.
12.	Reston, Va.	West Springfield, Va.
13.	Sharpstown, Tex.	Southwest Houston, Tex.
14.	Valencia, Calif.	Bouquet Canyon, Calif.
15.	Westlake Village, Calif.	Agoura–Malibu Junction, Calif.

Table A–1 summarizes information about the location, population, and acreage of the sample new communities at the start of the study, together with comparable data on the location and population of the paired conventional communities. Population estimates for the paired conventional communities are based on the whole community as defined for the respondents rather than for subselected tracts or neighborhoods from which the household sample was drawn. Vignettes describing the characteristics of the sample new communities and paired conventional communities are provided in Appendix B.

Selection of Retirement New Communities, Conventional Black Suburban Areas, and Subsidized Housing Projects in Conventional Communities

Six additional communities were selected to serve as controls and as another base of comparison with the responses of new community elderly residents, black residents, and low- and moderate-income residents of subsidized housing. Two of the communities were retirement new communities designed specifically for the elderly. Rossmoor Leisure World is located in the Laguna Hills section of Orange County, Calif. Sun City Center is located in Hillsborough County, south of Tampa, Fla. Two conventional communities, the Seat Pleasant area, Md., and Markham, Ill., contained predominantly black populations housed in single-family, detached subdivisions that provided housing similar to that available to black families in new communities. In two other communities, Laurel, Md., and Chicago Heights, Ill., federally subsidized housing projects were utilized as sampling frames to select low- and moderate-income households that could be compared to similar groups living in new communities.

The primary criterion used in the selection of these special comparison communities was that they be located in the vicinity of the sample new communities. This was done in order to limit regional variation and to facilitate comparisons among the communities. The special comparison communities are comparable to the other sample

Table A–1. Distance from Central Business District, Estimated Population, and Target Acreage for Sample New Communities and Their Paired Conventional Communities at Beginning of Study

Nonfederally Assisted New Communities/Paired Conventional Communities	New Communities and Conventional Communities				New Communities Only		
	Number of Miles from Metropolitan Central Business District[a]		Estimated Population		Percent of Target Population	Target Population	Target Acreage
	New Community	Conventional Community	New Community	Conventional Community			
Average for nonfederally assisted new and conventional communities	21.5	22.5	17,900	21,800	38.5	71,346	11,646
Columbia/Norbeck-Wheaton, Md.	19	15	24,000	20,000	22	110,000	18,000
Elk Grove Village/Schaumburg, Ill.	26	30	22,900	25,200	39	58,500	5,760
Forest Park/Sharonville, Oh.	15	15	17,000	11,000[c]	49	35,000	3,725
Foster City/San Mateo, Calif.	25	30	15,000	79,000[c]	42	36,000	2,600
Irvine/Fountain Valley, Calif.	8	11	20,000[d]	49,900	6	338,000	64,000
Laguna Niguel/Dana Point, Calif.	23	27	8,500	6,600	21	40,000	7,936
Lake Havasu City/Kingman, Ariz.	b	b	8,500	7,300[c]	14	60,000	16,630
North Palm Beach/Tequesta, Fla.	7	17	12,500	2,600[c]	42	30,000	2,362
Park Forest/Lansing, Ill.	29	27	30,600	25,800[c]	87	35,000	3,182
Reston/Springfield, Va.	18	13	20,000	35,000	27	75,000	7,400
Sharpstown/Southwest Houston, Tex.	10	12	35,000	10,000	100[e]	35,000	4,100
Valencia/Bouquet Canyon, Calif.	32	38	7,000	6,000	28	25,000	4,000

Westlake Village/Agoura/Malibu Junction, Calif.	40	35	13,000	5,000	26	50,000	11,709
Federally Assisted New and Paired Conventional Communities							
Jonathan/Chanhassen, Minn.	25	20	1,500	5,100	3	50,000	8,194
Park Forest South/Richton Park, Ill.	32	30	3,200	4,800	3	110,000	8,291

[a] Road distance from central business district of central city of Standard Metropolitan Statistical Area (as defined for the 1970 U.S. Census) in which community is located.

[b] Freestanding community (i.e., not in a Standard Metropolitan Statistical Area).

[c] Data from 1970 United States Census.

[d] Population data refer to the City of Irvine which includes residential areas not developed by The Irvine Company. Only areas developed by The Irvine Company were included in the household interview sample. At the time of our field work these areas had a population of about 12,300.

[e] Residential densities in Sharpstown have ended up being greater than initially planned, and its final population will probably exceed the initial target population by 5,000 to 10,000.

communities in terms of the age and price range of housing available. They were selected in much the same manner as the paired conventional communities—on the basis of site visits and consultations with local planning agencies and realtors.

THE HOUSEHOLD SURVEY

Residents living in the 36 new and conventional communities were interviewed during the period from February through May 1973. The interview schedule is reproduced in Appendix D. The number of households interviewed in each community is shown in Table A−2.

Selection of Sample Households and Respondents .

The universe sampled for the household survey included family heads and their spouses living in the 36 sample communities. The sample was selected in such a manner that every head or spouse who had moved into his or her dwelling before January 1, 1973 had a known probability of selection. The method of selecting the household sample was as follows:

Visits were made to all 36 sample communities between mid-October 1972 and mid-January 1973 to identify all occupied dwellings on large-scale maps showing lot lines for each community. These maps, with the location and number of occupied dwellings delineated, were used to outline clusters of from five to seven dwelling units. The number of units to be included in a cluster was chosen on the basis of projected field costs, expected response rate, and the number of clusters needed to generate a household sample representative of the sample communities. The eventual analysis of housing clusters was considered in delineating sample clusters. Accordingly, the clusters were outlined so as to include dwellings that faced one another across a street or common court. Dwellings strung out in a row were rarely defined as clusters.

For apartment buildings where the location of individual dwellings was unknown, the total number of units in the building was divided into a designated number of five-, six-, or seven-dwelling clusters. For buildings containing fewer than ten apartments, two or three neighboring buildings were grouped together and clusters were designated for all units in the group. Where the location of apartments within a building was known, it was possible to cluster these units directly as in the procedure described above.

After clusters were defined for a community, a probability sample of clusters was selected. The samples in paired conventional communities that had more than one type of dwelling unit available were stratified by dwelling unit type (single-family, detached houses, town-houses, or apartments) so that the proportion of selected clusters of each dwelling type approximated the proportions of dwelling unit types found in the paired new community. Overall, the selection of sample clusters was designed to obtain 200 interviews in each of the thirteen nonfederally assisted new communities and two federally assisted new communities, and 100 interviews in each of the paired conventional communities, retirement new communities, and conventional communities used to obtain interviews with subsidized housing and black residents.

Subsample of New Community Households Occupying Subsidized Housing. Five of the sample new communities (Columbia, Forest Park, Jonathan, Lake Havasu City, and Reston) had FHA Sections 235 (owner) or 221(d)3 or 236 (rental) subsidized housing occupied at the time of the sampling process. In each of these communities, the sampling frame was divided into two strata, one of subsidized housing units and one of nonsubsidized housing units. Separate random probability cluster samples were drawn from each stratum in the manner described above. Selection of clusters was designed to produce 50 interviews with households occupying subsidized housing and 200 interviews with households occupying nonsubsidized housing in each of the five communities.

Subsample of New Community Black Households. In each of the five sample new communities known to have more than 100 resident black households (Columbia, Forest Park, Park Forest, Park Forest South, and Reston) a special subsample of black households was selected to supplement those falling into the regular cluster samples. Lists suitable for use as sampling frames were not available in all five of the communities. Therefore, sampling frames were constructed by referrals from the random sample respondents. Addresses generated by the referral procedure were listed and duplications were eliminated. The five resulting lists were used as the sample frames from which simple random samples of addresses were drawn, aimed at producing 50 additional interviews with black households in each of the five communities.

It should be noted that because it is a referral sample this sub-sample of black households does not constitute a random sample representative of the population of black family heads and their spouses in these communities. However, comparison of black sub-sample respondent characteristics and attitudes with those of black

Table A-2. Number of Household Interviews

Communities	Total	Basic Sample	Number of Interviews Subsamples Subsidized Housing Residents	Black Residents	Young Adults
Total	6485	5087	274	150	974
Thirteen nonfederally assisted new communities	3546	2619	219	131	577
Thirteen paired conventional communities	1585	1321	NA	NA	264
Federally assisted new communities and paired conventional communities					
Jonathan, Minn. (NC)	219	152	55	NA	12
Chanhassen, Minn. (CC)	118	100	NA	NA	18
Park Forest South, Ill. (NC)	247	200	NA	19	28
Richton Park, Ill. (CC)	104	101	NA	NA	4
Two retirement new communities (NC)	204	204	NA	NA	NA
Two subsidized housing conventional communities (CC)	215	187	NA	NA	28
Two black conventional communities (CC)	246	203	NA	NA	43

Nonfederally assisted new communities and paired conventional communities

Community					
Columbia, Md. (NC)	341	213	61	37	30
Norbeck-Wheaton, Md. (CC)	151	123	NA	NA	28
Elk Grove Village, Ill. (NC)	258	199	NA	NA	59
Schaumburg, Ill. (CC)	116	102	NA	NA	14
Forest Park, Oh. (NC)	374	202	53	51	68
Sharonville, Oh. (CC)	145	115	NA	NA	30
Foster City, Calif. (NC)	202	176	NA	NA	26
West San Mateo, Calif. (CC)	112	93	NA	NA	19
Irvine, Calif. (NC)	239	202	NA	NA	37
Fountain Valley, Calif. (CC)	117	102	NA	NA	15
Laguna Niguel, Calif. (NC)	245	208	NA	NA	37
Dana Point, Calif. (CC)	139	105	NA	NA	34
Lake Havasu City, Ariz. (NC)	324	209	47	NA	68
Kingman, Ariz. (CC)	108	93	NA	NA	15
North Palm Beach, Fla. (NC)	245	202	NA	NA	43
Tequesta, Fla. (CC)	126	111	NA	NA	15
Park Forest, Ill. (NC)	253	200	NA	16	37
Lansing, Ill. (CC)	78	64	NA	NA	14
Reston, Va. (NC)	331	197	58	27	49
West Springfield, Va. (CC)	114	95	NA	NA	19
Sharpstown, Tex. (NC)	248	203	NA	NA	45
Southwest Houston, Tex. (CC)	134	108	NA	NA	26
Valencia, Calif. (NC)	235	202	NA	NA	33
Bouquet Canyon, Calif. (CC)	124	103	NA	NA	21
Westlake Village, Calif. (NC)	251	206	NA	NA	45
Agoura—Malibu Junction, Calif. (CC)	121	107	NA	NA	14

NC = New Community   CC = Conventional Community   NA = Not Applicable

respondents from the random sample of the five communities indicated that the two groups were very similar. See Table A−3. Therefore, responses from the black subsample were included with those of random sample blacks in the analysis presented in Chapter 6 to increase the reliability of estimates for new community blacks without introducing substantial sampling error. Interviews obtained from the referral sample are not included in community totals presented in other chapters.

Subsample of New Community and Conventional Community Young Adults. The universe for the young adult subsample included all persons fourteen through 20 years old (other than family heads and their spouses) found to be living in sample dwellings. If one such young adult was found at a sample dwelling, this person was selected for the sample. If two or more were found, the interviewer selected one of these at random using a random selection table stamped on the young adult questionnaire. Thus, choice of young adult respondents was specified for interviewers rather than left to their discretion.

Designation of the Household Survey Respondent. The prospective respondent was randomly designated as either the head of the family residing at the address or the spouse of the family head for each address in the regular cluster sample, the subsidizing housing subsample, and the black subsample prior to assignment of addresses to interviewers. The head was designated as the respondent for half of the addresses sampled in each community; the spouse was designated as the respondent for the remaining half. Interviews were allowed only with the designated respondent except where the spouse was designated and there was no spouse of family head living in the household. In such situations, the interview was to be taken with the family head. If a household was occupied by more than one family unit, the head or spouse of the head of each family unit was to be interviewed.

These procedures left no freedom to interviewers in the choice of respondents. The dwellings where interviews were to be taken and the individuals to be interviewed within the dwellings were specified.

Interviewing Methods
Interviewers were instructed to ask questions using the exact wording appearing in the questionnaire. When probing was necessary to obtain full answers to open-end questions, interviewers were to use

Table A–3. Comparison of Responses from Random Sample Blacks and the Nonrandom Black Subsample in Five Sample Communities

Characteristic or Attitude	Percentage of Black Respondents from[a]	
	Random Sample	Nonrandom Black Subsample
Number of persons in respondent's household		
One	2.2	2.7
Two	23.7	10.0
Three to five	62.6	70.7
Six or more	11.5	16.7
Number of children in respondent's household		
None	23.5	12.7
One	28.2	24.0
Two	28.3	30.0
Three or more	20.0	33.3
Age of family head		
Under 35	50.4	45.0
35–44	32.1	37.6
45–54	14.1	16.1
55 or older	3.5	1.3
Marital status of household head		
Married	89.9	86.7
Widowed	0.1	2.0
Divorced or separated	9.0	6.0
Never married	1.0	5.3
Education of household head		
High school graduate or less	39.7	33.6
Some college to college graduate	34.5	33.6
Graduate or professional training	25.9	32.9
Employment status of household head		
Employed	95.8	97.3
Retired	1.3	0.0
Not employed (not retired)	2.8	2.7
Family's total income in 1972 (before taxes)		
Under $10,000	13.2	15.6
$10,000–$14,999	23.9	13.6
$15,000–$24,999	42.1	44.9
$25,000 or more	20.8	25.9
Tenure		
Owns or buying	67.3	85.8
Rents	32.1	13.5
Other	0.6	0.7

Table A–3. continued

Characteristic or Attitude	Percentage of Black Respondents from[a]	
	Random Sample	Nonrandom Black Subsample
Length of residence in the community		
One year or less	47.2	32.4
Two or three years	31.8	30.4
Four or five years	17.2	27.0
Six or more years	3.9	10.1
Rating of recreational facilities		
Excellent	35.9	26.8
Good	32.9	36.9
Average	16.6	20.1
Below average or poor	14.5	16.1
Rating of the community overall		
Excellent	38.0	31.5
Good	44.6	58.4
Average	15.2	10.1
Below average or poor	2.2	0.0

[a] The responses of blacks falling into the random cluster sample in five sample communities known to have more than 100 resident black households at the time the sample was drawn are shown in the first column; the percentages are based on 95 interviews. Responses from blacks in the nonrandom referral subsamples in the same five communities are shown in the second column; the percentages are based on 150 interviews. The five communities are Columbia, Md., Forest Park, Oh., Park Forest, Ill., Park Forest South, Ill., and Reston, Va. To be statistically significant, differences between percentages in the table that are around 50 percent need to be at least 14.8 percent; differences between percentages around 30 percent or 70 percent need to be at least 13.6 percent; and differences between percentages around 10 percent or 90 percent need to be at least 8.9 percent.

nondirective probes (such as, "How do you mean?" or "Could you tell me more about that?") to avoid influencing the responses.

When recording responses to open-end questions, interviewers were to write the actual words spoken as nearly as possible and to indicate when they had probed for additional information. Recording of responses to closed-end questions simply required checking the appropriate precoded response in most cases.

In situations where the respondent could not be contacted on the first call at a sample household, interviewers were required to call back at the household up to six times in order to obtain the interview. These callbacks were to be made at different times of day and on different days of the week to maximize the chance of a contact. Addresses at which the designated individuals refused to be interviewed were generally reassigned to a second interviewer who contacted the individuals and attempted to persuade them to be interviewed.

No substitutions for sample households or sample respondents were allowed. The addresses of sample households (including apartment designations) were listed for each cluster, and the proper respondent (head or spouse of head) was designated for each address prior to assignment of clusters to interviewers. Interviewers were required to interview the designated individuals at the addresses listed.

Reliability of the Data

Sample surveys, even though properly conducted, are liable to several kinds of errors. These include response errors that arise in the reporting and processing of the data, nonresponse errors that arise from failure to interview some individuals selected in the sample, and sampling errors that arise from the random choice of individuals who may make the sample unrepresentative of the population from which it was drawn. Some evaluations of each of these types of error is necessary for the proper interpretation of any estimates from survey data.

Response Errors. Such errors include inaccuracies in asking and answering questions in the interview, recording responses, coding the recorded responses, and processing the coded data. They can be reduced by thoroughly pretesting field procedures and instruments, training interviewers and coders, and exercising quality controls throughout the data collection, coding, and editing phases of the research process.

The questionnaires and field procedures used in the household survey were pretested in the autumn of 1972.[b] Pretesting was carried out in a planned community, Crofton, Md. in the Washington, D.C. metropolitan area, with respondents similar to the populations in the sample. Analysis of pretest interviews resulted in some revisions, such as the rewording of questions to make their meaning clearer to respondents and interviewers.

Interviewer training included a question-by-question review of the household interview instrument, the taking of a practice interview, and discussion of this interview with the interviewer's supervisor. Supervisors reviewed interviewers' work with them throughout the field period.

The coding operation involved two procedures. Responses to

[b]The field and coding operations for the household survey were conducted by The Research Triangle Institute, Research Triangle Park, N.C. Members of the research team monitored all phases of these operations.

closed-end questions were scored directly on the household interview and young adult questionnaire forms which had been printed so that the scored responses could be machine read directly from the forms onto computer tape. Responses to open-end questions were hand coded onto coding forms and keypunched from these forms. Coders were trained in the codes and coding conventions used prior to the beginning of this work. Hand coding was checked by coding 10 percent of the interviews and questionnaires twice and comparing the two codings for discrepancies. Errors found were corrected.

Data tapes were checked for inconsistencies and incorrect codes and indicated corrections were made.

Nonresponse Errors. Some proportion of the sample in any survey fails to respond, usually because of refusals or the failure of the interviewers to contact potential respondents despite repeated attempts. In the random sample for the 36 communities there were a total of 7626 addresses at which there was an eligible respondent after elimination of those addresses whose occupants had moved in on January 1, 1973 or later, as well as addresses that were vacant, commercial establishments, and others at which no one lived permanently. Interviews were obtained with the selected respondent at 5361 of these addresses—an overall response rate of 70.3 percent. Response rates varied somewhat from community to community.

Because response rates were lower than anticipated (80 to 85 percent overall), a study was conducted to assess the extent to which nonrespondents differed systematically from respondents. First, response rates were computed by dwelling unit type and found to differ. Households living in higher density housing were somewhat underrepresented. Since residents in higher density areas tended to have fewer children, for example, and were thought likely to view the community and its facilities from a different perspective than residents of single-family, detached homes, interviews in each of the sample communities were weighted to give responses from residents of each of the three dwelling unit types a weight proportional to that of the dwelling unit type in the community's original sample.

In addition, a survey of nonrespondents was conducted to gather basic demographic and attitude date.[c] Analyses of these data in comparison with household survey data revealed no significant differences between respondent and nonrespondent households for eight of thirteen demographic items (including race, income, marital status,

[c]The nonrespondent follow-up survey, involving telephone interviews and mailback questionnaires, was carried out during February and March 1974 by Chilton Research Services, Radnor, Pa.

and employment status). For five of seven community and quality of life rating items, there were so significant differences between respondents and nonrespondents (including their overall rating of community livability, ratings of schools and recreational facilities, and satisfaction with life as a whole). The major differences between respondent and nonrespondent households included age of household, length of residence, and ratings of health care and shopping facilities. Since most of these differences could be explained by the length of time between the original survey and the nonrespondent follow-up survey, it is estimated that the lower than expected response rates obtained for the original households survey do not bias the study findings.

Sampling Errors.   If all family heads or their spouses living (as of January 1, 1973) in the sampled new and conventional communities had been interviewed, the percentages and other values reported in the text would be population values. Because a sample of persons was interviewed in a sample of communities, the reported statistics are estimates of the population values. Any distribution of individuals selected for a sample will differ by chance somewhat from the population from which it was drawn. If more than one sample were used under the same survey conditions, the estimates from one sample might be larger than the population value for a given variable while the estimates from another sample were smaller. The magnitude of random variability of sample statistics from population values (sampling error) can be calculated for any sample providing it is known exactly how and with what probability the sample was selected.

Sampling errors associated with observed percentages in a group (see Table A−4) can be used to determine a range around an observed percentage within which an analyst can be 95 percent sure that the population value would fall. Sampling errors associated with observed differences in percentages between subgroups (see Table A−5) indicate the minimum size of a percentage difference required for the difference to be considered statistically significant, that is, for it to reflect a true difference between the subgroups in the population rather than chance variation because of sampling. Estimates of average sampling errors based on experiences with other studies in urban areas were adjusted for the clustering in the sample to estimate the statistical significance of percentage differences. Conservative estimates of the sampling error in the sample have been used.

Table A–4. **Approximate Sampling Errors of Percentages** [a]
(expressed in percentages)

| | Number of Interviews | | | |
| | Thirteen New Communities 2600 | Thirteen Conventional Communities 1300 | New Community 200 | Conventional Community 100 |
Reported Percentages				
50	2.3	3.2	8.1	11.5
40 or 60	2.2	3.1	8.0	11.3
30 or 70	2.1	2.9	7.5	10.5
20 or 80	1.8	2.6	6.5	9.2
10 or 90	1.4	1.9	4.9	6.9

[a] The figures in this table represent two standard errors adjusted to take into account clustering in the sample. For items in the tables of the report, chances are 95 in 100 that the population value being estimated lies within a range equal to the reported percentages, plus or minus the sampling error.

Table A–5. **Approximate Sampling Errors of Differences between Subgroups** [a]
(expressed in percentages)

Size of Subgroup	Thirteen New Communities 2600	Thirteen Conventional Communities 1300	New Community 200	Conventional Community 100
	For percentages around 50 percent			
2600	3.2			
1300	3.9	4.5		
200	8.5	8.7	11.5	
100	11.7	11.9	14.1	16.3
	For percentages around 30 percent or 70 percent			
2600	2.9			
1300	3.6	4.1		
200	7.7	8.0	10.5	
100	10.7	10.9	12.9	14.9
	For percentages around 10 percent or 90 percent			
2600	1.9			
1300	2.3	2.7		
200	5.1	5.2	6.9	
100	7.0	7.2	8.4	9.8

[a] The values shown are the size of percentage differences required for significance (two standard errors adjusted for clustered sample) in comparing percentages derived from two different subgroups in a study.

DATA WEIGHTS

Before combining the nonfederally assisted new community and paired conventional community samples to produce estimates presented in this book, cases were weighted by factors that include adjustments for each community's probability of selection and expected number of interviews in the community (200 for new communities, 100 for less planned conventional communities, and 50 for subsidized housing subsample). Cases in the five communities having subsidized housing subsamples (Columbia, Forest Park, Jonathan, Lake Havasu City, and Reston) have also been weighted to adjust for oversampling of households in subsidized housing in the community. In addition, each case is weighted by the proportion of its dwelling unit type (single-family detached, townhouse or rowhouse, or apartment) in the original sample for its community to adjust for differential response rates among the three dwelling unit types.

Data presented for combined nonfederally assisted new communities and combined paired conventional communities are weighted to make all the adjustments listed above: each community's probability of selection, dwelling unit type, disproportionate selection of subsidized housing, and expected number of interviews. Data presented for individual communities exclude the weight for the community's probability of selection. Weights for subsidized housing have been applied only for the five new communities with a subsidized housing subsample and only when data for this sample are presented in combination with those from the basic random sample.

※ *Appendix B*

The New Communities and Their Paired Conventional Communities

The sampling procedures described in Appendix A resulted in the selection of a cross-section of new communities now under development in the United States. The new communities chosen for the study all meet basic criteria for new community status. They are large. Their development has been guided by comprehensive master plans and directed by unified development organizations. Each community contains a variety of housing types and land uses. At the same time, the communities selected differ in a number of important ways. The diversity among the new communities studied is highlighted by the following vignettes which describe the development status and selected characteristics of each community.

COLUMBIA, MARYLAND

Columbia is being developed on 18,000 acres in rural Howard County, Md. midway between the beltways surrounding Washington, D.C. and Baltimore. The idea for this new community was conceived by Baltimore mortgage banker and shopping center developer, James Rouse, in mid-1962 when he began secretly acquiring more than 140 ' parcels assembled for Columbia's development. On October 29, 1963 Rouse announced that he had acquired a tenth of the land in Howard County and proposed the building of an entirely new city. In mid-1965 the plans for Columbia were approved by Howard County, and the development site was rezoned in accordance with a recently completed new-town section of the county zoning ordinance. Construction began in June 1966, and the first homes in Columbia were occupied the following year.

Columbia's land use plan starts with a neighborhood of 2000 to 5000 people built around a neighborhood center consisting of an elementary school, park and playground, swimming pool, community center building, and, in some cases, a convenience store. Two to four neighborhoods are then combined to form a village of from 10,000 to 15,000 people. Village centers provide supermarkets and other convenience shopping facilities, community meeting facilities, land for middle and high schools, and major community recreational facilities. Nine villages surround a town center complex that will include a regional mall, office buildings, a hotel–motel, restaurants, theaters, and a 40-acre town center park and music pavilion. More than 20 percent of Columbia's development acreage will be set aside for open space, with another 20 percent reserved for business and industry.

When study of Columbia began in 1972, the population had grown to 24,000 of a projected 110,000 residents at full development. As shown in Table B–1, Columbia provided a relatively high proportion of rental housing (43 percent), and a variety of housing types, with over a third of the housing stock composed of apartments and townhouses. Twenty percent of the population was nonwhite, but Columbia residents, both white and nonwhite, tended to be middle class and affluent.

By 1972, Columbia's residents had access to a wide variety of community facilities and services. These included an assortment of recreational facilities—an indoor ice rink, two lakes for boating, an indoor swimming pool and eight outdoor neighborhood pools, two golf courses, an indoor tennis club and numerous outdoor courts, an athletic club, miniature golf, a professional dinner theater, an outdoor concert pavilion, several restaurants and lounges, and hundreds of acres of parks and open spaces. Shopping facilities included the Columbia Mall, a regional center with two department stores, and three village centers with supermarkets, banks, drug stores, gas stations, and assorted specialty shops. The Howard County Public Library operated a branch in Columbia, and four college-level institutions were present in the community. These included the two-year Howard Community College, the new four-year Dag Hammarskjold College, a branch of Antioch College, and Loyola College of Baltimore. Over 65 firms had located in the Columbia industrial parks. Total employment in the community was more than 15,000.

Columbia's growth and development had also been marked by a number of institutional innovations. Recreational facilities, early childhood educational programs, and a community transit system were operated by the Columbia Park and Recreation Association, a unique automatic membership homes association that was incorporated in 1965. The Protestant Columbia Cooperative Ministry was formed in 1966 to seek out new opportunities for mission and service. Catholics, Jews, and Protestants shared common religious facilities in The Interfaith Center, located in Wilde Lake Village. The Columbia Medical Plan, a prepaid group practice health care program provided by the Columbia Hospital and Clinics Foundation in affiliation with The Johns Hopkins Medical Institutions, was formed to meet community health care needs. Innovation in the schools, including operation of a model high school in Wilde Lake Village, had drawn national attention.

Norbeck—Wheaton, Maryland

Columbia was paired with the conventional community of Norbeck—Wheaton, located on the urban fringe of Montgomery County fifteen miles northwest of downtown Washington. Major facilities serving the community's 20,000 residents included the Aspen Hill and Rock Creek Village neighborhood shopping centers, Manor Country Club, four neighborhood parks, sections of the North Branch and Rock Creek (regional stream valley) parks, ten schools, and a public library. There were no hospital or medical facilities in Norbeck—Wheaton and only one major employment facility, Vitro Laboratories, which employed about 3600 persons. Although Norbeck—Wheaton did not have as large a minority population as Columbia, other characteristics of the population, including education, occupation, and income were similar (see Table B—1).

ELK GROVE VILLAGE, ILLINOIS

Elk Grove Village is being developed by the Centex Construction Company on a 5760-acre site located 26 miles northwest of Chicago's Loop. The original plan for Elk Grove Village, prepared by the Dallas firm of Phillips, Proctor, Bowers, and Associates, envisioned a community of neighborhood schools and parks surrounded by single-family subdivisions and apartments. Shopping needs were to be accommodated by a series of small community centers within easy access of residential neighborhoods. With room for over 450 establishments, the Centex Industrial Park in Elk Grove Village was designated to provide a major source of employment opportunities for community residents, as well as to assure an adequate tax base.

Table B-1. Housing and Population Characteristics, Spring 1973

Communities	Tenure % Own	Rent	Housing Type (%) Single Family	Townhouse	Apartment	Median Home Value
Columbia, Md. (NC)	57	43	57	14	29	$44,100
Norbeck-Wheaton, Md. (CC)	53	47	69	7	24	52,200
Elk Grove Village, Ill. (NC)	83	17	79	2	19	38,400
Schaumburg, Ill. (CC)	83	17	72	9	19	36,300
Forest Park, Oh. (NC)	88	12	85	6	9	27,300 ↑
Sharonville, Oh. (CC)	85	15	84	4	13	26,100
Foster City, Calif. (NC)	71	29	53	16	31	46,100
West San Mateo, Calif. (CC)	74	26	69	0	31	61,400
Irvine, Calif. (NC)	80	20	56	28	16	42,800
Fountain Valley, Calif. (CC)	84	16	59	24	17	36,200
Jonathan, Minn. (NC)	52	48	45	16	39	33,500
Chanhassen, Minn. (CC)	59	41	59	0	41	40,600
Laguna Niguel, Calif. (NC)	96	4	80	0	20	40,300 ↑
Dana Point, Calif. (CC)	95	5	100	0	0	36,100
Lake Havasu City, Ariz. (NC)	68	32	65	0	35	31,800
Kingman, Ariz. (CC)	74	26	70	0	30	20,900
North Palm Beach, Fla. (NC)	88	12	50	0	50	35,500
Tequesta, Fla. (CC)	98	2	50	0	50	40,300

continued below

Housing Characteristics[a]

Table B-1. continued

Communities	Population Characteristics			
	Race[b]	Education[c]	Occupation[c]	Median Income
	White (%)	Some College + (%)	White Collar (%)	
Columbia, Md. (NC)	80	83	89	$17,300
Norbeck-Wheaton, Md. (CC)	98	79	87	17,800
Elk Grove Village, Ill. (NC)	99	56	65	17,600
Schaumburg, Ill. (CC)	99	55	68	15,400
Forest Park, Oh. (NC)	91	60	58	16,400
Sharonville, Oh. (CC)	100	41	61	15,100
Foster City, Calif. (NC)	93	76	81	20,200
West San Mateo, Calif. (CC)	92	71	89	20,300
Irvine, Calif. (NC)	95	80	87	19,000
Fountain Valley, Calif. (CC)	97	75	76	17,500
Jonathan, Minn. (NC)	97	62	75	11,800
Chanhassen, Minn. (CC)	100	69	81	15,000
Laguna Niguel, Calif. (NC)	99	79	77	17,500
Dana Point, Calif. (CC)	99	73	70	15,300
Lake Havasu City, Ariz. (NC)	100	42	48	12,100
Kingman, Ariz. (CC)	98	40	46	12,800
North Palm Beach, Fla. (NC)	99	65	82	16,900
Tequesta, Fla. (CC)	99	61	83	17,500

(Table B-1. continued overleaf . . .)

Table B–1. continued

| Communities | Tenure (%) | | Housing Characteristics[a] | | | Median Home Value |
| | | | Housing Type (%) | | | |
	Own	Rent	Single Family	Townhouse	Apartment	
Park Forest, Ill. (NC)	78	22	63	35	2	24,800
Lansing, Ill. (CC)	80	20	79	0	21	30,300
Park Forest South, Ill. (NC)	68	32	48	12	40	30,600
Richton Park, Ill. (CC)	66	34	47	16	37	25,300
Reston, Va. (NC)	52	48	25	25	50	58,000
West Springfield, Va. (CC)	37	63	30	31	39	50,800
Sharpstown, Tex. (NC)	62	38	52	11	37	31,200
Southwest Houston, Tex. (CC)	74	26	56	4	40	30,800
Valencia, Calif. (NC)	82	18	80	0	20	37,500
Bouquet Canyon, Calif. (CC)	95	5	100	0	0	30,400
Westlake Village, Calif. (NC)	81	19	56	13	31	47,500
Agoura–Malibu Junction, Calif. (CC)	99	1	80	0	20	35,400

↑ continued below ↑

NC = New Community   CC = Conventional Community

[a] Housing characteristic data are based on household surveys in each of the study communities. Because respondents in the conventional communities were sampled to match the housing distribution in the paired new communities, housing characteristic data do not necessarily reflect housing characteristics of an entire conventional community.

[b] Refers to race of household survey respondents.

[c] Data refer to characteristics of household heads.

Table B–1. continued

Communities	Population Characteristics			
	Race[b] White (%)	*Education[c]* Some College + (%)	*Occupation[c]* White Collar (%)	*Median Income*
Park Forest, Ill. (NC)	91	67	75	16,100
Lansing, Ill. (CC)	100	50	63	12,800
Park Forest South, Ill. (NC)	90	74	73	16,800
Richton Park, Ill. (CC)	99	54	57	12,700
Reston, Va. (NC)	95	85	90	19,900
West Springfield, Va. (CC)	97	82	87	20,100
Sharpstown, Tex. (NC)	95	85	85	15,900
Southwest Houston, Tex. (CC)	100	79	90	17,600
Valencia, Calif. (NC)	97	79	81	19,000
Bouquet Canyon, Calif. (CC)	96	71	68	15,300
Westlake Village, Calif. (NC)	97	81	87	21,600
Agoura—Malibu Junction, Calif. (CC)	95	69	85	17,500

In order to free itself of Cook County zoning and subdivision controls and also to meet the need for municipal services, Centex incorporated Elk Grove Village in 1956, fully thirteen months before the first homes in the community were occupied. By 1972, the population stood at 22,900 and over 27,000 persons were employed in the industrial park. A relatively high proportion (41 percent) of Elk Grove Village's residents had migrated from Chicago. They were predominantly middle class and overwhelmingly white.

Major facilities in Elk Grove Village included the Alexian Brothers Hospital, a community high school and ten elementary and junior high schools, four neighborhood and community shopping centers, and a municipal center. The Elk Grove Village Park District, formed in 1966, operated recreational programs at nineteen park sites, including a large community recreational center and swimming pool complex. Village residents also had access to the adjacent 3800-acre Ned Brown Forest Preserve, which is owned and operated by the Cook County Forest Preserve District.

Schaumburg, Illinois

Paired with Elk Grove Village, the village of Schaumburg lies just to the west, some 30 miles from the Loop. Schaumburg also incorporated in 1956 and by 1970 had a population of 18,830 persons housed in a series of residential subdivisions, apartments, and condominium complexes. Schaumburg is the location of one of the largest regional shopping centers in the nation, the Woodfield Mall, which opened in 1971 with three levels, 215 shops, three department stores, and over two million square feet in its initial phase. Other facilities found in Schaumburg included a number of strip commercial shopping centers, five industrial parks, ten neighborhood and community parks, and a commuter bus service. Schaumburg residents also benefited from Cook County Forest Preserve District lands, which surrounded the community on three sides and provided some 10,000 acres for recreational use.

FOREST PARK, OHIO

Forest Park is located in Hamilton County, fifteen miles northwest of the city of Cincinnati. The development site was once part of a 6000-acre parcel acquired by the federal government in the early 1930s for the Greenbelt Program. In addition to building the town of Greenhills, the federal government used part of the land for a flood control project and gave some 2000 acres to Hamilton County for a regional park. In 1952, the remaining acreage was declared surplus, and the government began looking for a buyer.

In order to prevent the land from being developed in a piecemeal fashion, a group of Cincinnati leaders formed the Cincinnati Community Development Corporation to acquire 3400 acres from the federal government for a planned new community. In 1954, the Warner–Kanter Corporation acquired the site and retained the firm of Victor Gruen Associates to prepare a master plan which, according to the terms of its land sales agreement, the Community Development Corporation reviewed and approved. Gruen's plan featured a series of residential neighborhoods surrounding neighborhood elementary schools. Land was also reserved for industrial uses and for a community center.

The first residents moved to Forest Park in 1956. In 1961, the residents voted to incorporate, in part to ward off an annexation attempt by neighboring Greenhills. By 1972, the population of Forest Park had grown to 17,000, almost half of its target population of 35,000. Compared with most of the other new communities in the sample, Forest Park had attracted a larger black population (9 percent) and had a lower proportion of household heads who had attended college (60 percent) and who were employed in white collar occupations (58 percent). However, as is also shown in Table B–1, Forest Park was solidly middle class, with the median family income standing at $16,400. In addition, Forest Park had the highest proportion of residents (85 percent) among the study communities living in single-family, detached homes.

The major facilities found in Forest Park included a growing industrial park, which in 1972 had attracted twelve manufacturing firms, the corporate headquarters and home office of the Union Central Life Insurance Company, and a neighborhood shopping center. Educational needs were accommodated at a community high school located adjacent to a municipal center and central park, and at three elementary schools and a junior high school. Recreational facilities included a nonprofit community swimming pool and the Winton Woods regional park which was operated by the Hamilton County Park District.

Sharonville, Ohio

Forest Park was matched with the conventional town of Sharonville, located several miles to the east and twelve miles north of Cincinnati. Although the town was originally platted in 1818, it had barely 1000 residents in 1950, when it began a period of steady growth. Sharonville was in the path of major industrial growth out the Mill Creek Valley from Cincinnati. By the early 1970s, over 30 manufacturing plants with over 7000 employees had located in the community. This strong industrial base enabled the city of Sharonville to establish a park and open space system that included two community swimming pools and adjacent recreational centers. An additional amenity is the Sharon Woods regional park operated by the Hamilton County Park District. Compared with the residents of Forest Park, those living in Sharonville had similar socioeconomic characteristics. Sharonville, however, had no black residents.

FOSTER CITY, CALIFORNIA

Foster City is being developed on the west shore of San Francisco Bay, 25 miles south of San Francisco. The 2600-acre development site was acquired by T. Jack Foster and his three sons in 1959. Known as Brewer's Island, the land had been used as pasture by a dairyman early in the century and was later partially converted to evaporating ponds by the Leslie Salt Company. A unique feature of Foster City's development was the creation of the Estero Municipal Improvement District in 1960 to finance reclamation of the low-lying development site and to provide a vehicle for the provision of various urban services. During the first years of development, the district was controlled by the Fosters and caused considerable controversy in Foster City because of its high bonded indebtedness ($63.86 million in 1970) over which the residents had no control.

Foster City's general plan was prepared in 1961 by the firm of Wilsey, Ham and Blair. The plan laid out a series of nine residential neighborhoods, a town center, satellite shopping centers, and an industrial park. Each neighborhood was to be served by small parks and schools. A key feature of the plan was a lagoon system that was designed to provide a major recreational amenity and to serve as the key to successful marketing of the project.

By 1972, Foster City had grown to a community of 15,000 people living in six of the projected nine residential neighborhoods. Three shopping centers were in operation and a professional theater made its home in the community. However, the location of a nearby regional shopping center had slowed growth of Foster City's town center, and school construction was far behind schedule. In order to gain more control over the development process, the residents of Foster City voted to incorporate in April 1971. With incorporation, the Estero Municipal Improvement District was made a subsidiary of the new city government.

The residents of Foster City tended to be affluent (the median income was $20,200), and high proportions of the residents had attended college (76 percent of the household heads) and were working in white collar occupations (81 percent of the employed household heads). The community was racially integrated (3 percent black) and had attracted a number of families of Asian descent (4 percent).

West San Mateo, California

Foster City was paired with two residential subdivisions and adjacent apartment complexes located 30 miles south of San Francisco, at the western edge of the city of San Mateo, which borders Foster City. San Mateo had experienced its most rapid growth during the 1950s. While Foster City was developing during the 1960s on bayfill to the east, much of the remaining undeveloped land in San Mateo developed in the hills to the west.

San Mateo is an established city of 79,000 persons. In 1972, it had a well-developed downtown, a major regional shopping center, and an extensive municipal park system. Other amenities and facilities included the Bay Meadows Race Track, Peninsula Gulf and Country Club, the College of San Mateo, and the San Mateo County Hospital. Most of these facilities, however, were as accessible to Foster City residents as to the conventional subdivisions in West San Mateo. Although median home values were considerably higher in West San Mateo than in Foster City ($61,400 vs. $46,100), in most other respects the residents of these two communities were very similar (see Table B-1).

IRVINE, CALIFORNIA

The 88,000-acre Irvine Ranch is strategically located in the path of Southern California population growth, 40 miles south of Los Angeles in Orange County. Extending 22 miles inland from the Pacific Ocean, the Irvine Ranch will be the site of the nation's largest new community. A population of 430,000 is expected by 1990.

Planning for a new community at Irvine began in 1959 when 1000 acres were donated to the University of California for a new campus. William L. Pereira was retained by the university to plan the campus. Seeing the need for a supporting community, he was commissioned by The Irvine Company to prepare the plans for a 10,000-acre, university-oriented community in the central portion of the Irvine Ranch. Pereira's plan was subsequently incorporated into the South Irvine Ranch General Plan, which was approved by the Orange County Board of Supervisors in February 1964. This plan was then superceded by the 1970 Irvine General Plan, which proposed that a new city of 53,000 acres be developed in the central portion of the ranch. Incorporated in 1971 as the City of Irvine, this portion of the Irvine Ranch was selected for the study.

Originally encompassing 18,300 acres and a population of about 20,000 persons, the city of Irvine has since annexed over 7000 additional acres and has extended its long-range planning over an area of 64,000 acres constituting its approved sphere of influence. The city has adopted a plan that includes three growth options. Option 1 follows Irvine Company plans for a series of villages and environmental corridors, two large industrial complexes, and a new regional commercial center at the juncture of the Santa Ana and San Diego freeways. A midrange population of 337,800 is projected. Option 2 assumes maximum urbanization and projects a midrange population of 453,000. Option 3 is based on minimum urbanization assumptions, including reservation of a 10,000-acre section of coastal hills as open space, and projects a midrange population of 194,000.

When Irvine was selected for study in 1972, work was underway on five villages within the city limits: Walnut, Valleyview, New Culver, University Park, and Turtle Rock. The villages were composed of individual neighborhoods with neighborhood recreational facilities operated by homes associations. A neighborhood shopping center was operating adjacent to University Park, and another was ready for construction next to Walnut Village. The University of California at Irvine was in full operation, and a small town center building was open adjacent to the university. A public golf course has been constructed by The Irvine Company. Over 16,000 employees were working in the highly successful Irvine Industrial Complex, the first of the two industrial areas to be developed. As shown in Talbe B–1, Irvine residents were affluent (median income of $19,000) and overwhelmingly tended to be employed in white collar occupations. Eighty percent of the residents owned their own homes. The median home value was $42,800. Ninety-five percent of the residents were white.

Fountain Valley, California

Fountain Valley is located along the San Diego Freeway four miles north of Irvine. Although the community incorporated in 1957, residential tract development did not begin until January 1962 when the first 100 acres were approved for residential use. During the next ten years, approximately 2500 acres were zoned or developed for single-family homes and apartments. Population growth was equally spectacular, increasing from 597 persons when the community incorporated to 31,826 in 1970 and an estimated 49,000 in 1972. Fountain Valley contained a number of neighborhood shopping centers, a large industrial area, a county park with a golf course, and a community civic center. Ninety-seven percent of the population was white, with three fourths of the sampled household heads having attended college and about the same proportion (see Table B—1) employed in white collar occupations. The median income of the Fountain Valley households included in the study was $17,500.

JONATHAN, MINNESOTA

Jonathan was the first new community to be approved for assistance under the provisions of Title IV of the 1968 Housing and Urban Development Act. It is located in rural Carver County, 25 miles southwest of downtown Minneapolis within the Twin Cities Metropolitan Area. The planning area for the community encompassed 8166 acres of rolling hills interspersed with wooded areas along a ravine system that runs through the property. Jonathan is located a short distance north of an has been annexed by the farm-center town of Chaska, which had over 5000 residents when the study began in 1972.

The development of Jonathan was initiated in 1966 when the Ace Development Corporation (subsequently to become the Jonathan Development Corporation) was formed to manage the development and the Carver Company was organized to spearhead land acquisition for a new community envisioned by the late Henry T. McKnight, a former Minnesota State Senator with interests in downtown real estate, land development, and cattle ranching. Between 1965 and 1970, when a project agreement with the Department of Housing and Urban Development was signed, the concept for Jonathan evolved through three distinct phases. As originally planned, the community was to be developed on about 3000 acres in two upper- and middle-income residential villages. However, on the basis of a financial analysis and development program prepared by the firm of Robert Gladstone and Associates in 1966, the scope of the project was expanded to encompass 4800 acres with a target population of 41,300 after a 20-year development period. Finally, the project was further expanded when Jonathan finalized its application for a federal loan guarantee under Title IV. The project area was expanded to 6000 acres (and subsequently to over 8000 acres), projected population was increased to approximately 50,000, industrial acreage was expanded from 500 to 1989 acres, and a commitment was made to provide over 6500 housing units for low- and moderate-income families.

The design concept for Jonathan is shaped by the existing road system and a 1700-acre open space grid (21 percent of the site) following the natural ravines and drainage courses through the property. Within the matrix of existing highways and proposed open space, five villages, each to house approximately 7000 residents in a variety of housing types, were proposed. Village centers were to provide basic facilities for daily living, including shopping, post offices, municipal services, and elementary schools. A town center was to serve as a regional multifunctional center with major retail, medical, office, and entertainment facilities.

In 1972, when Jonathan was selected for the study, the population of the community stood at 1500 persons housed in 420 dwelling units, 148 of which were constructed under the FHA Section 235 and 236 subsidized housing programs. The initial phase of the first village center was in operation and provided some convenience shopping facilities. A man-made lake had been constructed adjacent to the village center, with an accompanying recreational pavillion. Walking paths connected homes to the village center, the lake, and a neighborhood park with a baseball diamond and tennis court. Although schools had yet to be constructed in Jonathan, the industrial park was growing, with 45 firms providing 1080 jobs by the end of 1973.

Reflecting the character of the Twin Cities area, Jonathan's population was predominantly (97 percent) white. However, because of the high proportion of subsidized housing, the median income of the Jonathan households, $11,800, was the lowest of any of the communities studied. Almost two-thirds of the household heads had attended college, and three-fourths were employed in white collar jobs.

Chanhassen, Minnesota

Jonathan was paired with the nearby village of Chanhassen, which was located adjacent to Jonathan's northeast and eastern planning boundaries. Encompassing 24 square miles, Chanhassen's population was estimated at 5100 in 1972. The community had a small downtown with a nationally known dinner theater, a 60-acre village park, an elementary school, and a high school. Housing included a series of scattered single-family, detached subdivisions and a number of apartment houses located near the downtown. The residents sampled in Chanhassen were somewhat more affluent than those in Jonathan (median income of $15,000 versus $11,800), but were similar in terms of educational attainment and occupation.

LAGUNA NIGUEL, CALIFORNIA

Laguna Niguel is being developed within and on the hills overlooking a valley extending seven miles from the Pacific Ocean to the San

Diego Freeway in southern Orange County. The 7936-acre development site, once part of the Moulton Ranch, was acquired in 1960 by the Boston firm of Cabot, Cabot & Forbes. Victor Gruen and Associates prepared the community master plan, which included a parkway running from the Pacific Coast Highway to the San Diego Freeway to serve as the spine of the community, with a series of residential neighborhoods located on either side. Nineteen schools and six neighborhood shopping centers were envisioned for an ultimate population of 80,000. A major civic and town center was planned in the heart of the community. An industrial area was to be located adjacent to the freeway and a resort complex adjacent to the Pacific beaches.

Because of slow sales throughout the 1960s, Laguna Niguel was sold to the Avco Corporation in 1971, after some 2300 homes had been completed. Since that time, Avco has invested heavily to speed the pace of development. However, concern for the fragile environment of the Southern California coastal hills and the increasing cost of developing hillside land has led to a sharp reduction in the projected population—to 43,000 residents by 1983.

In 1972, when Laguna Niguel was selected for the study, the community had 8500 residents. Most of them (96 percent) owned their own homes, and 80 percent of the households occupied single-family, detached dwellings. Like most of the other new communities studied, Laguna Niguel had attracted a middle class population. Median family income was $17,500, almost 80 percent of the household heads had attended college, and 77 percent were employed in white collar occupations. Laguna Niguel had also attracted a higher than average proportion of retired households (21 percent).

In spite of its slow development pace, Laguna Niguel residents had a variety of community facilities available for their use. These included three shopping centers, a medical office building, a golf course, a tennis club, and a beach club. Orange County had completed its South Coast Regional Civic Center in Laguna Niguel, located adjacent to the town center; Niguel Regional Park, which occupies a 167-acre site surrounding Niguel Lake; and a county beach park. Fifty-five firms had located in the Laguna Niguel Industrial Park, and North American Rockwell had completed construction of a 1,000,000-square foot building designed to house 7000 employees, which has since been acquired by the General Services Administration.

Dana Point–Capistrano Valley, California

This conventional community, located just to the south of Laguna Niguel, consists of several subdivisions of single-family, detached homes and a small shopping area located next to the Pacific Coast Highway. Major amenities in the area include the Dana Point Harbor and Marina, Doheny State Park and Beach, and a neighborhood park operated by the Capistrano Bay Park and Recreation District. The community, like Laguna Niguel, is in an unincorporated portion of Orange County. In 1972, its population was estimated to be 6600. Dana Point residents were somewhat less affluent than those living in Laguna Niguel. Median home value was $36,100 (versus $40,300 in Laguna Niguel) and the median family income was $15,300 (versus $17,500 in Laguna Niguel). Both Dana Point and Laguna Niguel were overwhelmingly white (99 percent).

LAKE HAVASU CITY, ARIZONA

Located 150 air miles northwest of Phoenix and 235 miles east of Los Angeles, Lake Havasu City is the only freestanding new community selected for the study. The idea of building an entirely new city in the Arizona desert originated with Los Angeles oilman and manufacturer, Robert P. McCulloch. In 1959, McCulloch acquired 3500 acres adjacent to Lake Havasu for an outboard motor testing site. Two years later, when he was unable to expand his outboard motor plant in Los Angeles, McCulloch turned to the Lake Havasu site as the location for a new plant and a new city. With C.V. Wood, the former general manager of Disneyland, McCulloch went about acquiring an additional 12,990 acres of desert in a complex series of transactions that required release of the federally owned land to the state of Arizona and its subsequent sale at a public auction. McCulloch was the only bidder, paying approximately $73 an acre.

The general plan for Lake Havasu City was drawn up by Wood. Some 22 miles of lakefront were set aside for community use and are being developed as part of Lake Havasu State Park. The rest of the land was divided into some 40,000 residential, commercial, and industrial building sites. In addition, 36 lots were set aside for neighborhood parks. Land sales have been conducted on a nationwide basis, with a private airline used to transport prospective lot purchasers to the community.

By 1972, Lake Havasu City had an estimated 8500 residents and most of the elements of a complete community. To bolster the economic base, McCulloch transferred his chain saw manufacturing operation (which has since been sold) to Lake Havasu City and bought the historic London Bridge and reassembled it in Lake Havasu City to bolster the tourist industry. Schools were provided by organizing an elementary school district from scratch (two elementary schools and a junior high school have been built) and by persuading the Mohave County Union High School District to build a community high school. Private investors have helped to build a thriving downtown, including a movie theater and bowling alley which were originally built by McCulloch and later sold to private operators. Two developer-owned golf courses are in operation. Lake Havasu City is also served by a weekly newspaper and a local radio station.

Lake Havasu City is the only one of the study new communities with less than a majority (42 percent) of the household heads with at least some college education and with less than a majority (48 percent) employed in white collar jobs. The median income of Lake Havasu City households was $12,100, well below the average ($17,500) of the thirteen nonfederally assisted new communities studied. Because it is a freestanding community, Lake Havasu City has had to provide housing for the workers employed in its manufacturing and service jobs. In addition, it has attracted a relatively high proportion of retired households (23 percent versus 10 percent for the entire sample of thirteen nonfederally assisted new communities).

Kingman, Arizona

Located 56 miles across the Arizona desert from Lake Havasu City, Kingman is the closest comparably sized community on the Arizona side of the Colorado River. Kingman was founded in the early 1880s but was not incorporated as a city until 1952. With a population of 7312 in 1970, Kingman had a small downtown clustered near the Mohave County Courthouse, a long strip commercial section running along U.S. Highway 66, and a series of residential neighborhoods that follow a grid pattern of development. The economy centers on government, transportation, and commercial services, with a small manufacturing sector. A golf course, three city parks, and a municipal pool provided recreational amenities for Kingman's residents. As shown in Table B−1, the socioeconomic characteristics of the residents interviewed in Kingman were similar to those of the Lake Havasu City respondents, though the median home value in Kingman was much lower ($20,900 versus $31,800).

NORTH PALM BEACH, FLORIDA

North Palm Beach is a 2362-acre waterfront community located along the intercoastal waterway, seven and one-half miles north of West Palm Beach. The development site was acquired by North Palm Beach Properties in 1955. Early land development operations included the dredging of a series of canals and the bulkheading of all waterfront properties. The overall planning of the community was honored by the National Association of Home Builders for its design, layout, restrictions, and facilities.

North Palm Beach Properties incorporated the community shortly after the development site was acquired and some months before the first homes were sold. The village government originally restricted its activities to public safety and housekeeping but has gradually increased its functions. In addition to the North Palm Beach Country Club, which was purchased from the developer in 1961, the village operates a public marina, library, art center, and a small park system.

In recent years, Palm Beach County has been one of the best housing markets in the country, and the village of North Palm Beach has the highest growth rate in the county. During the past five years, condominium apartment construction has soared. Commercial development is located in a series of shopping centers along U.S. Highway 1, the major north–south artery through the town. A small area is zoned for industrial use, but has not been occupied.

In 1972, the population was estimated to be 12,500, 42 percent of the 30,000 population projected at full development. Approximately half of the residents lived in apartments, though a high proportion (88 percent) owned their own dwelling units. North Palm Beach households tended to be white and middle class. The median family income was $16,900. A relatively high proportion of the household heads (27 percent) were retired.

Tequesta, Florida

North Palm Beach was paired with the small incorporated village of Tequesta, located nine miles to the north on the Loxahatchee River at Jupiter Inlet. This conventional community consisted of a patchwork of small subdivisions and condominiums. Community amenities include the Tequesta Country Club, the Community Public Library, and a small art institution, the Lighthouse Gallery. In 1970, the population of Tequesta was 2576, with 4323 persons living in adjacent unincorporated areas. As shown in Table B–1, Tequesta's residents were similar to those living in North Palm Beach in terms of socioeconomic characteristics. However, a higher proportion of the household heads (53 percent) were retired.

PARK FOREST, ILLINOIS

Park Forest is the oldest new community included in the study. The community was begun in 1947 on some 2200 acres of Illinois prairie in southeast Cook County by American Community Builders, Inc., a partnership consisting of Nathan Manilow, Phillip M. Klutznick, and

Jerrold Loebl. Land planning was under the direction of Elbert Peets, who had earlier designed the town of Glendale for the United States Housing Authority.

Because of the vast housing market created by returning war veterans and the availability of financing for rental housing for veterans, initial residential building consisted of 3010 rental townhouses grouped in courts near the center of Park Forest. Several years later these courts received national publicity as the home of William Whyte's "organization man." Families who occupied the rental housing units and the single-family subdivisions that were subsequently built provided customers for a large shopping center located at the geographical and population center of Park Forest. The shopping center was one of the first open malls in the country.

Park Forest incorporated as a village in 1949, and the village government assumed responsibility for various urban services in the community. The village established an aggressive park development program on land donated by the development company. In 1973, the village recreation and parks department maintained 275 acres of parks, operated a nine-hole golf course, and supervised and staffed some 80 recreational programs, ranging from preschool through adult activities. A nonprofit community swimming pool corporation built and operated an "aquatic center" open to all Park Forest residents.

Although industrial land was set aside in Park Forest, poor highway access limited its appeal to prospective firms. However, the community's location at the end of the Illinois Central's commuter rail line to the Loop meant that the developer did not have to rely on local employment as a source of housing demand. In fact, most of the community's early residents worked 29 miles away in downtown Chicago.

By 1960, Park Forest had a population of 30,000, just short of current numbers. American Community Builders, Inc. disbanded in 1959. Since that time, development has been limited. Park Forest had the lowest median home value ($24,800) of any of the new communities studied. Nevertheless, two-thirds of the household heads had attended college, and three-fourths were working in white collar occupations. The median family income of $16,100 was not too much lower than the median of $17,500 for all thirteen nonfederally assisted new communities studied. Nine percent of the households in Park Forest were nonwhite.

Lansing, Illinois
Park Forest was paired with the village of Lansing, located adjacent to the Indiana state line in southeastern Cook County, 26 miles from

Chicago's Loop. Although Lansing was incorporated as a village in 1893 (with a population of 200), major residential growth did not occur until after World War II. In 1950, both Lansing and Park Forest had populations between 8000 and 9000. Both communities more than doubled in population during the 1950s. Lansing, however, had somewhat greater success than Park Forest in attracting industrial development. In 1970, there were 30 manufacturing establishments and a total of 1000 manufacturing employees in the community. Major amenities in Lansing include a community park and swimming pool operated by the Lan-Oak Park District, a number of small neighborhood parks, and a section of the Cook County Forest Preserve adjacent to the community's southwest boundary. The population of Lansing was 25,218 in 1970.

PARK FOREST SOUTH, ILLINOIS

Park Forest South, the second federally assisted new community selected for the study, is located in Will County, 32 miles south of the Chicago Loop and immediately south of Park Forest. The idea for the community originated with the late Nathan Manilow, who was one of the principal partners involved in the building of Park Forest. When Park Forest's development company, American Community Builders, Inc., disbanded in 1959, Manilow retained control of the Park Forest Plaza shopping center through his wholly owned company, Park Forest Properties. In the mid-1960s, Nathan Manilow and his son Lewis saw the potential for the expansion of Park Forest to a community of some 60,000 residents and began to assemble the necessary acreage to the south in Will County.

In June 1967, the Manilows persuaded the residents of a small, bankrupt subdivision surrounded by Manilow land holdings to incorporate as the Village of Park Forest South. The Manilows then retained the firm of Carl L. Gardner and Associates to develop a comprehensive plan for the village and to prepare zoning and subdivision regulations. When these were completed, the Manilows requested annexation of 1200 acres of adjoining land which had been prezoned for a large, planned unit development. This was accomplished on January 26, 1968 in exchange for a promise by the Manilows to support village fire protection and police services.

In order to secure development capital and financing, the Manilows then proceeded on two fronts. First, additional equity participation in the venture was achieved in 1968 when Mid-America Improvement Corporation (owned by Illinois Central Industries, Inc.) became a partner in the new community and in 1969 when United States Gypsum Urban Development Corporation (owned by The United States Gypsum Company) was recruited. Each company took a 25 percent interest in the Park Forest South Development Company, with the Manilow Organization, Inc. acting as managing partner. Second, to generate the long-term capital required to develop a full-scale new community, assistance was sought from the Department of Housing and Urban Development under Title IV of the 1968 Housing and Urban Development Act. Park Forest South's participation in the federal new communities program was formally accomplished on March 17, 1971 when a project agreement with HUD was signed.

The Park Forest South planning area encompassed 8291 acres which were to be developed over a fifteen-year period for a target population of 110,000. Highlights of the development plan included the 753-acre campus of Governors State University, Governors Gateway Industrial Park, and a multifunctional town center. These three elements were to be connected by the "Main Drag"—a three-mile linear strip development containing major commercial, recreational, and municipal facilities served by a rapid transit system. Other commercial and institutional facilities were to be provided in a number of neighborhood centers designed to serve day-to-day needs. Rapid transit service to Chicago was to be initiated through an extension of the Illinois Central Gulf commuter rail line when 3000 dwelling units were occupied. A major hospital and medical complex with close connections with the university were planned. Almost 900 acres of major open space were to be provided, together with a more intimate open space network and path system running through individual neighborhoods. Finally, Park Forest South was expected to provide an estimated 4500 housing units to be constructed with assistance from federal low- and moderate-income housing subsidy programs and an employment base of over 28,000 jobs.

When Park Forest South was selected for the study in 1972, the community had a population of 3200 residents living in 1310 dwelling units. Recreational facilities were provided at two neighborhood swimming and recreational centers, which were operated by private automatic membership associations. An elementary school had been completed, as well as a small convenience shopping center and a commercial ice skating rink. Development was well underway in the industrial park, which had 34 firms employing 925 persons by the end of 1973.

Because subsidized housing had yet to be occupied in Park Forest South at the time of the household survey in the spring of 1973, the median family income in the community ($16,800) was considerably higher than that of Jonathan ($11,800). However, Park Forest South had attracted a number of nonwhite families (10 percent of the population).

Richton Park, Illinois

Richton Park is located directly north of Park Forest South and adjacent to the western boundary of Park Forest. In 1972, the community had an estimated 4800 residents and was undergoing rapid residential growth. Recently developed projects included a large subdivision of single-family, detached homes marketed under the FHA Section 235 subsidized home ownership program, as well as conventional single-family subdivisions, townhouses, and apartments. Major community facilities included an elementary school and a high school, strip commercial shopping centers, a golf course, and a neighborhood park and playground. Unlike Park Forest South, Richton Park's population was almost entirely white. However, the median income of residents was lower ($12,700), and lower proportions of the household heads had attended college (54 percent) and were working in white collar occupations (57 percent).

RESTON, VIRGINIA

Reston is being developed on 6750 acres located in Fairfax County, eighteen miles northwest of Washington, D.C. The development site was acquired in March 1961 by Robert E. Simon, Jr. after he and his family had sold Carnegie Hall in New York City. The Reston master plan was prepared by the New York architectural firm of Whittlesey and Conklin and was approved by the Fairfax County Board of Supervisors in June 1962. The plan assigned about 23 percent of the site for recreational areas, provided for a 970-acre industrial park, and for a variety of housing types and commercial areas. These land uses were organized in a series of seven villages, each with a projected population of 10,000 to 12,000 people. A town center was designated to serve Reston's projected 75,000 residents and some 50,000 people in the surrounding region.

Throughout its early years, Reston was plagued by a slow development pace and financial difficulties. These problems came to a head in September 1967, when the Gulf Oil Corporation, which had made a major loan to Simon for Reston's development, took over full financial and operational responsibility and formed Gulf-Reston, Inc. to manage the development process. Gulf increased its investment in Reston and by 1972 was able to report a positive cash flow.

In 1972, Reston had an estimated 20,000 residents living in two villages, Lake Anne and Hunters Woods. Over 50 tenants occupied the Lake Anne Village Center, which had attracted national attention because of its urbane design and mixture of shops and apartments. Two golf courses were operating, as well as a series of neighborhood swimming and tennis facilities and a riding stable. Medical and day care centers were functioning. Over 2000 persons were employed in Reston and construction was underway on a $54-million headquarters building for the United States Geological Survey.

Reston had one of the most educated and affluent populations of any of the new communities selected for the study. Eighty-five percent of the household heads had attended college, 90 percent were employed in white collar occupations, and the median income was $19,900. The median home value was $58,000. Reston was racially integrated (5 percent of the population was nonwhite) and economically integrated (11 percent of the housing stock consisted of subsidized units).

West Springfield, Virginia

This conventional community in Fairfax County is located eighteen miles southeast of Reston and thirteen miles southwest of downtown Washington. With almost 35,000 residents in 1972, the West Springfield community was served by four neighborhood and community shopping centers but made no provision for industrial development. Recreational facilities were provided at Lake Accotink, Cardinal Forest, and West Springfield Golf and Country Club and at facilities provided by individual tract and apartment developers. As shown in Table B—1, the socioeconomic characteristics of the West Springfield residents were very similar to those of the Reston residents, although a significantly higher proportion rented their homes (63 percent versus 48 percent).

SHARPSTOWN, TEXAS

Sharpstown, which began development in 1953 on a 4100-acre site, is located ten miles southeast of downtown Houston. The community master plan followed traditional patterns, with single-family subdivisions surrounding neighborhood elementary schools and small parks. Although little emphasis was placed on architectural merit, homes were built and marketed within the means of a broad spectrum of consumers.

In 1972, Sharpstown had over 11,000 homes and apartments. The Sharpstown Center, a regional shopping center occupying a 77-acre site in the heart of the community, had opened in 1960. Other projects completed in the 1960s included a boy's preparatory school operated by the Society of Jesus, Houston Baptist College, which occupied a 196-acre campus in Sharpstown, a branch of the Houston Public Library, the Memorial Baptist Hospital's Southwest Branch, and the Sharpstown General Hospital. Recreational and entertainment facilities included several neighborhood parks, the Sharpstown Country Club, a drive-in theater, a 2100-seat movie theater, and a 3000-seat professional theater. Employment opportunities were provided at the many commercial establishments in Sharpstown and by firms located in the 755-acre Sharpstown Industrial Park.

Sharpstown is a middle class community. Eighty-five percent of the household heads had attended college, and 85 percent were employed in white collar occupations. The median family income was $15,900. Five percent of the population was nonwhite.

Southwest Houston, Texas

This conventional community consists of three large subdivisions located southwest of Sharpstown at the edge of the Houston city limits. The subdivisions were developed gradually over a period of years and were tied together by a major thoroughfare and series of strip-commercial shopping centers. Major amenities and recreational facilities included the Braeburn Country Club, the Southwest Branch of the Houston YMCA, and the City of Houston's Southwest Tennis Center. Although the median income of households was higher than in Sharpstown ($17,600 versus $15,900), educational and occupation characteristics of the household heads were similar, as was the median home value.

VALENCIA, CALIFORNIA

Valencia is located 32 miles northeast of downtown Los Angeles in an unincorporated section of Los Angeles County. The community is being developed by the Newhall Land and Farming Company on a 4000-acre section of the 44,000-acre Newhall Ranch. The land was originally purchased by Henry Mayo Newhall in the 1870s.

The stimulus for the development of a new community on the Newhall Ranch was provided by approaching urbanization in the San Fernando Valley, seven miles to the south, and the Palmdale International Airport, which was proposed for nearby Antelope Valley. The general plan for Valencia was prepared by Thomas L. Sutton and Victor Gruen and Associates and was adopted by the Los Angeles County Regional Planning Commission in October 1965. The Valencia plan combines individual neighborhoods with schools and parks into a series of villages, each with its own shopping and recreational centers, high schools, library, and church. Paseos (pathways) connect superblocks of homes with neighborhood schools and parks. An open space system separates the villages. A major regional shopping and civic center is planned in the heart of the community, with employment opportunities to be provided at the 1000-acre Valencia Industrial Center.

By 1972, Valencia had an estimated 7000 residents living in over 2000 homes and garden apartments. The first village shopping center was in operation. Two educational institutions, California Institute of the Arts, a four-year art and music school conceived by Walt Disney, and College of the Canyons, a community college, had begun operation. In order to attract potential residents to Valencia, the Newhall Land and Farming Company had invested heavily in regional recreational and entertainment facilities. These included three golf courses, a $30-million family ride park called Magic Mountain, a public riding stable, a travel trailer park, and a dune buggy and motorcycle park. Some fifteen companies had located in the Valencia Industrial Center, thus creating an employment base approaching 3000 jobs.

The median income of Valencia residents was $19,000. Seventy-nine percent of the household heads had attended college and 81 percent were employed in white collar occupations. Ninety-seven percent of the residents were white.

Bouquet Canyon, California

The hills and valleys northeast of Valencia began to develop several years before Valencia's master plan was approved. The Bouquet Canyon community consists of a series of single-family, detached residential subdivisions on the canyon floor. Shopping facilities were available at two centers located near the mouth of Bouquet Canyon and its junction with San Francisquito Canyon. The community was also served by a small park operated by the Los Angeles County Park and Recreation Department. As shown in Table B—1, the Bouquet Canyon residents tended to be less affluent than those living in Valencia. The median family income was $15,300, $3700 less than in Valencia.

WESTLAKE VILLAGE, CALIFORNIA

Westlake Village is surrounded by mountains in the picturesque Conejo Valley, 40 miles northwest of the Los Angeles Civic Center. The community is being developed on the 11,709-acre Albertson Ranch which was acquired by shipping magnate Daniel K. Ludwig in 1964 after one year of litigation over title to the property. During 1964 and 1965, the Bechtel Corporation conducted master plan studies for Ludwig's American-Hawaiian Steamship Company, which was to manage the development process. Earthmoving began in 1966, and the first homes were occupied in 1967.

The Westlake Village master plan is based on interrelating a series of neighborhood clusters composed of homes, schools, parks, recreational facilities, and small neighborhood shopping centers. A major regional shopping center was planned along the Ventura Freeway, which bisects the community, and approximately 500 acres along the freeway were set aside for industrial use. Unique among American new communities, the Westlake Village plan also reserved a 170-acre parcel at the community's sourthern boundary for a cemetery. The theme for Westlake Village was established by a 150-acre artificial lake which cost $2 million to construct.

In 1972, Westlake Village had an estimated 13,000 residents. Major community facilities and amenities included a community shopping center and two satellite centers, a motel–restaurant complex, an 18-hole, night-lighted golf course and tennis club, individual neighborhood swimming pools and recreational centers, two riding stables, a marina at Lake Westlake, and a community hospital. A number of nationally known firms had located in the industrial parks. Employment in Westlake Village was estimated to be 4500. Nevertheless, Westlake Village was in financial difficulty. In 1969, the Prudential Insurance Company converted a $30-million land loan into an equity investment in Westlake Village's development. By late in 1972, disagreements between Prudential and the American-Hawaiian Steamship Company led to dissolution of the partnership, Prudential keeping the undeveloped acreage in the community and American-Hawaiian the income property. Prudential has completed a second golf course and is proceeding with development.

Westlake Village had the highest median family income of the new communities studied ($21,600) and the second highest median home value ($47,500). Eighty-one percent of the household heads had attended college, and 87 percent were employed in white collar occupations. Ninety-seven percent of the residents were white.

Agoura—Malibu Junction, California
The Malibu hills and canyons between Westlake Village and the new community of Calabassas Park, several miles to the south along

the Ventura Freeway, have been steadily developing since the late 1960s. This conventional community of some 5000 residents consisted of a series of unrelated and widely separated subdivisions located on either side of the freeway. Shopping facilities were provided at a small convenience center located just off of the freeway. A 12-acre park site is owned by the Simi Valley Recreation and Park District, and several subdivisions had neighborhood recreational facilities operated by home associations. The residents were affluent (median income of $17,500), and high proportions of the household heads had attended college (69 percent) and were employed in white collar occupations (85 percent). Ninety-five percent of the residents were white.

*   *Appendix C*

Supplementary Tables

Table C–1.   Community Component Ratings in New Communities (percentage distributions)

Component[a]	Nonfederally Assisted New Communities												Federally Assisted New Communities			Thirteen Nonfederally Assisted New Communities	Thirteen Conventional Communities
	Columbia	Reston	Irvine	Valencia	Park Forest	Westlake Village	Elk Grove Village	Foster City	Laguna Niguel	Lake Havasu City	Sharpstown	Forest Park	North Palm Beach	Jonathan	Park Forest South		
A. Dwelling unit																	
1. Completely satisfied	28	28	43	39	22	51	35	52	52	45	29	29	42	28	29	40	39
2.	29	36	29	35	34	32	29	23	26	20	28	32	31	35	33	30	29
3.	23	21	19	16	20	10	22	14	14	19	20	17	16	18	22	17	17
4.	9	9	5	11	13	4	9	5	5	11	12	13	7	10	9	8	8
5.	5	4	1	1	7	1	3	2	1	3	6	8	2	3	3	3	4
6.	3	2	1	0	3	0	1	1	1	2	3	1	1	4	4	1	1
7. Completely dissatisfied	3	1	1	0	1	1	1	2	1	0	2	2	1	1	1	1	1
B. Health care																	
1. Excellent	21	9	11	3	21	47	42	28	26	3	40	13	31	26	12	26	18
2. Good	38	38	28	27	53	42	39	31	49	21	43	42	52	47	37	40	37
3. Average	20	34	26	30	21	10	17	16	19	24	16	29	14	22	25	20	24
4. Below average	13	13	25	26	4	1	2	12	4	37	1	12	2	4	16	9	11
5. Poor	9	6	9	13	2	0	1	13	3	15	0	4	1	2	11	5	9

C. *Homeowners association*

1. Completely satisfied	10	4	19	22	15	31	—	35	6	—	—	—	35	10	16	21	28
2.	18	17	42	36	27	19	—	30	43	—	—	—	42	13	37	29	19
3.	33	29	24	26	27	20	—	9	19	—	—	—	12	23	28	23	19
4.	27	33	8	11	27	17	—	8	13	—	—	—	3	33	13	16	18
5.	6	10	3	1	4	7	—	9	12	—	—	—	9	13	6	6	8
6.	3	4	2	4	0	3	—	9	4	—	—	—	0	7	0	3	5
7. Completely dissatisfied	1	1	1	0	0	4	—	0	4	—	—	—	0	2	0	2	3
(Number of respondents rating homeowners association)[b]	(191)	(133)	(149)	(98)	(24)	(134)	—	(24)	(50)	—	—	—	(39)	(183)	(29)	(704)	(151)

D. *Microneighborhood*

Scale score:																	
3. Highest ratings	30	34	36	35	21	57	31	31	42	28	21	28	37	29	21	34	30
4–5.	25	33	31	38	30	25	33	34	35	30	33	29	29	35	36	32	34
6–7.	34	23	26	20	35	12	24	25	15	25	25	27	21	18	30	23	25
8–15. Lowest ratings	11	11	7	7	15	6	12	10	8	17	20	15	13	18	13	11	11

E. *Recreation facilities*

1. Excellent	49	49	46	42	27	66	39	28	39	37	15	27	41	55	24	38	26
2. Good	42	36	39	39	48	23	43	39	35	38	38	42	48	39	32	39	37
3. Average	6	9	10	16	20	6	13	15	12	16	31	16	9	5	25	14	21
4. Below average	1	3	4	3	3	3	3	12	10	6	8	10	2	1	10	6	9
5. Poor	1	3	1	0	3	2	3	5	3	3	8	4	1	0	10	3	7

F. *Religious facilities*

Can find those wanted?																	
1. Yes	76	78	69	82	91	91	89	45	72	92	86	76	88	54	62	80	81
5. No	24	22	31	18	9	9	11	55	28	8	14	24	12	46	38	20	19
(Number of respondents)[c]	(162)	(152)	(155)	(166)	(182)	(158)	(172)	(149)	(144)	(184)	(188)	(176)	(187)	(172)	(158)	(2177)	(1075)

(Table C–1. continued overleaf . . . .)

Table C-1. continued

Component[a]	Nonfederally Assisted New Communities											Federally Assisted New Communities				Thirteen Nonfederally Assisted New Communities	Thirteen Conventional Communities
	Columbia	Reston	Irvine	Valencia	Park Forest	Westlake Village	Elk Grove Village	Foster City	Laguna Niguel	Lake Havasu City	Sharpstown	Forest Park	North Palm Beach	Jonathan	Park Forest South		
G. School attended by child																	
1. Excellent	30	37	48	30	29	32	48	27	41	18	26	35	21	28	25	33	36
2. Good	48	49	41	57	44	43	45	53	42	39	39	47	41	40	43	46	45
3. Average	15	13	10	12	26	18	6	15	12	34	32	12	35	24	26	17	16
4. Below average	5	1	1	0	2	7	2	4	5	7	0	3	3	7	6	3	2
5. Poor	2	0	0	1	0	0	0	1	0	2	3	3	1	1	0	1	1
(Number of respondents rating school)[d]	(83)	(90)	(89)	(88)	(94)	(95)	(115)	(92)	(86)	(76)	(69)	(114)	(70)	(66)	(77)	(1175)	(616)
H. Shopping facilities																	
1. Excellent	32	23	30	3	43	20	55	31	25	2	54	60	41	8	14	34	32
2. Good	47	39	32	16	45	27	29	41	34	19	36	30	41	31	38	33	33
3. Average	16	21	19	18	10	28	10	17	14	32	9	8	16	28	21	16	15
4. Below average	4	10	15	41	2	18	3	7	17	38	0	2	2	20	18	12	11
5. Poor	1	7	4	23	0	7	3	3	9	10	1	0	1	13	9	6	9

I. *Transportation*

Scale score:

2. Highest rating	32	21	23	23	22	27	24	23	14	49	28	28	34	26	9	26	22
3.	23	12	16	21	20	20	18	24	17	12	16	20	22	15	20	19	18
4.	30	42	39	37	39	33	31	39	35	21	37	37	28	41	34	35	34
5.	11	16	15	14	10	12	13	11	18	5	9	9	10	15	22	12	13
6. Lowest rating	4	9	7	5	9	8	14	4	17	12	10	7	5	5	15	9	13

[a] Questionnaire items for each of the community components are detailed in the notes of Table 3–5. Except as noted below, the number of responses for each of the items was at or near the number of interviews listed in the basic sample column of Table A–2.

[b] Homeowner association membership was not universal, hence the reduced *N*'s in some communities.

[c] Respondents who said they "did not care" about religious facilities were not included in the base for these percentages.

[d] The school evaluation question was asked only of respondents who had a child attending school.

Table C-2. Microneighborhood Attribute Ratings in New Communities *(percentage distributions)*

	Nonfederally Assisted New Communities													Federally Assisted New Communities			
Attribute	Columbia	Reston	Irvine	Valencia	Park Forest	Westlake Village	Elk Grove Village	Foster City	Laguna Niguel	Lake Havasu City	Sharpstown	Forest Park	North Palm Beach	Jonathan	Park Forest South	Thirteen Assisted New Communities	Thirteen Conventional Communities
Satisfaction scale components																	
A. 1. Attractive	39	47	47	55	31	68	44	46	51	38	34	38	48	42	40	47	42
2.	37	34	40	34	37	25	41	41	34	28	35	35	29	30	35	34	39
3.	21	16	11	9	25	5	12	11	13	27	24	20	19	18	21	15	16
4.	3	3	1	2	6	2	3	2	2	6	5	5	2	9	3	3	3
5. Unattractive	1	1	1	1	1	*	0	1	1	1	2	2	1	2	2	1	1
B. 1. Pleasant	57	60	62	55	46	73	51	53	66	64	48	54	56	60	54	57	56
2.	32	29	26	35	39	19	33	30	23	24	29	30	31	24	33	29	29
3.	10	9	10	9	12	8	13	15	9	10	22	13	11	15	12	12	12
4.	1	2	1	1	2	1	2	2	1	2	1	3	3	2	1	2	2
5. Unpleasant	0	*	1	1	2	0	1	0	1	*	1	*	0	0	1	1	1
C. 1. Very good place to live	51	58	64	62	45	75	55	57	76	48	44	49	64	52	41	59	57
2.	34	30	29	31	38	19	37	29	18	33	39	34	27	36	43	30	34
3.	11	11	6	6	14	4	5	14	5	17	15	14	7	10	15	9	8
4.	3	*	1	0	2	2	1	1	1	2	2	3	2	1	2	1	1
5. Very poor place to live	1	1	1	1	1	1	2	0	0	1	1	*	0	0	0	1	1

Microneighborhood attributes

D. 1. Convenient	57	42	48	44	58	52	53	57	46	47	62	65	61	45	29	54	50
2.	28	37	29	31	31	28	28	28	25	25	30	22	27	26	29	28	26
3.	10	15	17	21	9	14	14	12	22	23	6	10	11	23	25	14	17
4.	3	5	4	4	1	5	4	1	6	2	2	2	0	4	12	3	5
5. Inconvenient	1	1	3	1	1	2	1	3	2	4	0	1	*	2	5	1	2
E. 1. Enough privacy	44	41	52	52	41	57	46	55	62	64	46	45	54	39	43	51	50
2.	26	31	29	24	21	22	28	16	22	17	22	19	21	25	29	23	23
3.	14	16	7	10	19	9	16	9	8	13	17	13	10	13	19	12	14
4.	9	6	8	8	13	9	6	12	3	5	9	13	11	13	5	9	7
5. Not enough privacy	7	6	5	5	7	4	3	8	4	2	6	10	5	10	4	6	6
F. 1. Friendly	45	40	43	45	42	49	40	42	54	53	33	43	52	52	42	45	42
2.	30	37	31	37	31	26	35	30	24	24	35	28	27	30	36	30	29
3.	20	18	20	15	19	23	21	21	15	16	26	22	15	15	18	19	21
4.	4	4	4	3	5	2	2	6	4	5	4	4	5	3	2	4	5
5. Unfriendly	*	2	3	1	3	1	2	1	2	1	3	3	1	0	2	2	2
G. 1. People like me	17	13	18	20	16	29	28	16	29	33	17	21	27	20	20	22	24
2.	22	27	25	32	37	23	33	26	25	20	29	33	28	25	28	28	28
3.	45	45	42	33	36	34	31	46	33	38	36	34	32	43	40	36	35
4.	12	10	11	10	6	9	5	7	10	6	11	8	8	9	7	9	9
5. People not like me	5	6	4	5	6	4	3	5	4	3	8	5	6	3	5	5	5
H. 1. Quiet	39	35	43	41	38	46	39	34	62	58	36	34	43	39	41	42	41
2.	30	34	26	33	27	28	29	37	26	18	22	32	25	25	28	29	26
3.	20	16	19	19	21	17	20	14	7	15	26	24	22	21	23	19	21
4.	7	9	8	5	11	6	7	7	3	5	11	7	6	10	5	7	8
5. Noisy	5	6	4	3	3	3	4	9	2	4	6	3	5	5	3	4	4
I. 1. Safe	34	48	58	37	47	62	53	49	67	59	32	49	59	70	55	51	51
2.	37	37	30	42	38	25	38	30	21	24	35	33	29	20	31	32	31
3.	19	10	9	14	11	11	6	18	8	16	26	13	9	8	10	13	14
4.	9	6	3	7	4	1	2	2	2	1	6	4	2	0	4	3	3
5. Unsafe	1	1	1	1	3	2	2	2	2	1	2	1	1	2	0	1	1

Table C–2. continued overleaf . . .)

Table C–2. continued

Attribute	Columbia	Reston	Irvine	Valencia	Park Forest	Westlake Village	Elk Grove Village	Foster City	Laguna Niguel	Lake Havasu City	Sharpstown	Forest Park	North Palm Beach	Jonathan	Park Forest South	Thirteen Nonfederally Assisted New Communities	Thirteen Conventional Communities
					Nonfederally Assisted New Communities									Federally Assisted New Communities			
J. 1. Uncrowded	36	27	34	38	37	39	31	33	47	73	30	32	30	39	26	36	38
2.	26	29	23	34	20	22	33	23	24	11	26	23	28	20	32	26	24
3.	22	26	28	19	28	23	27	29	18	11	24	27	22	18	29	23	22
4.	11	11	12	7	10	12	6	12	8	3	16	13	13	16	11	11	11
5. Crowded	5	6	3	3	5	5	4	3	3	2	4	5	6	7	3	4	5
K. 1. Well kept up	51	44	53	59	41	69	56	55	48	47	41	42	48	50	46	51	47
2.	31	34	33	27	42	23	29	33	34	29	33	33	33	24	39	31	33
3.	11	13	10	11	13	6	13	6	13	20	18	17	14	19	12	12	14
4.	6	7	4	3	4	3	3	4	5	3	5	5	4	5	1	4	4
5. Poorly kept up	2	1	1	1	0	0	0	2	1	1	4	3	1	2	3	1	2

*Less than 0.5 percent.

Table C-3. Dwelling Unit Attribute Ratings in New Communities *(percentage distributions)*

Attribute [a]	Nonfederally Assisted New Communities													Federally Assisted New Communities		Thirteen Nonfederally Assisted New Communities	Thirteen Assisted New Communities	Thirteen Conventional Communities
	Columbia	Reston	Irvine	Valencia	Park Forest	Westlake Village	Elk Grove Village	Foster City	Laguna Niguel	Lake Havasu City	Sharpstown	Forest Park	North Palm Beach	Jonathan	Park Forest South			
A. Indoor space																		
More than needed	13	16	11	20	7	18	10	12	11	15	10	11	12	8	13	13	13	11
About right	62	54	68	62	63	69	57	65	70	61	57	65	65	63	62	63	63	66
Too little	26	31	21	18	30	14	32	24	19	24	33	23	24	29	25	24	24	23
B. Outdoor space																		
More than needed	9	7	7	5	6	8	8	6	10	15	4	6	9	11	6	7	7	8
About right	72	75	76	74	79	78	80	72	79	73	63	65	75	75	72	74	74	71
Too little	20	17	17	21	15	14	12	23	11	12	33	30	17	14	22	19	19	22
C. Outdoor privacy																		
Yes	42	54	77	69	42	71	58	61	77	58	59	35	50	48	37	59	59	60
No	58	46	23	32	58	29	43	39	23	42	42	66	50	52	63	41	41	40
D. Investment compared to other dwellings																		
Better	72	77	77	71	41	77	68	88	78	55	54	56	75	64	63	70	70	73
Same	25	18	20	23	46	19	30	12	21	42	39	38	25	31	29	27	27	24
Worse	2	5	3	6	14	3	2	0	1	3	7	6	0	5	8	3	3	3
(Number of homeowners responding)	(109)	(93)	(145)	(153)	(128)	(145)	(157)	(129)	(174)	(121)	(108)	(163)	(160)	(98)	(124)	(1863)	(953)	

[a] Questionnaire items are detailed in the notes of Table 4–5. Except for the rating of the home as an investment (panel D) which was asked only of homeowners, the number of responses for these items was at or near the numbers listed in the "basic sample" column of Table A–2.

Table C–4. Life Satisfaction and Life Domain Ratings in New Communities (percentage distributions)

Domain[a]	Nonfederally Assisted New Communities													Federally Assisted New Communities				
	Columbia	Reston	Irvine	Valencia	Park Forest	Westlake Village	Elk Grove Village	Foster City	Laguna Niguel	Lake Havasu City	Sharpstown	Forest Park	North Palm Beach	Jonathan	Park Forest South	Thirteen Nonfederally Assisted New Communities	Thirteen Conventional Communities
Overall life satisfaction																	
1. Completely satisfied	21	20	28	25	27	39	31	41	36	38	23	33	28	31	27	31	31
2.	36	41	40	42	32	33	38	28	37	32	37	31	42	33	36	36	35
3.	20	24	21	20	26	19	20	20	20	16	27	19	21	21	22	21	21
4.	14	8	7	6	11	5	9	5	4	11	7	8	8	8	8	7	8
5.	5	6	3	3	3	2	2	3	2	3	5	6	1	4	5	3	3
6.	3	1	1	3	1	1	0	3	1	*	1	1	0	3	2	1	2
7. Completely dissatisfied	1	0	1	1	1	0	1	0	0	0	0	1	1	0	0	1	1
Life domains																	
A. *Community*																	
1. Excellent	40	55	52	57	28	75	42	50	61	31	27	32	59	41	21	49	42
2. Good	42	39	43	37	55	21	49	36	35	48	57	50	34	50	56	41	45
3. Average	14	5	5	6	14	2	9	10	3	15	16	15	7	9	20	9	12
4. Below average	3	1	0	1	2	*	1	2	1	4	0	3	*	0	3	1	1
5. Poor	1	1	0	0	2	1	0	2	0	3	1	1	0	*	1	1	1

B. *Dwelling unit*

1. Completely satisfied	28	28	43	39	22	51	35	52	52	45	29	29	42	28	29	40	39
2.	29	36	29	35	34	32	29	23	26	20	28	32	31	35	33	30	29
3.	23	21	19	16	20	10	22	14	14	19	20	17	16	18	22	17	17
4.	9	9	5	11	13	4	9	5	5	11	12	13	7	10	9	8	8
5.	5	4	1	1	7	1	3	2	1	3	6	8	2	3	3	3	4
6.	3	2	1	0	3	0	1	1	1	1	3	1	1	4	4	1	1
7. Completely dissatisfied	3	1	1	0	1	1	1	2	1	*	2	2	1	1	1	1	1

C. *Family life*

1. Agree strongly	44	47	53	51	54	61	54	54	60	60	53	60	61	60	49	56	57
2. Agree somewhat	37	39	35	37	29	29	29	36	29	33	34	29	30	27	33	32	31
3. Disagree somewhat	17	12	10	11	15	8	15	8	10	7	9	10	9	12	15	10	11
4. Disagree strongly	3	3	1	1	3	1	2	3	1	1	3	2	1	1	3	2	2

D. *Health*

1. Completely satisfied	47	46	54	43	44	56	49	55	54	55	49	48	51	52	49	50	45
2.	30	29	27	32	28	21	22	28	25	20	29	28	26	31	30	27	28
3.	11	10	10	11	15	11	13	11	12	11	9	11	8	10	9	11	12
4.	7	6	4	9	5	6	9	3	6	12	9	7	9	1	6	7	10
5.	2	4	1	2	3	3	4	2	3	1	3	4	3	5	3	3	3
6.	3	3	2	1	2	1	1	1	0	1	1	1	0	0	1	1	1
7. Completely dissatisfied	1	2	1	3	3	1	1	1	1	0	1	1	3	*	2	1	2

E. *Housework*

1. Agree strongly	22	23	30	25	34	33	28	32	31	33	37	34	29	25	24	31	31
2. Agree somewhat	38	45	36	41	40	34	42	25	41	44	36	45	41	42	44	39	40
3. Disagree somewhat	23	19	23	21	16	18	20	25	16	13	17	13	21	22	22	19	20
4. Disagree strongly	17	14	11	13	10	15	11	18	13	10	11	8	9	11	9	12	10

(Table C–4. continued overleaf . . .)

Table C-4. continued

Domain[a]	Nonfederally Assisted New Communities													Federally Assisted New Communities			
	Columbia	Reston	Irvine	Valencia	Park Forest	Westlake Village	Elk Grove Village	Foster City	Laguna Niguel	Lake Havasu City	Sharpstown	Forest Park	North Palm Beach	Jonathan	Park Forest South	Thirteen Nonfederally Assisted New Communities	Thirteen Conventional Communities
F. Job																	
1. Completely satisfied	33	31	45	24	44	59	41	61	47	47	34	40	46	41	36	43	41
2.	27	31	28	36	23	22	23	19	21	20	35	26	26	31	30	26	24
3.	18	13	13	21	16	12	16	11	11	17	17	20	14	15	15	16	17
4.	8	9	5	10	10	1	9	4	10	12	7	8	7	5	7	7	7
5.	8	7	4	3	7	1	5	3	2	1	2	3	3	3	4	3	4
6.	3	4	4	2	0	4	5	1	8	0	1	2	1	1	3	3	3
7. Completely dissatisfied	4	4	1	4	0	1	2	1	2	3	3	2	3	5	5	2	3
(Number of responses)[b]	(157)	(130)	(127)	(133)	(127)	(102)	(143)	(139)	(110)	(109)	(135)	(133)	(105)	(150)	(142)	(1636)	(798)
G. Leisure time																	
1. Completely satisfied	21	22	24	24	29	38	25	42	35	41	27	29	36	17	24	31	29
2.	18	23	27	22	23	20	16	17	24	22	17	19	22	21	17	20	18
3.	28	21	21	16	20	16	23	18	22	16	26	22	18	31	27	20	18
4.	14	17	13	19	14	15	18	14	9	12	15	16	15	15	15	15	18
5.	9	9	12	11	7	5	7	5	8	5	9	9	4	7	9	8	9
6.	7	2	3	3	4	3	5	1	2	2	3	4	3	2	4	3	4
7. Completely dissatisfied	5	7	1	5	3	3	6	3	1	1	3	2	3	7	4	3	3

H. *Marriage*

1. Completely satisfied	54	55	64	66	67	64	61	66	74	64	63	65	67	61	64	66
2.	30	28	24	22	19	23	23	21	16	18	23	21	23	26	22	23
3.	6	8	5	5	7	8	9	9	3	9	8	7	4	5	8	5
4.	7	5	3	2	3	3	3	2	5	4	0	2	2	5	3	3
5.	1	4	3	1	1	1	1	1	1	2	2	1	1	1	3	1
6.	1	0	1	1	2	1	1	1	1	2	1	1	1	0	1	1
7. Completely dissatisfied	1	*	1	2	3	1	3	1	2	2	2	2	2	2	2	2

(Number of respondents rating marriage)c (150)(151)(153)(178)(165)(167)(168)(151)(168)(151)(175)(149)(185)(162)(139)(171)(2140)(1080)

I. *Microneighborhood*

Scale score:

3. Highest rating	30	34	36	35	21	57	31	31	42	28	21	28	37	29	21	34	30
4–5.	25	33	31	38	30	25	33	34	35	30	33	29	29	35	36	32	34
6–7.	34	23	26	20	35	12	24	25	15	25	25	27	21	18	30	23	25
8–15. Lowest ratings	11	11	7	7	15	6	12	10	8	17	20	15	13	18	13	11	11

J. *Standard of living*

1. Completely satisfied	29	32	32	35	20	43	36	47	46	42	33	29	46	29	27	38	36
2.	35	33	30	33	31	27	27	25	30	23	28	30	29	26	28	29	27
3.	16	18	24	17	22	21	20	18	13	16	24	24	23	23	21	19	19
4.	11	9	8	9	15	7	11	7	5	15	9	11	9	12	9	11	11
5.	7	6	6	5	7	2	3	1	4	2	5	3	6	8	3	4	4
6.	2	2	1	1	3	1	1	1	0	1	2	2	2	2	1	1	1
7. Completely dissatisfied	*	1	1	0	2	0	2	1	1	1	1	1	5	1	1	1	1

*Less than 0.5 percent.

aQuestionnaire items for each of the life domains are detailed in the notes of Table 5–2. Except as noted below, the number of responses for each of the items was at or near the number of interviews listed in the basic sample column of Table A–2.

bOnly respondents who were self-employed or were working full or part-time were asked this item.

cNonmarried respondents were not asked to respond to this item.

Table C–5.   Facilities Wanted within One-Half Mile of Home in New Communities *(percentage selecting facility as one of three most wanted)*[a]

Facility[b]	Nonfederally Assisted New Communities												Federally Assisted New Communities			Thirteen Nonfederally Assisted New Communities	Thirteen Conventional Communities
	Columbia	Reston	Irvine	Valencia	Park Forest	Westlake Village	Elk Grove Village	Foster City	Laguna Niguel	Lake Havasu City	Sharpstown	Forest Park	North Palm Beach	Jonathan	Park Forest South		
1. Library	26	31	35	25	28	39	27	18	49	14	30	31	32	30	18	31	25
2. Supermarket	30	25	31	31	34	22	35	20	28	25	41	22	40	19	44	30	31
3. Quiet place to walk and sit outdoors	31	38	20	32	30	34	24	16	29	20	28	22	25	36	20	27	27
4. Outdoor swimming pool	29	29	22	21	12	22	20	35	30	20	21	27	18	20	21	24	26
5. Playground with swings and slides	21	16	14	18	31	11	22	21	24	22	16	27	14	22	29	19	23
6. Post office substation	14	6	20	10	14	29	10	9	16	18	14	16	25	11	19	16	13
7. Teenage recreation center	7	18	17	14	21	9	14	17	13	19	12	21	13	7	12	15	17
8. Indoor movie theater	28	17	16	6	5	32	13	26	5	3	11	16	6	16	16	14	12
9. Drug store	9	10	34	12	20	11	23	6	9	17	14	10	23	8	22	14	15

10. Convenience grocery store	21	17	13	15	25	8	15	13	7	18	12	17	17	17	9	14	11
11. Tennis courts	10	13	15	17	7	19	6	28	11	9	15	8	7	13	10	13	14
12. Picnic area	7	6	8	9	10	13	7	8	14	11	16	16	9	10	13	11	13
13. Gasoline service station	8	10	20	10	11	7	15	8	9	8	13	8	17	13	4	11	11
14. Bus stop	6	13	4	4	8	12	15	13	10	11	8	8	15	19	4	10	13
15. Private medical clinic	4	10	7	9	11	4	15	4	8	8	12	7	17	8	16	9	12
16. Bowling alley	14	8	7	5	8	6	7	14	9	4	7	7	3	14	6	7	7
17. Public health clinic	10	7	2	6	6	1	8	5	4	7	6	7	5	5	13	6	5
18. Roller skating rink	6	4	1	9	6	1	7	4	3	8	3	9	2	6	4	5	5
19. Nursery school	5	4	3	5	5	3	5	5	3	1	5	12	1	4	7	4	4
20. Laundromat	4	5	5	1	4	5	4	2	2	5	6	3	4	5	2	4	3
21. Bar or tavern	4	6	4	1	1	1	4	5	3	1	3	2	1	8	2	3	2
22. Day care center	4	3	2	3	2	3	3	4	1	1	2	3	1	7	5	2	3
23. Billiard parlor	2	1	2	2	1	1	1	2	2	2	3	2	1	2	2	2	2

a The question was "We have asked you a number of questions about the facilities and services you've used in the last year or so. Now here is a list of some of these same facilities as well as some new ones we've added. (HAND CARD I) Whether or not you have them now, if you had your choice, which *three* of these facilities would you most prefer to have in your neighborhood, that is, within one-half mile of your home?"

b Listed in order of frequency of mention in the thirteen nonfederally assisted new community sample.

✳ *Appendix D*

Household Survey
Interview Schedule

I. D. NUMBER

⓪⓪⓪⓪⓪⓪⓪
①①①①①①①
②②②②②②②
③③③③③③③
④④④④④④④
⑤⑤⑤⑤⑤⑤⑤
⑥⑥⑥⑥⑥⑥⑥
⑦⑦⑦⑦⑦⑦⑦
⑧⑧⑧⑧⑧⑧⑧
⑨⑨⑨⑨⑨⑨⑨

A NATIONAL STUDY OF ENVIRONMENTAL PREFERENCES AND THE QUALITY OF LIFE
JANUARY – APRIL 1973

OFFICE USE ONLY

Supporting Agency:	National Science Foundation Research Applied to National Needs Division of Social Systems and Human Resources Research Grant Number GI-34285		
Research Organization	Center for Urban and Regional Studies, University of North Carolina at Chapel Hill	Field Work Subcontractor	Research Triangle Institute Research Triangle Park, North Carolina

A.   Sample Cluster Number: _____ - _____   B.   Sample Line Number: _____

C.   Street Address: _____

D.   City or Town: _____

E.   Respondent Designated on Cluster Listing Sheet: ○ Head   ○ Spouse

F.   Hello, I'm _____ representing the Research Triangle Institute, a not-for-profit national research organization and the University of North Carolina. We are conducting a survey about the attitudes, preferences, living conditions, and activities of people in a number of communities across the United States. Since your household falls into our sample in this community, I would like to ask you a few questions. All the answers you give will be strictly confidential and will be used only in statistical tables where your name can in no way be connected with your answers. Of course, no one is required to participate, but I hope very much that you will, and I think you'll find it interesting.

G.   Before we start, however, I need to know if you and your family have moved to this address since the first of the year (1973) or if you've been living here longer than that.
        ○ SINCE FIRST OF YEAR - - THANK RESPONDENT AND TERMINATE INTERVIEW
        ○ "LONGER THAN THAT" - - CONTINUE WITH HOUSEHOLD LISTING

H.   Time is now: _____

I.   Good. Now first, I need some information about the people who live here with you. I don't need the names, just the relationships of the people who live here. Let's start with the adults. What is the age of the head of household? (PAUSE. OBTAIN ALL INFORMATION ABOUT HEAD OF HOUSEHOLD AND CONTINUE WITH OTHER HOUSEHOLD MEMBERS.) Have we missed anyone -- a roomer, someone who lives here but who is away right now?

IF HEAD AND SPOUSE ARE LIVING IN A HOUSEHOLD, INTERVIEW PERSON INDICATED ON CLUSTER LISTING SHEET (AND TRANSFERRED TO ITEM E ABOVE). IF HEAD IS NOT NOW MARRIED, OR SPOUSE IS NOT LIVING IN HOUSEHOLD, INTERVIEW HEAD.

ADULTS

All Persons:
* 21 or Older
   or
* Married, any Age
   or
* Under 21 and Living Away From Parents

List All Adults By Relation to the Head	Sex	Age	Marital Status	Indicate R "X"
1. Head of Household				
2.				
3.				
4.				

NCS Trans-Optic S388C-321

List All Children By Relation to the Head	Sex	Age	In School? * (Circle)	Indicate Child Selected With "X"
1.			Y N	
2.			Y N	
3.			Y N	
4.			Y N	
5.			Y N	

* "IN SCHOOL" DOES NOT INCLUDE NURSERY SCHOOL OR COLLEGE. INDICATE CHILD SELECTED FOR SCHOOL QUESTIONS (Q 29–38) AFTER REFERRING TO RANDOM SELECTION TABLE BELOW.

```
RANDOM SELECTION TABLE IF MORE THAN ONE CHILD IN SCHOOL
                    (FOR QUESTIONS 29-38)
Number of Children In School          Child Selected In Sample

           2                          _____

           3                          _____

           4                          _____

           5                          _____

           6                          _____
```

1. There's quite a bit of talk these days about the overall "quality" of people's lives. What does the phrase "quality of life" mean to you -- that is, what would you say are the main things the overall "quality" of your own life depends on?

_____

_____

1a. Anything else? _____

_____

2. Compared to the last community you lived in, would you say that for you yourself, moving to this community has improved the quality of your life, has made it worse, or hasn't made much difference?

① Improved   ⑤ Worse   ③ Not much difference - Go to Q. 3

2a. How is that?

3. And what year was it you moved to this address?

YEAR: _____

4. Was your previous residence here in this community, or in another part of this metropolitan area, or outside this metropolitan area?

① Outside Metro area   ⑤ Same community
        ③ Same Metro area

> **4c. What year was it you moved to this community?**
>
> Year: _____   ⓪①②③④⑤⑥⑦⑧⑨   (Go to
>   ⓪①②③④⑤⑥⑦⑧⑨   Q. 5)

4a. What city, county, and state was that?

City: _____   County: _____

State: _____

4b. Did you live within the city limits, outside the city in a built up area, outside the city in the open country, or on a farm?

                  ① In city   ② Out – built up   ③ Out – open   ④ Farm

5. Just before you moved to this (house/apartment), did you live in a single family house on its own lot, a townhouse or row house, an apartment, or what?

① Single family   ② Townhouse/Row house   ③ Apartment   ④ Other (specify): _____   ⑤   ⑥

6. How many rooms were there in that (house/apartment), not counting bathrooms?

① One   ③ Three   ⑤ Five   ⑦ Seven
② Two   ④ Four   ⑥ Six   ⑧ Eight or more

7. Did you own that place, rent it, or what?

① Own   ② Rent   ③ Other (specify): _____

8. Would you please tell me which of the reasons listed on this card (HAND CARD A) were important in your decision to move out of your previous place? (MARK ALL THAT APPLY)

Yes   No   Yes   No
①   ⑤ Job change or transfer   ①   ⑤ Recent retirement
①   ⑤ Forced moved because of fire, eviction, condemnation, etc.   ①   None of these
①   ⑤ Recent marriage, divorce, separation, or widowhood

9. What (other) factors were important in your decision to move out of your previous place?

_____

_____

9a. Anything else? _____

_____

10. Here is a list of things that people often consider when they move. (HAND CARD B) Thinking of what attracted you to this place, could you tell me which **three** of these factors were <u>most</u> important in your (family's) decision to move to this community (originally)?

11. Now, I'd like you to compare this community to the one you lived in just before you moved here. For each item on CARD B, please tell me if where you're living now is better, not as good, or about the same as where you lived before.

Yes	No		Better	Same	Not As Good
①	⑤ a.	Layout and space of the dwelling and lot	a. ①	③	⑤
①	⑤ b.	Construction of the place	b. ①	③	⑤
①	⑤ c.	Cost of buying (and financing) or renting the dwelling	c. ①	③	⑤
①	⑤ d.	Nearness to outdoors and the natural environment	d. ①	③	⑤
①	⑤ e.	Appearance of the immediate neighborhood	e. ①	③	⑤
①	⑤ f.	Public Schools.	f. ①	③	⑤
①	⑤ g.	Health and medical services.	g. ①	③	⑤
①	⑤ h.	Shopping facilities	h. ①	③	⑤
①	⑤ i.	Recreational facilities	i. ①	③	⑤
①	⑤ j.	Opportunity for participation in community life	j. ①	③	⑤
①	⑤ k.	Good place to raise children	k. ①	③	⑤
①	⑤ l.	Cost of living in the community	l. ①	③	⑤
①	⑤ m.	Safety from crime	m. ①	③	⑤
①	⑤ n.	Finding a job here in this community.	n. ①	③	⑤
①	⑤ o.	Convenience to work; ease of commuting	o. ①	③	⑤
①	⑤ p.	Ease of getting around the community	p. ①	③	⑤
①	⑤ q.	Climate	q. ①	③	⑤
①	⑤ r.	Type of people living in the neighborhood	r. ①	③	⑤
①	⑤ s.	Overall planning that went into the community	s. ①	③	⑤
①	⑤ t.	Other (specify):	t. ①	③	⑤

---

12. | Response to Question 11r, "Type of people -- neighborhood": (MARK AS 11r ANSWERED)
① Better -- Continue with Q. 13   ③ Same -- Go to Q. 14   ⑤ Not as good -- Continue with Q. 13

13. When you said that the "type of people living in the neighborhood" was (better/not as good) what, specifically, did you have in mind? (MARK ALL THAT APPLY)

13a. If better:

Yes	No	
①	⑤	Friendly here
①	⑤	Same race as respondent here
①	⑤	Same age, family life cycle here
①	⑤	Same (better) class, income, education, SES level here
①	⑤	Other (specify): _____

13b. If not as good:

Yes	No	
①	⑤	Not as friendly here
①	⑤	Not same race here
①	⑤	Not same age, family life cycle here
①	⑤	Not same (as good) class, income, education, SES level here
①	⑤	Other (specify): _____

---

14. | Response to Question 11s, "Overall planning -- into community": (MARK AS 11s ANSWERED)
① Better -- Continue with Q. 15   ③ Same -- Go to Q. 16   ⑤ Not as good -- Continue with Q. 15

15. (And) when you said that the "overall planning that went into the community" was (better/not as good) what, specifically, did you have in mind?

_____

_____

16. At the time you were deciding to move to this community, did you seriously consider moving to another community instead?

① Yes   ⑤ No – Go to Q. 19

> **16a.** Where was that?
> NAME OF COMMUNITY: _____
>
> **16b.** What was the single most important reason you did not move there?
>
> _____

17.
> Respondent lives in: (MARK ONE)
> ○ Control community; did not mention planned community in Q. 16a – Continue with Q. 18.
>
> ○ Control community; mentions planned community in Q. 16a – Go to Q. 19.
> ○ Planned community – Go to Q. 19.

18. Did you consider moving to (NAME OF PLANNED COMMUNITY)?

① Yes   ⑤ No – Go to Q. 19

> **18a.** What was the single most important reason you did not move there?
>
> _____

19. I'd like to ask you how you feel now about this area as a place to live -- I mean the area outlined on the map (SHOW MAP). From your own personal point of view, would you rate this area as an excellent place to live, good, average, below average, or poor?

① Excellent   ② Good   ③ Average   ④ Below average   ⑤ Poor

> **19a.** Why do you say that? _____
>
> _____

20.
> If respondent makes any voluntary comments about the appropriateness of the mapped area, please note them.
> ① Mapped area too small   ② Mapped area too large   ③ Mapped area wrong shape   ④ Don't understand it
>
> ⑦ Other (specify): _____

21.
> Household includes: (MARK ONE)
> ⑤ No child under 21 -- Go to Q. 39   ③ No children age 12-20 -- Go to Q. 23
> ① Child(ren) age 12-20 – Continue with Q. 22

22. From the teenagers' point of view, how would you expect them to rate this community as a place to live -- would they say it was excellent, good, average, below average, or poor?

① Excellent   ② Good   ③ Average   ④ Below average   ⑤ Poor

23.
> Household includes: (MARK ONE)
> ⑤ No children under 12 -- Go to Q. 28   ① Child(ren) under 12 – Continue with Q. 24

24. As a place to raise children under 12, how would you rate this area -- would you say it was excellent, good, average, below average, or poor?

① Excellent   ② Good   ③ Average   ④ Below average   ⑤ Poor

25. How do you feel about the places right near your home for children under 12 to play out of doors -- would you say they are excellent, good, average, below average, or poor?

① Excellent   ② Good   ③ Average   ④ Below average   ⑤ Poor

     25a. Why do you say that? _____

_____

_____

26. Is there a park or playground near here where young children can play?

   ① Yes   ⑤ No -- Go to Q. 27

     26a. Where is that?

            NAME OF PARK OR PLAYGROUND: _____

            NEAREST INTERSECTION: _____

                                        (Street)   (Cross Street)

     26b. About how many minutes would it take a child to walk there from your front door? _____ MINUTES

     26c. And when the weather is good, do(es) your child(ren) -- those under 12 -- play there every day, several times a week, once a week, once or twice a month, or less often?

         ⑤ Every day   ④ Several times a week   ③ Once a week   ② Once or twice a month   ① Less often

27. When your child(ren) -- those under 12 -- play(s) outdoors where do(es) (they/he/she) usually play? (HAND CARD C)

   ① Your yard/apartment or townhouse grounds   ② Neighbor's yard   ③ Park or playground   ④ Street/parking areas

   ⑤ Vacant lots   ⑥ Woods or open space away from your yard/apartment grounds

   ⑦ Somewhere else (specify): _____

28. ENTER PROPER INFORMATION FROM HOUSEHOLD LISTING ON PAGE 2 FOR SELECTED CHILD. ASK Q. 29 - 38 ABOUT SELECTED CHILD AND SCHOOL THAT CHILD ATTENDS.

Relationship to Family Head	Sex	Age

   ⓪ No eligible child -- Go to Q. 39

29. We would also like to know your feelings about different aspects of the schools around here. First, would you tell me the name of the school your (AGE OF CHILD) year old (son/daughter) attends?

NAME OF SCHOOL: _____

30. What town is (NAME OF SCHOOL) in? _____

31. How does your child usually get to that school?

   ① Walk   ② Bicycle   ③ Car   ④ School bus   ⑤ Other

32. And about how many minutes does it take (him/her) to get there? _____ MINUTES

33. Here is a list of problems that sometimes come up in schools. (HAND CARD D) For each of the items on the list would you tell me if, in your opinion, it is a serious problem at (NAME OF SCHOOL), somewhat of a problem, or not a problem?

    a) Students disrupting school or causing trouble.
      ① Serious   ③ Somewhat   ⑤ Not a problem

    b) Racial conflict or hostility.
      ① Serious   ③ Somewhat   ⑤ Not a problem

    c) Students using drugs during or after school hours.
      ① Serious   ③ Somewhat   ⑤ Not a problem

    d) Students drinking during or after school hours.
      ① Serious   ③ Somewhat   ⑤ Not a problem

34. Do you think (NAME OF SCHOOL) spends too much time on new kinds of teaching methods and courses, not enough time on that sort of thing, or is it about right?

    ① Too much   ③ About right   ⑤ Not enough

35. Would you say that most of the teachers your child has at that school are excellent, good, average, below average, or poor?

    ① Excellent   ② Good   ③ Average   ④ Below average   ⑤ Poor

36. And how would you rate how well your child is doing in school -- is (he/she) doing well above average, above average, average, below average, or well below average?

    ① Well above   ② Above   ③ Average   ④ Below   ⑤ Well below

37. In general, how do you think your child feels about going to school -- do you think (he/she) dislikes it very much, dislikes it somewhat, likes it somewhat, likes it very much, or doesn't care about it one way or the other?

    ④ Dislikes very much   ③ Dislikes somewhat   ② Likes somewhat   ① Likes very much   ⑤ Doesn't care

38. All things considered, how would you rate (NAME OF SCHOOL) -- do you think it's excellent, good, average, below average, or poor?

    ① Excellent   ② Good   ③ Average   ④ Below average   ⑤ Poor

39. I have one (more) question about schools. In the last year, have you yourself gone to a local public school - - - - - - - -

    Yes No
    ① ⑤ To attend a school function (play, open house, athletic event)?
    ① ⑤ To attend a meeting of the parent-teachers association?
    ① ⑤ To attend a meeting of some other club or organization?
    ① ⑤ To make use of any of the school's indoor or outdoor recreation facilities?

40. Now we have some questions about your health and health care. Of course, most people get sick now and then, but overall, how satisfied are you with your own health? (HAND CARD E) Here is a card I'd like you to use to answer this question. If you are completely satisfied with your health, you would say "one." If you are completely dissatisfied, you would say "seven." If you are neither completely satisfied nor completely dissatisfied, you would put yourself somewhere from two to six; for example, four means that you are just as satisfied as you are dissatisfied.

    Completely Satisfied ① ② ③ ④ ⑤ ⑥ ⑦ Completely Dissatisfied

41. Have you had a routine check-up in the past year, that is, since (MONTH) 1972?
   ① Yes   ⑤ No

42. Do you have routine check-ups as often as you feel you should?
   ① Yes   ⑤ No

43. Do you have a regular doctor or clinic you go to?
   ① Doctor   ③ Clinic   ⑤ No -- Go to Q. 44

> 43a. Where is (his/her office/the clinic) located?
>
>   NAME OF DOCTOR/CLINIC: _____
>
>   NEAREST INTERSECTION: _____ _____ TOWN: _____
>   (Street)   (Cross Street)
>
> 43b. How long does it usually take to
>   get there from here? _____ MINUTES
>
> 43c. The last time you went to that (doctor/clinic), did you find anything annoying or inconvenient about - - -
>   Yes No
>   ①   ⑤ Arranging appointments?
>   ①   ⑤ Arranging transportation to get there?
>   ①   ⑤ The way you and other patients were treated?
>   ①   ⑤ The cost of the visit for treatment received?
>
> 43d. Overall, how satisfied are you with the quality of the medical care you usually receive from that (doctor/clinic)?
>   (HAND CARD E) Which number comes closest to how you feel?
>   Completely Satisfied ① ② ③ ④ ⑤ ⑥ ⑦ Completely Dissatisfied

44. Altogether, how many different times have you been to see doctors, other than dentists, in their offices or in clinics about
   your own health in the past 12 months -- that is, since (MONTH) 1972?
                          _____ TIMES

45. And during the last 12 months, did you ever really want to see or talk to a doctor but didn't for some reason?
   ① Yes   ⑤ No -- Go to Q. 46.

> 45a. The last time that happened, why didn't you?
>
>   _____
>
>   _____

46. Do you belong to a prepaid medical plan or have any other kind of medical or hospital insurance?

   ① Yes -- Prepaid plan only   ③ Yes -- Both   ⑤ No -- Go to Q. 47.
   ② Yes -- Insurance only   ④ Yes -- Not sure/don't know which

> 46a. What is the name of the (plan/insurance)?
>
>   NAME(S): _____
>
> 46b. (Does this/Do these) cover your doctor's bills in full, in part, or not at all?
>   ① In full   ③ In part   ⑤ Not at all
>
> 46c. (Does it/Do they) cover your hospital expenses in full, in part, or not at all?
>   ① In full   ③ In part   ⑤ Not at all

47. Here is a list of services available in many communities. [HAND CARD F] We'd like to know, first, if such services are available in this community or its vicinity, and second, if you would be willing to recommend those that are here as good places to go for help.

	SERVICE AVAILABLE			SERVICE NOT AVAILABLE	DON'T KNOW IF SERVICE AVAILABLE
	Would Recommend	Not Sure	Would Not Recommend		
a. Emergency medical care	①	②	③	⑤	⑧
b. Hospital care	①	②	③	⑤	⑧
c. Family planning	①	②	③	⑤	⑧
d. Prenatal care	①	②	③	⑤	⑧
e. Health care for children	①	②	③	⑤	⑧
f. Dental care	①	②	③	⑤	⑧
g. Convalescent or nursing home care	①	②	③	⑤	⑧
h. Public assistance or welfare services	①	②	③	⑤	⑧
i. Family and marital counseling	①	②	③	⑤	⑧
j. Help with a legal problem	①	②	③	⑤	⑧
k. Help with a drug problem	①	②	③	⑤	⑧
l. Help with an emotional problem	①	②	③	⑤	⑧
m. Help with a drinking problem	①	②	③	⑤	⑧

48. Overall, how good would you say health care facilities and services are for people who live in this community -- excellent, good, average, below average, or poor?

① Excellent   ② Good   ③ Average   ④ Below average   ⑤ Poor

49. We are also interested in where people in this area go shopping. First, what about day to day items, such as milk and bread that you need between trips to the supermarket. Where do you usually go for these -- or do you get all that sort of thing at the supermarket?

[Ask 49a–g for convenience store, then ask Q. 50a–g for supermarket, and then ask Q. 51a–g for shopping center used most often.]

○ Supermarket only – Go to Q. 50

	49. Where do you usually go for day to day items?	50. What supermarket do you usually go to?	51. What shopping center or mall do you use most often?
a. Name of store (shopping center)			
b. Location	Name: _____ Nearest Intersection: _____ Street / Cross Street Town: _____	Name: _____ Nearest Intersection: _____ Street / Cross Street Town: _____	Name: _____ Nearest Intersection: _____ Street / Cross Street Town: _____
c. How often do you usually go there?	① More than once a week ② Once a week ③ 2-3 times a month ④ Less often	① More than once a week ② Once a week ③ 2-3 times a month ④ Less often	① More than once a week ② Once a week ③ 2-3 times a month ④ Less often
d. How do you usually get there?	① Walk ② Bicycle ③ Car ④ Bus ⑤ Taxi ⑥ Other	① Walk ② Bicycle ③ Car ④ Bus ⑤ Taxi ⑥ Other	① Walk ② Bicycle ③ Car ④ Bus ⑤ Taxi ⑥ Other
e. And how many minutes does it take to get there?	⓪①②③④⑤⑥⑦⑧⑨ ⓪①②③④⑤⑥⑦⑧⑨ MINUTES:	⓪①②③④⑤⑥⑦⑧⑨ ⓪①②③④⑤⑥⑦⑧⑨ MINUTES:	⓪①②③④⑤⑥⑦⑧⑨ ⓪①②③④⑤⑥⑦⑧⑨ MINUTES:
f. Would you say you like, dislike like, or neither like nor dislike shopping at (NAME OF STORE OR SHOPPING CENTER)?	① Like shopping ③ Neither ⑤ Dislike shopping	① Like shopping ③ Neither ⑤ Dislike shopping	① Like shopping ③ Neither ⑤ Dislike shopping
g. (HAND CARD G) What are the main reasons you go there to shop? (UP TO 3 ITEMS MAY BE CHECKED IN EACH COLUMN)	ⓐ Convenient location ⓑ Variety of goods ⓒ Prices ⓓ Hours open ⓔ Friendly service ⓕ Place to sit and rest ⓖ Cleanliness ⓗ Parking space ⓘ Attractive store ⓙ Place to meet or shop with friends	ⓐ Convenient location ⓑ Variety of goods ⓒ Prices ⓓ Hours open ⓔ Friendly service ⓕ Place to sit and rest ⓖ Cleanliness ⓗ Parking space ⓘ Attractive store ⓙ Place to meet or shop with friends	ⓐ Convenient location ⓑ Variety of goods ⓒ Prices ⓓ Hours open ⓔ Friendly service ⓕ Place to sit and rest ⓖ Cleanliness ⓗ Parking space ⓘ Attractive store ⓙ Place to meet or shop with friends

52. Thinking over everything we've mentioned about shopping facilities, overall, how good would you say they are for people who live in this community -- excellent, good, average, below average, or poor?

① Excellent ② Good ③ Average ④ Below Average ⑤ Poor

53. We are also interested in what people do in their spare time. What is your favorite type of leisure or recreational activity to do outside the house? ⓪ No favorite activity -- Go to Q. 54

FAVORITE ACTIVITY: _____

53a. About how often did you (ACTIVITY) last year, not counting when you were on vacation? (ACCEPT RANGES)

_____ TIMES ⓪①②③④⑤⑥⑦⑧⑨
⓪①②③④⑤⑥⑦⑧⑨

53b. Where do you go most often?

NAME OF FACILITY: _____

NEAREST INTERSECTION: _____ TOWN: _____
STREET   CROSS STREET

53c. The last time you went (ACTIVITY) there, did you go and (ACTIVITY) by yourself or with someone else? (PAUSE) Who (ACTIVITY) with you? (MARK ALL THAT APPLY)

Yes	No		Yes	No		Yes	No	
ⓐ	ⓐ Self only		ⓒ	ⓒ Child(ren)		ⓔ	ⓔ Friend(s)	
ⓑ	ⓑ Spouse		ⓓ	ⓓ Other relative		ⓕ	ⓕ Other	

53d. Overall, how satisfied are you with that place as a place to (ACTIVITY)? Which number comes closest to how you feel?

CARD E   Completely Satisfied ① ② ③ ④ ⑤ ⑥ ⑦ Completely Dissatisfied

---

54. Here is a list of recreational activities. (HAND CARD H) I'd like to know which of these you have taken part in within the last year, not counting when you were on vacation. (COMPLETE Q. 54a FOR ALL FIVE ACTIVITIES, THEN COMPLETE b FOR EACH ACTIVITY, THEN COMPLETE c-f FOR EACH ACTIVITY THAT IS NOT R'S FAVORITE.)

	GOLF ① Yes ⑤ No	SWIMMING ① Yes ⑤ No
a. Participate?		
b. Interviewer: (CHECK ONE) If activity is - - - - - - - - - ▸	① Favorite, go to next activity ⑤ Not favorite, complete column	① Favorite, go to next activity ⑤ Not favorite, complete column
c. About how often did you (ACTIVITY) last year, not counting when you were on vacation?	TIMES: ⓪①②③④⑤⑥⑦⑧⑨ ⓪①②③④⑤⑥⑦⑧⑨	TIMES: ⓪①②③④⑤⑥⑦⑧⑨ ⓪①②③④⑤⑥⑦⑧⑨
d. Where did you go (most often)?	NAME OF PLACE: NEAREST INTERSECTION: STREET CROSS STREET TOWN: _____	NAME OF PLACE: NEAREST INTERSECTION: STREET CROSS STREET TOWN: _____
e. The last time you went (ACTIVITY) there did you go and (ACTIVITY) by yourself or with someone else? Who (ACTIVITY) with you? (MARK ALL THAT APPLY)	Yes No Yes No ①⑤ Self only ①⑤ Other relative ①⑤ Spouse ①⑤ Friend(s) ①⑤ Child(ren) ①⑤ Other	Yes No Yes No ①⑤ Self only ①⑤ Other relative ①⑤ Spouse ①⑤ Friend(s) ①⑤ Child(ren) ①⑤ Other
f. Overall, how satisfied are you with that place as a place to (ACTIVITY)? Which number comes closest to how you feel? HAND CARD E	Completely Satisfied ① ② ③ ④ ⑤ ⑥ ⑦ Completely Dissatisfied	Completely Satisfied ① ② ③ ④ ⑤ ⑥ ⑦ Completely Dissatisfied

54. (Continued)

TENNIS	BICYCLING	WALKING AND HIKING
① Yes ⑤ No	① Yes ⑤ No	① Yes ⑤ No
① Favorite, go to next activity ⑤ Not favorite, complete column	① Favorite, go to next activity ⑤ Not favorite, complete column	① Favorite, go to next activity ⑤ Not favorite, complete column
TIMES: ⓪①②③④⑤⑥⑦⑧⑨ ⓪①②③④⑤⑥⑦⑧⑨	TIMES: ⓪①②③④⑤⑥⑦⑧⑨ ⓪①②③④⑤⑥⑦⑧⑨	TIMES: ⓪①②③④⑤⑥⑦⑧⑨ ⓪①②③④⑤⑥⑦⑧⑨
NAME OF PLACE:	NAME OF PLACE:	NAME OF PLACE:
NEAREST INTERSECTION:		NEAREST INTERSECTION:
STREET CROSS STREET		STREET CROSS STREET
TOWN: _____	TOWN: _____	TOWN: _____
Yes No Yes No ①⑤ Self only ①⑤ Other relative ①⑤ Spouse ①⑤ Friend(s) ①⑤ Child(ren) ①⑤ Other	Yes No Yes No ①⑤ Self only ①⑤ Other relative ①⑤ Spouse ①⑤ Friend(s) ①⑤ Child(ren) ①⑤ Other	Yes No Yes No ①⑤ Self only ①⑤ Other relative ①⑤ Spouse ①⑤ Friend(s) ①⑤ Child(ren) ①⑤ Other
Completely Satisfied ① ② ③ ④ ⑤ ⑥ ⑦ Completely Dissatisfied	Completely Satisfied ① ② ③ ④ ⑤ ⑥ ⑦ Completely Dissatisfied	Completely Satisfied ① ② ③ ④ ⑤ ⑥ ⑦ Completely Dissatisfied

55. All things considered, how good would you say the recreational facilities in this community and its immediate vicinity are for the people who live here -- excellent, good, average, below average, or poor?

① Excellent   ② Good   ③ Average   ④ Below average   ⑤ Poor

56. We'd like to ask you about other types of leisure activities too. For example, how many different days in the last week did you spend an hour or more:

DO NOT MARK

a. watching television?	_____	DAYS	⓪	①	②	③	④	⑤	⑥	⑦
b. reading a book in your spare time?	_____	DAYS	⓪	①	②	③	④	⑤	⑥	⑦
c. working at a hobby?	_____	DAYS	⓪	①	②	③	④	⑤	⑥	⑦
d. playing cards with friends?	_____	DAYS	⓪	①	②	③	④	⑤	⑥	⑦
e. reading newspapers and/or magazines?	_____	DAYS	⓪	①	②	③	④	⑤	⑥	⑦
f. doing community volunteer work?	_____	DAYS	⓪	①	②	③	④	⑤	⑥	⑦

57. Overall, how satisfied are you with the ways you spend your spare time? (HAND CARD E) Which number comes closest to how you feel?

Completely Satisfied   ①   ②   ③   ④   ⑤   ⑥   ⑦   Completely Dissatisfied

58. We have asked you a number of questions about the facilities and services you've used in the last year or so. Now here is a list of some of these same facilities as well as some new ones we've added. (HAND CARD I) Whether or not you have them now, if you had your choice, which three of these facilities would you most prefer to have in your neighborhood, that is, within one-half mile of your home?

	Yes	No	
a.	①	⑤	Bar or tavern
b.	①	⑤	Billiard parlor
c.	①	⑤	Bowling alley
d.	①	⑤	Bus stop
e.	①	⑤	Convenience grocery store
f.	①	⑤	Day care center
g.	①	⑤	Drug store
h.	①	⑤	Gasoline service station
i.	①	⑤	Indoor movie theatre
j.	①	⑤	Laundromat
k.	①	⑤	Library
l.	①	⑤	Nursery school
m.	①	⑤	Outdoor swimming pool
n.	①	⑤	Picnic area
o.	①	⑤	Playground with swings and slides
p.	①	⑤	Post office substation
q.	①	⑤	Private medical clinic
r.	①	⑤	Public health clinic
s.	①	⑤	Quiet place to walk and sit outdoors
t.	①	⑤	Roller skating rink
u.	①	⑤	Supermarket
v.	①	⑤	Teenage recreation center
w.	①	⑤	Tennis courts

* *

This next section goes better if you fill it out yourself. (HAND R THE SELF—ADMINISTERED QUESTIONNAIRE.) Here are some statements that some people agree with and others disagree with. Please mark each one according to whether you agree or disagree and how strongly. (EXPLAIN BY USING FIRST ONE AS AN EXAMPLE IF NECESSARY. CONTINUE WITH Q. 59 WHEN SELF—ADMINISTERED QUESTIONNAIRE IS COMPLETED.)

* *

IDENTIFICATION
NUMBER

INTERVIEWER'S NAME _____

SAMPLE CLUSTER NO. _____ — _____ LINE NO. _____

A NATIONAL STUDY OF
ENVIRONMENTAL PREFERENCES
AND THE QUALITY OF LIFE
JANUARY – APRIL 1973

Supporting Agency:	National Science Foundation Research Applied to National Needs Division of Social Systems and Human Resources Research Grant Number GI-34285

Research Organization:	Center for Urban and Regional Studies, University of North Carolina at Chapel Hill	Field Work Subcontractor	Research Triangle Institute Research Triangle Park North Carolina

SELF-ADMINISTERED SECTION

Please indicate for each of the following sentences whether you agree or disagree with it and how much. Do this by placing a mark in the appropriate circle under the sentence.

1. All things considered, the people who live in this community are pretty much the same.
   ① Agree Strongly   ② Agree Somewhat   ③ Disagree Somewhat   ④ Disagree Strongly

2. I am much more interested in national affairs than I am in local affairs.
   ① Agree Strongly   ② Agree Somewhat   ③ Disagree Somewhat   ④ Disagree Strongly

3. I can live the way I please in this community without social pressures for me to act in particular ways.
   ① Agree Strongly   ② Agree Somewhat   ③ Disagree Somewhat   ④ Disagree Strongly

4. As often as not, I actually enjoy cooking, cleaning, and doing other chores around the house.
   ① Agree Strongly   ② Agree Somewhat   ③ Disagree Somewhat   ④ Disagree Strongly

5. I am able to see my close friends about as much as I want these days.
   ① Agree Strongly   ② Agree Somewhat   ③ Disagree Somewhat   ④ Disagree Strongly

6. I don't believe that public officials care about what people like me think.
   ① Agree Strongly   ② Agree Somewhat   ③ Disagree Somewhat   ④ Disagree Strongly

7. It is quite safe for women and children to be out alone at night in this community.
   ① Agree Strongly   ② Agree Somewhat   ③ Disagree Somewhat   ④ Disagree Strongly

8. It is harder to call on my neighbors in time of need in this community than where I used to live.
   ① Agree Strongly   ② Agree Somewhat   ③ Disagree Somewhat   ④ Disagree Strongly

9. It is worth considerable effort to assure one's self of a good name with important people.
   ① Agree Strongly   ② Agree Somewhat   ③ Disagree Somewhat   ④ Disagree Strongly

NCS Trans-Optic S388A-321

– CONTINUED –

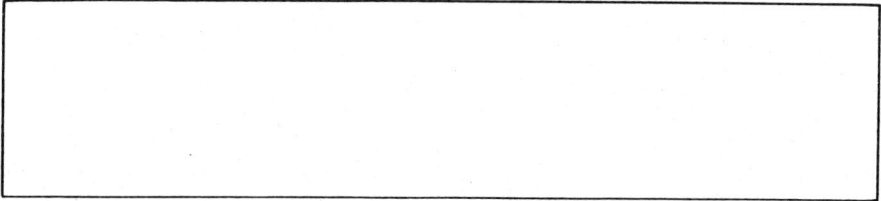

SELF-ADMINISTERED SECTION (Continued)

10. These days a person doesn't really know whom he can count on.
    ① Agree Strongly   ② Agree Somewhat   ③ Disagree Somewhat   ④ Disagree Strongly

11. Despite all the newspaper and television coverage, national and international happenings rarely seem as interesting as events that occur right in the local community in which one lives.
    ① Agree Strongly   ② Agree Somewhat   ③ Disagree Somewhat   ④ Disagree Strongly

12. Most local officials are primarily concerned with looking out for themselves.
    ① Agree Strongly   ② Agree Somewhat   ③ Disagree Somewhat   ④ Disagree Strongly

13. The major advantage of living in a highly planned community is that you don't have to worry that the character of your neighborhood will change for the worse.
    ① Agree Strongly   ② Agree Somewhat   ③ Disagree Somewhat   ④ Disagree Strongly

14. As far as I can tell, black families are treated just as well in this community as anyone else.
    ① Agree Strongly   ② Agree Somewhat   ③ Disagree Somewhat   ④ Disagree Strongly

15. Sometimes politics and government seem so complicated that a person like me can't really understand what's going on.
    ① Agree Strongly   ② Agree Somewhat   ③ Disagree Somewhat   ④ Disagree Strongly

16. People like me are always treated fairly by the police and other law enforcement officers in this community.
    ① Agree Strongly   ② Agree Somewhat   ③ Disagree Somewhat   ④ Disagree Strongly

17. All things considered, I am very satisfied with my family life — the time I spend and the things I do with members of my family.
    ① Agree Strongly   ② Agree Somewhat   ③ Disagree Somewhat   ④ Disagree Strongly

18. The social needs of the citizens are the responsibility of themselves and their families and not the community.
    ① Agree Strongly   ② Agree Somewhat   ③ Disagree Somewhat   ④ Disagree Strongly

19. There doesn't seem to be much connection between what people like me want and what town officials do.
    ① Agree Strongly   ② Agree Somewhat   ③ Disagree Somewhat   ④ Disagree Strongly

20. The raising of one's social position is one of the more important goals in life.
    ① Agree Strongly   ② Agree Somewhat   ③ Disagree Somewhat   ④ Disagree Strongly

21. In spite of what some people say, the lot of the average man is getting worse.
    ① Agree Strongly   ② Agree Somewhat   ③ Disagree Somewhat   ④ Disagree Strongly

22. There are a lot more interesting things to do around this town than there were in the last place I lived.
    ① Agree Strongly   ② Agree Somewhat   ③ Disagree Somewhat   ④ Disagree Strongly

23. I don't feel much a part of what goes on in this town.
    ① Agree Strongly   ②Agree Somewhat   ③ Disagree Somewhat   ④ Disagree Strongly

24. Religious groups in this community are too involved in social concerns and neglect spiritual matters.
    ① Agree Strongly   ② Agree Somewhat   ③ Disagree Somewhat   ④ Disagree Strongly

SELF-ADMINISTERED SECTION (Continued)

25. White people have a right to keep black people out of their neighborhoods.
① Agree Strongly   ② Agree Somewhat   ③ Disagree Somewhat   ④ Disagree Strongly

26. Hardly anything to do with local government in this town takes place behind closed doors; everything is pretty much above board.
① Agree Strongly   ② Agree Somewhat   ③ Disagree Somewhat   ④ Disagree Strongly

27. Being a member of a church or synagogue should be part of any well-rounded life.
① Agree Strongly   ② Agree Somewhat   ③ Disagree Somewhat   ④ Disagree Strongly

28. Police and other law enforcement officers in this community are not doing a very good job.
① Agree Strongly   ② Agree Somewhat   ③ Disagree Somewhat   ④ Disagree Strongly

29. It is very easy to make new friends in this community.
① Agree Strongly   ② Agree Somewhat   ③ Disagree Somewhat   ④ Disagree Strongly

30. If a man has an important job, he ought to be very careful about the kind of neighborhood he lives in.
① Agree Strongly   ② Agree Somewhat   ③ Disagree Somewhat   ④ Disagree Strongly

31. Most people around here would like to spend more time with their neighbors.
① Agree Strongly   ② Agree Somewhat   ③ Disagree Somewhat   ④ Disagree Strongly

32. All things considered, how satisfied are you with your marriage? Which number comes closest to how you feel?

Completely Satisfied ①   ②   ③   ④   ⑤   ⑥   ⑦ Completely Dissatisfied

(◯ Not Applicable)

33. There has recently been a great deal of talk about building homes for low and moderate income families in suburban areas. We would like to know what you think about putting homes for the following types of families here in this neighborhood, say within a half mile of your home. Please place a mark in the circle which indicates whether you think homes in this neighborhood for each type of family would greatly improve, improve, not effect, harm, or greatly harm your neighborhood.

Homes for:

	Greatly Improve	Improve	Not Effect	Harm	Greatly Harm
a. Retired white families with incomes under $5000 a year	①	②	③	④	⑤
b. White families with incomes under $5000 a year	①	②	③	④	⑤
c. White families with incomes of $5000-$10,000 a year	①	②	③	④	⑤
d. White families with incomes of $10,000-$15,000 a year	①	②	③	④	⑤
e. White families with incomes of $15,000 or more a year	①	②	③	④	⑤
f. Retired black families with incomes under $5000 a year	①	②	③	④	⑤
g. Black families with incomes under $5000 a year	①	②	③	④	⑤
h. Black families with incomes of $5000-$10,000 a year	①	②	③	④	⑤
i. Black families with incomes of $10,000-$15,000 a year	①	②	③	④	⑤
j. Black families with incomes of $15,000 or more a year	①	②	③	④	⑤

34. Below are some words and phrases which we would like you to use to describe this <u>neighborhood</u> as it seems to you. By neighborhood, we mean roughly the area near here which you can see from your front door – that is, the five or six homes nearest to yours around here. For example, if you think the neighborhood is noisy, please put a mark in the circle right next to the word "noisy." If you think it is quiet, please put a mark in the circle right next to the word "quiet." If you think it is somewhere in between, please put a mark where you think it belongs.

<u>YOUR NEIGHBORHOOD</u>

Noisy	O	O	O	O	O	Quiet
Attractive	O	O	O	O	O	Unattractive
Unfriendly people	O	O	O	O	O	Friendly people
Enough privacy	O	O	O	O	O	Not enough privacy
Poorly kept up	O	O	O	O	O	Well kept up
People who are like me	O	O	O	O	O	People who are not like me
Pleasant	O	O	O	O	O	Unpleasant
Convenient	O	O	O	O	O	Inconvenient
Very poor place to live	O	O	O	O	O	Very good place to live
Safe	O	O	O	O	O	Unsafe
Bad reputation	O	O	O	O	O	Good reputation
Crowded	O	O	O	O	O	Uncrowded

DO NOT MARK IN THIS BOX

⓪ ⓪ ⓪ ⓪ ⓪
① ① ① ① ①
② ② ② ② ②
③ ③ ③ ③ ③
④ ④ ④ ④ ④
⑤ ⑤ ⑤ ⑤ ⑤
⑥ ⑥ ⑥ ⑥ ⑥
⑦ ⑦ ⑦ ⑦ ⑦
⑧ ⑧ ⑧ ⑧ ⑧
⑨ ⑨ ⑨ ⑨ ⑨

59. **A number of people have indicated that one of the more important things about a neighborhood is how well kept up it is. As far as you're concerned, what would the __main reason__ be that a well kept up neighborhood is important? (CARD J)**

① Helps keep the property values up
② Indicates that the people there would probably be good neighbors
③ Makes the neighborhood look better and more attractive

④ Something else (specify): _____   ⑤   ⑥

60. Sometimes a source of concern for people living in residential areas is the type and the cost of housing going up in their vicinity. If a builder were able to buy up a tract of land within half a mile or so of your home, would you care what kind of housing he built there?

① Yes   ⑤ No -- Go to Q. 61

60a. Would you be opposed to any of the following types of housing being built there? (HAND CARD K; MARK ALL THAT APPLY)

Yes No   ◯ Opposed to none   Yes No
①   ⑤ Single family detached homes   ①   ⑤ Garden apartments
①   ⑤ Townhouses or rowhouses   ①   ⑤ High rise apartments

60b. How about the cost of such housing – would you object if new homes were sold for: (ASK EACH RANGE)

	Would Object	Would Not Object
1) Under $25,000?	1) ①	⑤
2) $25,000 up to $30,000?	2) ①	⑤
3) $30,000 up to $35,000?	3) ①	⑤
4) $35,000 up to $45,000?	4) ①	⑤
5) $45,000 or more?	5) ①	⑤

60c. What if the housing were rental apartments -- would you object if they rented for - - - - -
◯ (RESPONDENT VOLUNTEERS THAT HE/SHE OBJECTS TO ALL RENTAL HOUSING REGARDLESS OF COST: MARK HERE AND GO TO Q. 61.)

	Would Object	Would Not Object		Would Object	Would Not Object
1) Under $150/month?	①	⑤	3) $200-$250/month?	①	⑤
2) $150-$200/month?	①	⑤	4) Over $250/month?	①	⑤

---

61. If (NAME OF DEVELOPER IF STILL ACTIVE/a builder) were considering locating a facility or type of housing within half a mile or so of your home which in your opinion would seriously damage the residential character of this neighborhood, do you think that there is anything you could do to prevent it?

① Yes   ⑤ No   ⑧ Don't Know

61c. Why is that? _____

(Go to Q. 62)

61a. What could you do? _____

61b. What do you think your chances for success would be -- would you have a:
① very good chance of success,   ② a good chance,   ③ a limited chance, or
④ no chance at all for success?

62. When you moved to this place, were you aware of any plans for the development of the area around your neighborhood, say, within a half a mile or so of your home?

① Yes   ⑤ No -- Go to Q. 63

62a. Has the area been developed in accordance with these plans?   ① Yes   ⑤ No

63. Since you've been living here, do you think you have been adequately informed about plans for future developments, such as shopping centers, apartment houses and other facilities in the vicinity of your home?
    ① Yes   ⑤ No

64. What has been the most reliable source for the information that you have gotten? (HAND CARD L)
    ① Local newspaper   ② Friends/neighbors/family   ③ Radio/TV   ④ Developer

    ⑤ Community/homeowners' association   ⑥ Other (specify):_____

65. As far as you're concerned, do you think it's a good idea for neighborhoods -- and here I'm thinking of clusters of five or six homes -- to have people of different religious backgrounds or the same religious backgrounds, or doesn't it matter?
    ① Good if different   ⑤ Good if same   ③ Doesn't matter

66. And as far as you're concerned, do you think it's a good idea for neighborhoods to have people with quite different levels of education or roughly the same levels of education, or doesn't it matter?
    ① Good if different   ⑤ Good if same   ③ Doesn't matter

67. And do you think it's a good idea for neighborhoods to have people of different racial backgrounds or the same racial background, or doesn't it matter?
    ① Good if different   ⑤ Good if same   ③ Doesn't matter

68. | Race of Respondent: (MARK ONE)   ⑤ Respondent is black – Go to Q. 71   ① Respondent is not black -- continue with Q. 69

69. If a black family moved into this neighborhood, do you think that that would upset all, most, a few, or none of the families already living here?
    ④ All   ③ Most   ② A few   ① None

70. Which of the reasons on this card comes closest to how you would feel about it? (HAND CARD M) Would you: (READ CATEGORIES)
    ① a. wish they hadn't moved in and try to encourage them to leave;
    ② b. wish they hadn't moved in but try to be nice to them anyway;
    ③ c. not think about their race very much one way or the other and treat them like any other neighbor; or
    ④ d. go out of your way to make sure they were made to feel a part of the neighborhood?

71. Which of the following statements on this card (HAND CARD N) would best describe the relationships you have with your nearest neighbor? (READ CATEGORIES)
    ① a. Often visit one another in each other's homes, or
    ② b. Frequent casual chatting in the yard or if you happen to run into each other in the street, or
    ③ c. Occasional casual chatting in the yard or if you happen to run into each other in the street, or
    ④ d. Hardly know your neighbors?

72. Next, would you tell me how many of your five or six closest friends live here in this community -- all of them, most of them, one or two, or none of them?
    ④ All   ③ Most   ② One or two   ① None -- Go to Q. 74

73. How often do you get together with any of these friends -- every day, several times a week, once a week, 2-3 times a month, or once a month or less?
    ⑤ Every day   ④ Several times a week   ③ Once a week
    ② 2-3 times a month   ① Once a month or less

74. What about your relatives -- how many of the relatives you feel closest to live in this community -- all of them, most of them, one or two, or none of them?
    ④ All   ③ Most   ② One or two   ① None -- Go to Q. 76

75. And how often do you get together with any of these relatives -- every day, several times a week, once a week, 2-3 times a month, or once a month or less?
⑤ Every day   ④ Several times a week   ③ Once a week
② 2-3 times a month   ① Once a month or less

76. All things considered, would you like to see your relatives a lot more than you do now, somewhat more than now, about as often as you have been seeing them, or somewhat less often than now?
① A lot more than now   ② Somewhat more than now   ③ About as have been seeing them   ④ Less often than now

77. If a close relative or friend asked you if they should consider moving to this community, would you tell them that this would be a particularly good community to move to, that it's pretty much like other communities around here, or that they could probably do better somewhere else?
① It's particularly good here   ② It's like other communities   ③ Could probably do better

78. In your opinion, what are the most important issues or problems facing the community as a whole at the present time?

_____

_____

78a. Anything else? _____

_____

79. How often do you discuss local government or community policy matters with other people -- would you say several times a week, once a week, once or twice a month or less often than that?
① Several times a week   ② Once a week   ③ Once or twice a month   ④ Less often

80. There are a number of ways people become involved in local community matters. (HAND CARD O) Have you engaged in any of these activities in this community during the past year? Please tell me which ones. (PAUSE) Anything not on the list?
                    ○ None
Yes No
①   ⑤ Written to a local political leader or public official
①   ⑤ Written to a local newspaper about a community problem or issue
①   ⑤ Attended a meeting or gathering in which local government or community policy matters were a major subject or consideration
①   ⑤ Given money to help in a local political campaign or issue
①   ⑤ Been a candidate for and/or held local elective office
①   ⑤ Spoken to a local political leader or public official
①   ⑤ Contributed time in a local political campaign
①   ⑤ Contributed time in support of or opposition to a local issue
①   ⑤ Served in a local appointive office

①   ⑤ Other (specify): _____

81. People have different feelings about the responsiveness of local officials. Which of the following statements do you think best applies to (MOST LOCAL GOVERNMENTAL UNIT) officials in this area? Do you think:
① they do pretty much what the majority of the citizens want, or
② they do what a few of the more influential citizens want, or
③ they tend to do what they themselves think best?
④ (DON'T KNOW)

82. | DOES R LIVE IN NEW COMMUNITY OR RETIREMENT COMMUNITY STILL UNDER ACTIVE DEVELOP-MENT? (MARK ONE)

① Yes -- Continue with Q. 83   ⑤ No -- Go to Q. 84

83. How about officials of (NAME OF DEVELOPER)? Do you think:
   ① they do pretty much what the majority of the citizens want, or
   ② they do what a few of the more influential citizens want, or
   ③ they tend to do what they themselves think best?
   ④ (DON'T KNOW)

84. RESIDENCE OF R: (MARK ONE)
   ① Columbia, Md. – Go to Q. 86   ④ Sun City Center, Fla. – Go to Q. 86
   ② Jonathan, Minn. – Go to Q. 86   ⑤ Other Community – Continue with Q. 85
   ③ Reston, Va. – Go to Q. 86

85. Did you automatically become a member of a group such as a community, homeowners, property owners, townhouse, or condominium association when you moved here?
   ① Yes   ③ Not sure   ⑤ No – Go to Q. 98

   85a. What is the name of the association(s)?
   _____ (Go to Q. 87)

86. Now I have some questions about the (Columbia Park and Recreation Association/Jonathan Association/Reston Homeowners' Association/Sun City Center Civic Association).

87. Here is a list of services such associations often provide for their members. (HAND CARD P) Which of the services on this list do you believe your association provides? (PAUSE) Does your association do anything that is not on this list?

88. (ASK FOR EACH SERVICE R BELIEVES IS PROVIDED) Are you very satisfied, somewhat satisfied, somewhat dissatisfied, or very dissatisfied with the way your association handles (SERVICE)?

	87. PROVIDES?			88. SATISFACTION			
	NO	DON'T KNOW	YES	VERY SATIS.	SOME SATIS.	SOME DISSAT.	VERY DISSAT.
a. Architectural control	⑤	③	①→ a.	①	②	③	④
b. Maintenance of open space and common facilities	⑤	③	①→ b.	①	②	③	④
c. Provision of recreation facilities	⑤	③	①→ c.	①	②	③	④
d. Representation of residents' views to local government	⑤	③	①→ d.	①	②	③	④
e. Representation of residents' views to developer or builder	⑤	③	①→ e.	①	②	③	④
f. Social activities for members	⑤	③	①→ f.	①	②	③	④
g. Other (specify): _____			①→ g.	①	②	③	④

(IF R LIVES IN COLUMBIA, MD. SAY: "NOW I HAVE SOME QUESTIONS ABOUT YOUR VILLAGE ASSOCIATION.")

89. Do you attend all the meetings of { your village association / the Jonathan Association / the Reston Homeowners' Association / the Sun City Center Civic Association / your association }

most of them, a few of them, or none of them?
④ All   ③ Most   ② A few   ① None

90. Have you ever served on a committee or been an officer of that association?

① Yes   ⑤ No

91. Did you vote in the last election of officers for the association?

① Yes   ⑤ No

92. How satisfied are you with the amount of voice you have in your association – would you say you are very satisfied, somewhat satisfied, somewhat dissatisfied or very dissatisfied?

① Very satisfied
② Somewhat satisfied
③ Somewhat dissatisfied
④ Very dissatisfied

93. Which of the following statements do you think best applies to the officers of your association? Do you think:

① they do pretty much what the majority of the members want, or
② they do what a few of the more influential members want, or
③ they tend to do what they themselves think best?
④ (DON'T KNOW)

94. How do you feel about the dues and assessments of your association – do you think they are too high, too low, or just about right?

① Too high
③ Just about right
⑤ Too low

95. | DOES RESPONDENT LIVE IN NEW COMMUNITY OR RETIREMENT COMMUNITY STILL UNDER ACTIVE DEVELOPMENT? (MARK ONE)

① Yes – Continue with Q. 96
⑤ No – Go to Q. 97

96. What do you think of the role of (NAME OF DEVELOPER) in your association? Would you say that they generally have too much control over the affairs of the association, generally have too little control, or does it depend more on the issues involved?

① Too much
⑤ Too little
③ Depends

97. Based on your experience, how satisfied are you with the overall performance of your association? (HAND CARD E) Which number comes closest to how you feel?

Completely Satisfied   ①   ②   ③   ④   ⑤   ⑥   ⑦   Completely Dissatisfied

98. Here is a list of other types of clubs and organizations that many people belong to. (HAND CARD Q) Please look at each of the groups on the list and tell me which of these organizations you yourself belong to. (PAUSE) Are there any others that aren't on this list?
⓪ Belongs to no organizations – Go to Q. 102

99. Does the (TYPE OF ORGANIZATION) meet or hold its activities here in this community?

MARK AT LEFT EACH KIND OF ORGANIZATION R BELONGS TO, <u>THEN</u> ASK Q. 99 FOR EACH ORGANIZATION MENTIONED.

98. Mark if belongs		**99.** In community?
Yes No		Yes No
a. ① ⑤ Church or synagogue	a. ① ⑤
b. ① ⑤ Church-connected group (but not the church itself)	b. ① ⑤
c. ① ⑤ Charity or welfare organization	c. ① ⑤
d. ① ⑤ Civic or business group	d. ① ⑤
e. ① ⑤ College alumni (alumnae) association	e. ① ⑤
f. ① ⑤ Country club	f. ① ⑤
g. ① ⑤ Fraternal lodge or organization	g. ① ⑤
h. ① ⑤ Hobby club	h. ① ⑤
i. ① ⑤ Labor union	i. ① ⑤
j. ① ⑤ Nationality or ethnic club or organization	j. ① ⑤
k. ① ⑤ Parent-teachers association	k. ① ⑤
l. ① ⑤ Political club or organization	l. ① ⑤
m. ① ⑤ Professional group or association	m. ① ⑤
n. ① ⑤ Regular card playing group	n. ① ⑤
o. ① ⑤ Senior citizens organization	o. ① ⑤
p. ① ⑤ Sport team or athletic club	p. ① ⑤
q. ① ⑤ Youth group (Girl Scout leader, Little League manager, etc.)	q. ① ⑤
r. ① ⑤ Voluntary homeowners, neighborhood, or community association	r. ① ⑤
s. ① Other (specify): _____	s. ① ⑤
t. ① Other (specify): _____	t. ① ⑤

---

100. With which one of the organizations you belong to (including the AUTOMATIC HOMEOWNERS' ASSOCIATION) do you usually spend the most time?

TYPE OF ORGANIZATION: _____

101. How active is this organization in dealing with important issues, problems, or projects facing this community -- would you say very active, somewhat active, or not active at all?
① Very active   ③ Somewhat active   ⑤ Not active at all

102. How many cars or trucks do you have for family use?
① One   ② Two   ③ Three or more   ⓪ None -- Go to Q. 103

> **102a.** In the last twelve months, about how many miles has the car (have the cars) been driven? (ACCEPT APPROXIMATION)
>
> 1st CAR: _____ MILES   2nd CAR: _____ MILES   3rd CAR: _____ MILES
>
> ⓪①②③④⑤⑥⑦⑧⑨   ⓪①②③④⑤⑥⑦⑧⑨   ⓪①②③④⑤⑥⑦⑧⑨
> ⓪①②③④⑤⑥⑦⑧⑨   ⓪①②③④⑤⑥⑦⑧⑨   ⓪①②③④⑤⑥⑦⑧⑨

103. Is there a bus stop within a 10 minute walk of your home?
① Yes   ⑤ No -- Go to Q. 104   ⑨ Don't know -- Go to Q. 104

> **103a.** How often do you or someone in your family use the bus?
> ⑤ Daily or almost every day (5-7 days a week)   ② One day a month or less
> ④ 1-4 days a week   ① Never
> ③ 2-3 days a month

104. Here is a list of facilities and services. **(HAND CARD R)** Some we have talked about already, others we have not. For each, I want you to tell me whether you think about the right amount of money is now being spent on the facility or service in this community or whether there should be more money spent, or less money spent than there is now. (ASK Q. 104 FOR ALL ITEMS; <u>THEN</u> GO TO Q. 105)

105. FOR EACH ITEM FOR WHICH R SAID "MORE" IN Q. 104 ASK: Would you be willing to pay more in taxes or assessments to help pay for greater expenditures for (FACILITY OR SERVICE)? (MARK RESPONSE AT FAR RIGHT BELOW)

	104. SPEND				105. TAXES	
	DON'T KNOW	LESS	SAME	MORE	YES	NO
a. Schools	⑧	①	③	⑤→ a.	①	⑤
b. Fire protection	⑧	①	③	⑤→ b.	①	⑤
c. Police protection	⑧	①	③	⑤→ c.	①	⑤
d. Outdoor recreation facilities	⑧	①	③	⑤→ d.	①	⑤
e. Community upkeep and maintenance	⑧	①	③	⑤→ e.	①	⑤
f. Public Health facilities	⑧	①	③	⑤→ f.	①	⑤
g. Teen club or recreation center	⑧	①	③	⑤→ g.	①	⑤
h. Building housing for low-income families	⑧	①	③	⑤→ h.	①	⑤
i. Public transportation	⑧	①	③	⑤→ i.	①	⑤
j. Community advertising and promotion	⑧	①	③	⑤→ j.	①	⑤

106. All in all, would you say that your taxes and assessments are too high, too low, or about right to pay for the facilities and services that are needed in this community?
① Too high   ③ About right   ⑤ Too low

107. Which of the items on this card (HAND CARD S) best describes the employment status of the head of this household?
① Employed full time -- Go to Q. 108
┌② Employed part time   ┌⑤ Retired but still working for pay   ┌⑦ Student -- not employed
├③ Not employed   ├⑥ Disabled   └⑧ Student -- employed
└④ Retired

> 107a. Is (HEAD) presently looking for full or part-time work?
>   ① Yes, full   ③ Yes, part   ⑤ No -- Go to Q. 108
>
> 107b. Would you say there is a good chance or not that (HEAD) will be able to find a job right here
>   in this community or the immediate vicinity?
>   ① Good chance   ③ Don't know   ⑤ Not good chance

108. What (is/was) (HEAD'S) <u>main</u> job (when HEAD last worked)? (PROBE CAREFULLY FOR SPECIFIC JOB AND DUTIES)
⓪ Never worked -- Go to Q. 116

MAIN JOB: _____

108a. What kind of business or industry (is/was) that in? (MAIN JOB)

BUSINESS OR INDUSTRY: _____

109. Is (HEAD) now working? (MARK ONE)
                    ① Yes -- Ask Q. 110-115   ⑤ No -- Go to Q. 116

110. Where is (HEAD'S) job located? (IF UNKNOWN, PROBE FOR COMPANY NAME AND GENERAL LOCATION)

CITY OR TOWN: _____

111. Does (HEAD) usually make the entire trip to work by car or in a car pool, usually go part way by car and part way by public transportation, usually make the entire trip by public transportation or usually go some other way?
① Car/car pool   ② Part car, part public   ③ Public   ④ Walk

⑤ Other (specify):_____

112. How many minutes does it usually take (HEAD) to get to work? (ACCEPT APPROXIMATIONS)   _____ MINUTES

113. Does (HEAD) have a second job at this time or second source of income from work (HEAD) does, in addition to the one we've just been talking about?
① Yes   ⑤ No

114. On the average, about how many hours a week does (HEAD) work altogether?   _____ HOURS

115. All things considered, how satisfied is (HEAD) with (his/her) main job? (HAND CARD E) Which number comes closest to how satisfied or dissatisfied (HEAD) feels?
Completely Satisfied ①   ②   ③   ④   ⑤   ⑥   ⑦   Completely Dissatisfied

116. How many years of school did (HEAD) complete?
① 0–8 grades
② 9–11 grades, some high school
③ 9–11 grades, plus vocational training
④ 12 grades, high school graduate
⑤ 12 grades, plus vocational training
⑥ 13–15 years, some college
⑦ 16 years, college graduate
⑧ 17 or more, graduate or professional training

117. Head has: (MARK ONE)   ⑤ No spouse living at home – Go to Q. 123
① Spouse living at home – Continue with Q. 118

118. Which of the items on the card (HAND CARD S) best describes the employment status of (SPOUSE OF HEAD)?
① Employed full time -- Go to Q. 120
② Employed part time
③ Not employed
④ Retired
⑤ Retired but still working for pay
⑥ Disabled
⑦ Student -- not employed
⑧ Student -- employed

118a. Is (SPOUSE) presently looking for full or part-time work?
① Yes, full   ③ Yes, part   ⑤ No -- Go to Q. 119

118b. Would you say there is a good chance or not that (SPOUSE) will be able to find a job right here in this community or the immediate vicinity?
① Good chance   ③ Don't know   ⑤ Not good chance

119. Is (SPOUSE) now working? (MARK ONE)
① Yes -- Continue with Q. 120   ⑤ No -- Go to Q. 122

120. On the average, about how many hours a week does (SPOUSE) work altogether?   _____ HOURS

121. All things considered, how satisfied is (SPOUSE) with (SPOUSE'S) main job? (HAND CARD E) Which number comes closest to how satisfied or dissatisfied (SPOUSE) feels?
Completely Satisfied ①   ②   ③   ④   ⑤   ⑥   ⑦   Completely Dissatisfied

122. How many years of school did (SPOUSE) complete?
① 0–8 grades
② 9–11 grades, some high school
③ 9–11 grades, plus vocational training
④ 12 grades, high school graduate
⑤ 12 grades, plus vocational training
⑥ 13–15 years, some college
⑦ 16 years, college graduate
⑧ 17 or more, graduate or professional training

123. **Please tell me the letter of the group on this card (HAND CARD T) that would indicate about what the total income for you and your family was last year -- 1972 -- before taxes, that is.**

Ⓐ Under $5,000   Ⓓ $12,500 – $14,999   Ⓖ $20,000 – $24,999   Ⓙ $40,000 – $49,999

Ⓑ $5,000 – $9,999   Ⓔ $15,000 – $17,499   Ⓗ $25,000 – $29,999   Ⓚ $50,000 and over

Ⓒ $10,000 – $12,499   Ⓕ $17,500 – $19,999   Ⓘ $30,000 – $39,999

    123a. Does that include the income of everyone in the family who was living here in 1972?

       ① Yes   ⑤ No – Ask for "EVERYONE'S INCOME", make corrections above

124. The things people have -- housing, car, furniture, recreation and the like -- make up their standard of living. Some people are satisfied with their standard of living, others feel it is not as high as they would like. How satisfied are you with your standard of living? (HAND CARD E)

       Completely Satisfied   ①   ②   ③   ④   ⑤   ⑥   ⑦   Completely Dissatisfied

125. All things considered, how often do you find that you don't have enough money to do the things you would like because of what it costs just to live here -- fairly often, once in a while, or almost never?

     ① Often   ③ Once in a while   ⑤ Never

126. Do you own this (house/apartment), are you renting it or what?

     ① Owns or buying   ② Rents   ③ Other

> 126e. How is that? _____
>
> _____
>
>   **(Go to Q. 127)**

> 126c. (HAND CARD V) Could you tell me the letter of the group on this card that would indicate about how much the rent is on this (apartment/house) each month, not including utilities?
>
> Ⓐ Under $100   Ⓔ $250 – $299   Ⓘ $450 – $499
>
> Ⓑ $100 – $149   Ⓕ $300 – $349   Ⓙ $500 and over
>
> Ⓒ $150 – $199   Ⓖ $350 – $399
>
> Ⓓ $200 – $249   Ⓗ $400 – $449
>
> 126d. All things considered, how good a (landlord/resident manager) would you say you have -- good, neither good nor bad or not very good?
>
> ① Good   ③ Not good or bad   ⑤ Not good
>
> ◯ R says he/she has no real landlord
>
> **(Go to Q. 127)**

126a. (HAND CARD U) Could you tell me the letter of the group on this card that would indicate about what the present value of this house/apartment is? What would it bring if you sold it today?

Ⓐ Under $20,000   Ⓓ $30,000 - $34,999   Ⓖ $45,000 - $49,999   Ⓙ $70,000 - $79,999

Ⓑ $20,000 - $24,999   Ⓔ $35,000 - $39,999   Ⓗ $50,000 - $59,999   Ⓚ $80,000 and over

Ⓒ $25,000 - $29,999   Ⓕ $40,000 - $44,999   Ⓘ $60,000 - $69,999

126b. Compared to other homes you considered at the time you were buying, do you think that this home will be a better financial investment, a worse financial investment, or about the same?

     ① Better   ③ Same   ⑤ Worse

127. When was this (house/building) built? (ACCEPT GUESSES)

             YEAR BUILT _____

128. How many rooms do you have in this (house/apartment), not including bathrooms?

     ① One   ③ Three   ⑤ Five   ⑦ Seven

     ② Two   ④ Four   ⑥ Six   ⑧ Eight or more

129. Do you have more space indoors in this (house/apartment) than you and your family need, too little space or about the right amount?
① More than need ③ About right ⑤ Too little

130. How do you feel about the amount of outdoor space near your home which members of your family can use for their different activities – do you have more space than you need, too little space, or about the right amount?
① More than need ③ About right ⑤ Too little

131. Do you have a place where you can be outside and feel that you really have privacy from your neighbors if you want it?
① Yes ⑤ No

132. Now, overall how do you feel about the (house/apartment) as a place to live? (HAND CARD E) Which number comes closest to how satisfied or dissatisfied you feel?
Completely Satisfied ① ② ③ ④ ⑤ ⑥ ⑦ Completely Dissatisfied

133. How likely are you to move from this place in the next two or three years? Are you certain to move, will you probably move or do you plan to stay here?
① Certain to move ② Probably move ③ Don't know ④ Plan to stay – Go on to Q. 134

133a. Why are you thinking of moving?

134. Do you have a religious preference? That is, do you consider yourself Protestant, Roman Catholic, Jewish or something else?
① Protestant ② Roman Catholic ③ Jewish ④ Other (what) _____ ⑤ No preference

135. Is being a member of a church or synagogue an important part of your life?
① Yes ⑤ No

136. Can you find the kinds of church and religious activities you want in this community?
① Yes ③ Don't care about that ⑤ No

137. Generally speaking, do you usually think of yourself as a Democrat, a Republican, an Independent, or what?
① Democrat
  Republican
② Independent or other

137b. Do you think of yourself as closer to the Democratic Party, the Republican Party or not very close to either party?
③ Closer to Democrat
④ Closer to Republican
⑧ Not close to either
(Go to Q. 138)

137a. Would you call yourself a strong (Democrat/Republican) or not?
① Strong Democrat
② Not strong Democrat
⑤ Not strong Republican
⑥ Strong Republican

138. We have talked about various parts of your life; now I want to ask you about your life as a whole. How satisfied are you with your life as a whole these days? (HAND CARD E) Which number on the card comes closest to how you feel?
Completely Satisfied ① ② ③ ④ ⑤ ⑥ ⑦ Completely Dissatisfied

139. Finally, what do you think this community will be like in five years? Will it be a better place to live than it is now, not as good, or about the same?

① Better   ③ Same   ⑤ Not as good

139a. Why do you say that? _____

_____

139b. What do you think could be done to make it better?

_____

_____

140. In case we have to get in touch with you to clarify any of these answers which sometimes happens in research of this kind, could I please have your telephone number? Thank you.

TELEPHONE NUMBER: _____ ○ NO PHONE   ○ REFUSED

(ASK Q. 141 ONLY OF RESPONDENTS LIVING IN COLUMBIA, MD.; RESTON, VA.; FOREST PARK, OHIO; PARK FOREST, ILL.; PARK FOREST SOUTH, ILL.)

141. I've been asked to ask you one more thing. When the responses to these interviews are analyzed, we would like to be able to look at the reactions of black people living in (NAME OF COMMUNITY) separately. At this point, however, we can't be sure that the sample of houses that was selected includes enough black respondents. In case we do need to contact more black residents, would you give me the names and addresses of two friends or acquaintances who live in (NAME OF COMMUNITY) who are black? We'd be asking them the same questions I've just asked you. You don't have to give me any information, or course, and I can assure you that we wouldn't mention you to them.

FIRST FRIEND/ACQUAINTANCE   SECOND FRIEND/ACQUAINTANCE

NAME _____   NAME _____

ADDRESS _____   ADDRESS _____

TOWN   ⓪①②⑨   TOWN _____

TIME IS NOW: _____

THANK RESPONDENT FOR HIS/HER TIME. FILL IN POST-INTERVIEW ITEMS DIRECTLY AFTER LEAVING HOUSEHOLD.

POST INTERVIEW ITEMS

P1. Race of respondent:

① White   ② Black   ③ Oriental   ④ Other (specify): _____

P2. Type of dwelling in which respondent lives.
① Single family detached house
② Duplex
③ Rowhouse; townhouse
④ Walk-up apartment building

⑤ Elevator apartment building
⑥ Store with dwelling above or behind
⑦ House converted to rooms or apartments

Ⓐ Other (specify): _____

P3. Number of floors in respondent's building, <u>not</u> counting basement.

FLOORS _____   ⊚①②③④⑤⑥⑦⑧⑨
⊚①②③④⑤⑥⑦⑧⑨

P4. Floor on which respondent's apartment is found:
(⊚ Respondent does not live in apartment)
○ Basement   ○ 1st (ground) floor

○ Above ground floor
(specify floor): _____

⊚①②③④⑤⑥⑦⑧⑨
⊚①②③④⑤⑥⑦⑧⑨

P5. Respondent's rowhouse or townhouse is:
① At the end of a row   ⑤ Not at the end of a row   (⊚ Respondent does not live in rowhouse/townhouse)

P6. Condition of exterior of building:
① Well kept up
② Requires some maintenance -- in need of paint or minor repair
③ Requires extensive maintenance - in need of major repair, structural deterioration; many minor repairs

P7. Condition of lawn and property:
① Well kept up
② Requires some maintenance -- lawn needs cutting, shrubs need pruning
③ Requires extensive maintenance -- parts (all) of lawn and shrubs need replacement; a lot of litter

P8. Foundation planting (shrubs, bushes) in front of building:
① Exists   ⑤ Does not exist

P9. Sidewalk or pathway in front of, beside, or behind respondent's house/apartment house:
① Exists   ⑤ Does not exist

P10. Utilities in respondent's immediate neighborhood are:
① Underground   ② Overhead behind homes (on back lot line, etc.)   ③ Overhead along street

P11. Curb and gutter in front of respondent's house/apartment house:
① Exists   ⑤ Does not exist

P12. Street serving respondent's house/apartment house:
① In good state of repair   ⑤ Requires some maintenance -- bumps, holes, serious cracks, etc.

P13. I certify that the respondent was informed at the start of the interview of the purpose of the survey and the safeguards being taken to keep his replies confidential and that I obtained the respondent's verbal consent to proceed with the interview.

_____
INTERVIEWER'S SIGNATURE

DATE OF INTERVIEW: _____|_____
             Month   Day

LENGTH OF INTERVIEW: _____ MINUTES

TODAY'S DATE		
Mo.		Day	
⊚	⊚	⊚	⊚
①	①	①	①
②	②	②	②
③	③	③	③
④	④	④	④
⑤	⑤	⑤	⑤
⑥	⑥	⑥	⑥
⑦	⑦	⑦	⑦
⑧	⑧	⑧	⑧
⑨	⑨	⑨	⑨

LENGTH OF INTERVIEW (Minutes)		
⊚	⊚	⊚
①	①	①
②	②	②
③	③	③
④	④	④
⑤	⑤	⑤
⑥	⑥	⑥
⑦	⑦	⑦
⑧	⑧	⑧
⑨	⑨	⑨

Bibliography

Alston, Jon P. and Dudley, Charles J. 1973. "Age, Occupation, and Life Satisfaction," *The Gerontologist*, Vol 13 (Spring), pp. 58–61.

Alston, Jon P., Lowe, George D., and Wrigley, Alice. 1974. "Socioeconomic Correlates for Four Dimensions of Self-Perceived Satisfaction, 1972," *Human Organization*, Vol. 33 (Spring), pp. 99–102.

Andrews, Frank M. and Withey, Stephen B. 1973. "Developing Measures of Perceived Life Quality: Results from Several National Surveys." Ann Arbor: The University of Michigan, Institute for Social Research. Prepared for presentation to the annual convention of the American Sociological Association, New York City, August.

Andrews, Frank M. and Withey, Stephen B. 1974. "Assessing the Quality of Life as People Experience It." Ann Arbor: The University of Michigan, Institute for Social Research. Prepared for presentation to the annual convention of the American Sociological Association, Montreal, August.

Bracy, James H. 1976. "The Quality of Life Experience of Black People." Chapter 13 in Angus Campbell, Philip E. Converse, and Willard Rodgers, *The Quality of American Life*. New York: Russell Sage Foundation, pp. 443–469.

Bradburn, Norman M. 1969. *The Structure of Psychological Well-Being.* Chicago: Aldine Publishing Company.

Bradburn, Norman M. and Caplovitz, David. 1965. *Reports on Happiness.* Chicago: Aldine Publishing Company.

Burby, Raymond J., III. 1976. *Recreation and Leisure in New Communities.* Cambridge, Mass.: Ballinger Publishing Company.

Burby, Raymond J., III. and Donnelly, Thomas G. 1977. *Schools in New Communities.* Cambridge, Mass.: Ballinger Publishing Company.

Burby, Raymond J., III and Weiss, Shirley F. with Donnelly, Thomas G., Kaiser, Edward J., Zehner, Robert B. and Lewis, David F., Loewenthal, Norman H., McCalla, Mary Ellen, Rodgers, Barbara G., and Smookler, Helene V. 1976. *New*

Communities U.S.A. Lexington, Mass.: D.C. Heath and Company, Lexington Books.

Burby, Raymond J., III, Weiss, Shirley F., and Zehner, Robert B. "A National Evaluation of Community Services and the Quality of Life in American New Towns," *Public Administration Review*, Vol. 35 (May–June 1975), pp. 229–239.

Butler, Edgar W., Chapin, F. Stuart, Jr., Hemmens, Geroge C., Kaiser, Edward J., Stegman, Michael A., and Weiss, Shirley F. 1969. *Moving Behavior and Residential Choice: A National Survey.* Washington: Highway Research Board, National Academy of Sciences—National Academy of Engineering.

Campbell, Angus, Converse, Philip E., and Rodgers, Willard L. 1976. *The Quality of American Life.* New York: Russell Sage Foundation.

Chapin, F. Stuart, Jr. 1974. *Human Activity Patterns in the City: Things People Do in Time and in Space.* New York: John Wiley and Sons.

Clark, Terry Nicholas. 1973. "Community Social Indicators: From Analytic Models to Policy Applications," *Urban Affairs Quarterly*, Vol. 9 (September), pp. 3–36.

Clemente, Frank and Sauer, William J. 1976. "Life Satisfaction in the United States," *Social Forces*, Vol. 54 (March), pp. 621–631.

Dillman, Don A. and Dobash, Russell P. 1972. "Preferences for Community Living and Their Implications for Population Distribution." Pullman: Washington State University, Washington Agricultural Experiment Station, College of Agriculture, November.

Duncan, Otis Dudley. 1969. *Toward Social Reporting: Next Steps.* New York: Russell Sage Foundation.

Durand, Roger and Eckart, Dennis R. 1973. "Social Rank, Residential Effects and Community Satisfaction," *Social Forces*, Vol. 52 (September) pp. 74–85.

Easterlin, Richard A. 1973. "Does Money Buy Happiness?" *The Public Interest*, No. 30 (Winter), pp. 3–10.

Environmental Protection Agency, Office of Research and Monitoring, Environmental Studies Division. 1973. *The Quality of Life Concept: A Potential New Tool for Decision Makers.* Washington: The Agency.

Erskine, Hazel. 1973. "The Polls: Hopes, Fears and Regrets." *The Public Opinion Quarterly*, Vol. 37 (Spring), pp. 132–145.

Flax, Michael J. 1972. *A Study in Comparative Urban Indicators: Conditions in 18 Large Metropolitan Areas.* Washington: The Urban Institute.

Francis, Walton J. 1973. "A Report on Measurement and Quality of Life." Washington: U.S. Department of Health, Education, and Welfare, January.

Gans, Herbert J. 1968. *People and Plans: Essays on Urban Problems and Solutions.* New York: Basic Books, Inc.

Gans, Herbert J. 1966. *The Levittowners.* New York: Pantheon Books, A Division of Random House.

Goldsmith, Harold F. and Munsterman, Janice. 1967. "Neighborhood Homogeneity and Community Satisfaction," Paper presented at the annual meeting of the Rural Sociological Association, San Francisco, August.

Gurin, Gerald, Veroff, Joseph, and Feld, Shiela. 1960. *Americans View Their Mental Health*. New York: Basic Books, Inc.

Halkett, Ian P. B. 1976. *The Quarter-Acre Block*. Canberra: Australian Institute of Urban Studies.

Hammer, Philip G., Jr. and Chapin, F. Stuart, Jr. 1972. *Human Time Allocation: A Case Study of Washington, D.C.* A Technical Monograph. Chapel Hill, N.C.: The University of North Carolina, Center for Urban and Regional Studies, March.

Howard, Ebenezer. 1965. *Garden Cities of Tomorrow*. Cambridge, Mass.: The MIT Press (originally published in 1898).

James, L. Douglas, Brogan, Donna R., Laurent, Eugene A., and Baltimore, Henri Etta. 1974. *Community Well-Being as a Factor in Urban Land Use Planning*. Atlanta: Georgia Institute of Technology, Environmental Resources Center.

Kaiser, Edward J. 1976. *Residential Mobility in New Communities: An Analysis of Recent In-movers and Prospective Out-movers*. Cambridge, Mass.: Ballinger Publishing Company.

Keller, Suzanne. 1968. *The Urban Neighborhood: A Sociological Perspective*. New York, Random House.

Lansing, John B. 1966. *Residential Location and Urban Mobility: The Second Wave of Interviews*. Ann Arbor: The University of Michigan, Institute for Social Research.

Lansing, John B., Marans, Robert W., and Zehner, Robert B. 1970. *Planned Residential Environments*. Ann Arbor: The University of Michigan, Institute for Social Research.

Lansing, John B., Mueller, Eva with Barth, Nancy. 1964. *Residential Location and Urban Mobility*. Ann Arbor: The University of Michigan, Institute for Social Research.

Lewis, David F. 1974. "Dwelling Unit Satisfaction in New Communities." Chapel Hill: The University of North Carolina, Center for Urban and Regional Studies, December.

Loewenthal, Norman H. and Burby, Raymond J., III. 1976. *Health Care in New Communities*. Cambridge, Mass.: Ballinger Publishing Company.

Marans, Robert W. 1975. "The Perceived Quality of Residential Environments: Some Methodological Issues." Ann Arbor: The University of Michigan, Institute for Social Research. Paper prepared for research workshop on Perceived Environmental Quality Indices at The University of Massachusetts, Amherst, April.

Marans, Robert W. and Mandell, Lewis. 1972. "The Relative Effectiveness of Density-Related Variables," *Proceedings of the American Statistical Association Meetings*, pp. 360–363.

Marans, Robert W. and Rodgers, Willard L. 1972. "Towards an Understanding of Community Satisfaction." Ann Arbor: The University of Michigan, Institute for Social Research, December.

Markley, O.W. and Bagley, Marilyn, D. 1975. "Minimum Standards for Quality of Life," Prepared for the Environmental Protection Agency by the Stanford Research Institute. Springfield, Va.: U.S. Department of Commerce, National Technical Information Service, May.

Menchik, Mark D. 1971. *Residential Environmental Preferences and Choice.* Madison, Wis.: The University of Wisconsin, Institute for Environmental Studies.

Michelson, William H. 1970. *Man and His Urban Environment: A Sociological Approach.* Reading, Mass.: Addison-Wesley.

Murray, James R. 1974. "Causes of Satisfaction." Continuous National Survey, National Opinion Research Center, May.

National Capital Development Commission (Australia). 1975. "Residential Satisfaction and Design Effectiveness of Two-Storey Flats." Technical Paper No. 10, Canberra: The Commission, July.

Norcross, Carl. 1966. *Open Space Communities in the Marketplace.* Washington: Urban Land Institute, Technical Bulletin 57, December.

Office of Program Analysis and Evaluation, Office of the Assistant Secretary for Policy Development and Research, Department of Housing and Urban Development. 1975. *Evaluation of the New Communities Program.* Washington: The Department, April.

Palmore, Erdman and Luikart, Clark. 1972. "Health and Social Factors Related to Life Satisfaction." *Journal of Health and Human Behavior*, Vol. 13 (March), pp. 68–80.

Prestridge, James A. 1973. *Case Studies of Six Planned New Towns in the United States.* Lexington, Ky.: University of Kentucky Research Foundation, Institute for Environmental Studies.

Rabinovitz, Francine F., and Lamare, James. 1970. "After Suburbia What?: The New Communities Movement in Los Angeles." Los Angeles: The University of California at Los Angeles, Institute of Government and Public Affairs.

Real Estate Research Corporation. 1974. *The Costs of Sprawl: Detailed Cost Analysis.* Washington: U.S. Government Printing Office.

Reynolds, Ingrid and Nicholson, Charles with Crouther, Sylvia, Birley, Rosalind, and Bell, Ann. 1972. *The Estate Outside the Dwelling: Reactions of Residents to Aspects of Housing Layout.* Department of the Environment Design Bulletin 25. London: Her Majesty's Stationery Office.

Robinson, John P. and Shaver, Phillip R. 1969. *Measures of Social Psychological Attitudes.* Ann Arbor: The University of Michigan, Institute for Social Research.

Rossi, Peter H. 1955. *Why Families Move.* Glencoe, Ill.: The Free Press.

Savitzky, Joseph. 1973. "Columbia Neighborhood Evaluation Survey: Preliminary Report." Columbia, Md.: The Rouse Company, Evaluation Section, September.

Spreitzer, Elmer and Snyder, Eldon E. 1974. "Correlates of Life Satisfaction Among the Aged." *Journal of Gerontology*, Vol. 13 (Spring), pp. 58–61.

Stretton, Hugh. 1974. *Housing and Government: 1974 Boyer Lectures by Hugh Stretton.* Sydney: The Australian Broadcasting Commission.

Troy, Patrick N. 1971. *Environmental Quality in Four Sydney Suburban Areas.* Canberra: Australian National University, Urban Research Unit, September.

Tunstall, Daniel B. 1973. *Social Indicators, 1973.* Washington: U.S. Government Printing Office.

Van Arsdol, Maurice, Jr., Sabagh, Georges, and Butler, Edgar W. 1968. "Retrospective and Subsequent Residential Mobility," *Demography*, Vol. 5, pp. 249–267.

Varady, David P. 1973. "Moving Intentions and Behavior in the Cincinnati Model Neighborhood," Paper presented at the annual conference of the American Institute of Planners, Atlanta, October.

Werthman, Carl, Mandel, Jerry S., and Dienstfrey, Ted. 1965. *Planning and the Purchase Decision: Why People Buy in Planned Communities*. Berkeley: The University of California at Berkeley, Institute of Regional Development, Center for Planning and Development Research, Preprint No. 10.

Zehner, Robert B. 1970. *Satisfaction with Neighborhoods: The Effects of Social Compatibility, Residential Density, and Site Planning*, Ph.D. dissertation, The University of Michigan. Ann Arbor: University Microfilms.

Zehner, Robert B. 1971. "Neighborhood and Community Satisfaction in New Towns and Less Planned Suburbs," *Journal of the American Institute of Planners*, Vol. 37 (November) pp. 379–385.

Zehner, Robert B. 1977. *Access, Travel, and Transportation in New Communities*. Cambridge, Mass.: Ballinger Publishing Company.

Zehner, Robert B. and Chapin, F. Stuart, Jr. with Howell, Joseph T. 1974. *Across the City Line: A White Community in Transition*. Lexington, Mass.: D.C. Heath and Company, Lexington Books.

Zehner, Robert B. and Marans, Robert W. 1973. "Residential Density, Planning Objectives, and Life in Planned Communities," *Journal of the American Institute of Planners*, Vol. 39 (September), pp. 337–345.

Zehner, Robert B., Burby, Raymond J., III and Weiss, Shirley F. 1974. "Evaluation of New Communities in the United States." Chapel Hill: The University of North Carolina, Center for Urban and Regional Studies. Prepared for presentation at the Annual Meeting of the American Sociological Association, Montreal, August.

Zehner, Robert B. and McCalla, Mary Ellen. 1974. "Household Interview Response Rates and Non-Response Tabulations." Chapel Hill: Center for Urban and Regional Studies, The University of North Carolina, May.

Ziegler, Joseph A. and Britton, Charles R. 1975. "A Comparative Analysis of Socio-Economic Variations in Measuring the Quality of Life." Fayetteville, Ark.: The University of Arkansas, Department of Economics. Paper prepared for the annual meeting of the Regional Science Association, Cambridge, Massachusetts, November.

Zill, Nicholas. 1974. "Developing Indicators of Effective Life Management." Washington: Center for Social Indicators, Social Science Research Council, January.

Index

Agoura-Malibu, Calif.: response to moving, 26

Alston, J.P., et al., 120

amenities: Columbia, 50; and life satisfaction, 113; need for shopping facilities, 75; neighborhood inventory, 81; role of community services in quality of life, 67; shopping facilities and resident rating, 45

Andrews, F.M. and Withey, S.B.; determinants of satisfaction, 4; data interpretation, 128; satisfaction domains, 111; quality of life, 38

blacks: life satisfaction, 120; Park Forest and Forest Park, 73; and quality of life scale, 19

Bouquet Canyon, Calif., 109

Bradburn, N.M., 4

Campbell, A.: life satisfaction; —Converse, P. and Rodgers, W., 38, 101

Columbia, Maryland: amenities, 87; attribute rating, 28; compared with pair, 39; dwelling type, 11; facilities, 50; importance of community planning, 46; leisure, 109; life satisfaction, 101, 113; neighborhood satisfaction, 80; renters, 70; response to moving, 26; in Savitzky, 42; settlement, 10

community life: attribute rating, 32; as indicator, 20; inventory, 47; rating, 28; role of in resident rating, 18

community planning: attribute rating, 32; importance in ratings, 44; rank, 26; in resident evaluation, 17; role of in quality of life, 15

conventional communities: amenities, 81; analysis of community attributes, 28; as basis of comparison, 14; dwelling satisfaction, 92, 98; implications of life satisfaction data, 134; inventory of facilities, 47; life satisfaction, 102; moving intentions, 66; resident attitudes, 76; resident evaluation, 17; resident response on quality of life items, 19; respondents' definition of quality of life, 24

Dana Point, Calif., 81

density: lack of and importance in resident rating, 44; private outdoor space, 96; and resident concern, 71; and resident rating, 17; and satisfaction with neighborhood, 18, 84; townhouse/apartments, 92; and zoning, 75

developer: control and resident concern, 73; implications of good maintenance, 89; implications of resident satisfaction rating, 64;

✳

About the Author

Robert B. Zehner is Lecturer in the School of Town Planning at The University of New South Wales where he spent 1975 as Fulbright Senior Scholar and Honorary Visiting Fellow. He was co-principal investigator of the NSF/RANN New Communities Project while a senior research associate at the Center for Urban and Regional Studies of The University of North Carolina at Chapel Hill. He received the A.M. and Ph.D. in Sociology from The University of Michigan. Dr. Zehner is co-author of *Planned Residential Environments* and *Across the City Line: A White Community in Transition*, as well as articles on neighborhood and community satisfaction and the methodology of survey research.